Department of International Economic and Social Affairs

ST/ESA/SER.A/102/Add.2

Population Studies · No. 102/Add.2

World Population Policies

Volume III

Oman to Zimbabwe

 United Nations   New York, 1990

NOTE

The designations employed and the presentation of the material in this publication do not imply the expression of any opinion whatsoever on the part of the Secretariat of the United Nations concerning the legal status of any country, territory, city or area or of its authorities, or concerning the delimitation of its frontiers or boundaries.

The term "country" as used in the text of this report also refers, as appropriate, to territories or areas.

The designations "developed" and "developing" economies are intended for statistical convenience and do not necessarily express a judgement about the stage reached by a particular country or area in the development process.

The printing of this volume was made possible by a publications grant from the United Nations Population Fund.

ST/ESA/SER.A/102/Add.2

UNITED NATIONS PUBLICATION

Sales No. E.90.XIII.2

ISBN 92-1-151188-7

PREFACE

The information contained in the present report is based on the continuous monitoring of population policies by the Population Division of the Department of International Economic and Social Affairs of the United Nations Secretariat as part of its programme of work. World Population Policies presents, in three volumes, comparable and up-to-date information on the population policies of the 170 State Members of the United Nations and non-Member States. The countries are arranged in alphabetical order: volume I (United Nations publication, Sales No. E.87.XIII.4) covering countries from Afghanistan to France, volume II (United Nations publication, Sales No. E.89.XIII.3) from Gabon to Norway, and volume III from Oman to Zimbabwe. The present publication replaces Population Policy Briefs: The Current Situation in Developing Countries, 1985 (ST/ESA/SER.R/62), Population Policy Briefs: The Current Situation in Developed Countries, 1985 (ST/ESA/SER.R/63) and Population Policy Compendium.

Responsibility for this report rests with the United Nations Secretariat; however, the assessment was facilitated to a great extent by the close co-operation among the United Nations bodies. In particular, the contribution of the United Nations Population Fund in support of this publication is gratefully acknowledged.

Except where otherwise noted, the demographic estimates and projections cited in this report are based on the eleventh round of global demographic assessments undertaken by the Population Division.

For additional information and data relating to demographic estimates and projections, reference should be made to World Population Prospects, 1988 (United Nations publication, Sales No. E.88.XIII.7).

CONTENTS

Annexes

EXPLANATORY NOTES

Symbols of United Nations documents are composed of capital letters combined with figures.

Reference to "dollars" ($) indicates United States dollars, unless otherwise stated.

Reference to "tons" indicates metric tons, unless otherwise stated.

The term "billion" signifies a thousand million.

A hyphen between years (e.g., 1984-1985) indicates the full period involved, including the beginning and end years; a slash (e.g., 1984/85) indicates a financial year, school year or crop year.

A point (.) is used to indicate decimals.

The following symbols have been used in the tables:

Three dots (...) indicate that data are not available or are not separately reported.

A dash (--) indicates that the amount is nil or negligible.

A hyphen (-) indicates that the item is not applicable.

A minus sign (-) before a number indicates a deficit or decrease, except as indicated.

Details and percentages in tables do not necessarily add to totals because of rounding.

INTRODUCTION

The realization that population is a vital component of the development process has led an increasing number of countries to formulate and implement policies to influence either directly or indirectly the demographic character of their population. To meet the growing demand for information on national population policies, this publication presents in a systematic and comparable manner, for developed and developing countries, an overview of the Governments' perceptions and policies in relation to such factors as population growth and age structure, mortality and morbidity, fertility and the family, international migration, spatial distribution and urbanization and the status of women.

In order to place the Government's perceptions and policies within the proper context, the relevant demographic indicators are also provided. The definitions of the various indicators may be found in annex I. In addition, the institutional arrangements for the formulation and implementation of such policies are also described.

The major sources of information for this report were the Population Policy Data Bank maintained by the Population Division of the Department of International Economic and Social Affairs, Population Policy Compendium (now discontinued) and the six United Nations population inquiries among Governments. The Population Policy Data Bank contains, among other things, government documents and publications, such as development plans and position papers, speeches and publications of other international organizations. The status of the responses to the six inquiries is indicated in annex II.

OMAN

DEMOGRAPHIC INDICATORS	CURRENT PERCEPTION
SIZE/AGE STRUCTURE/GROWTH	The Government considers the rate of population growth to be <u>unsatisfactory</u> and <u>too low</u>.

Population:	1985	2025
(thousands)	1 242	4 309
0-14 years (%)	44.3	38.0
60+ years (%)	4.1	5.9

Rate of:	1980-85	2020-25
growth	4.7	2.3
natural increase	33.1	23.3

	CURRENT PERCEPTION
MORTALITY/MORBIDITY	The Government considers the mortality and morbidity levels to be <u>unacceptable</u>. A special concern is infant mortality.

	1980-85	2020-25
Life expectancy	52.3	71.0
Crude death rate	14.6	4.9
Infant mortality	117.0	27.0

	CURRENT PERCEPTION
FERTILITY/NUPTIALITY/FAMILY	The fertility level is viewed as <u>satisfactory</u>.

	1980-85	2020-25
Fertility rate	7.2	3.6
Crude birth rate	47.7	28.2
Contraceptive prevalence rate	...	...
Female mean age at first marriage	...	...

	CURRENT PERCEPTION
INTERNATIONAL MIGRATION	The level of immigration is considered to be <u>significant</u> and <u>too high</u>, while emigration is <u>not significant</u> and <u>satisfactory</u>.

	1980-85	2020-25
Net migration rate	0.0	0.0
Foreign-born population (%)	...	...

	CURRENT PERCEPTION
SPATIAL DISTRIBUTION/URBANIZATION	The spatial distribution pattern of the population is felt to be <u>partially appropriate</u>.

Urban	1985	2025
population (%)	8.8	31.6

Growth rate:	1980-85	2020-25
urban	8.4	4.9
rural	4.3	1.3

GENERAL POLICY FRAMEWORK

Overall approach to population problems: Government policies attach high priority to developing local human resources and improving their capability to contribute to the national economy. The Government also aims to distribute national investments among geographical regions with a view to spreading prosperity and progress to all regions of the Sultanate, reducing differences in the standard of living among these regions and assigning a special priority to the least developed areas.

Importance of population policy in achieving development objectives: While Oman lacks an explicit comprehensive population policy, some population issues, such as those dealing with settlements and internal migration, have been integrated within the five-year national development plans.

INSTITUTIONAL FRAMEWORK

Population data systems and development planning: No census has ever been conducted in Oman and as of 1989, none had been planned. There are no vital registration data. The only major statistical sources are the 1975 Socio-Demographic Survey in Five Cities and the 1977-1979 Socio-Demographic Survey in Eleven Towns. The First Five-Year Development Plan covered the period 1976-1980, followed by the Second Five-Year Plan for 1981-1985. The Third Five-Year Plan, 1986-1990, is currently in effect.

Integration of population within development planning: Since 1970, Oman has made considerable progress in its efforts to give structure to its economic and social development; this has been achieved through development plans and programmes. Development planning, which is the responsibility of the Development Council, has included sectoral programmes dealing with urbanization and internal migration.

POLICIES AND MEASURES

Changes in population size and age structure: The Government would like to raise the rate of population growth, given the relatively small size of the population. Information on the status of pension schemes is not readily available.

Mortality and morbidity: The Government's health policy aims to achieve, as rapidly as possible, the level of health care among its population that conforms to the goal of Health for All by the Year 2000. Development of health services is an integral part of national development plans and elements of national strategy emphasizing primary health care have been incorporated into the Third Five-Year Plan. Included among the health priorities specified by the Government are the strengthening of curative services particularly in urban areas, strengthening of preventive services with emphasis on common communicable diseases, immunizing children against the six target diseases, expanding primary health care and intensifying national health manpower resources. The Government indicated in 1985 that maternal and child health care had not reached the village level and that while the provision of safe water and adequate sanitary facilities has been expanded, there is still low coverage in rural areas. The Government intends to strengthen adult education, especially of mothers. In July 1987, a Gulf Co-operation Council ban on cigarettes with a high nicotine and tar content went into effect. Also in July 1987, the country held its first workshop on the acquired immunodeficiency syndrome (AIDS) in order to make medical staff aware of the problem.

Fertility and the family: The Government would like to maintain the rate of fertility. Programmes aiming to improve maternal and child care have been implemented. Abortion is not permitted, except to save the life of the woman. Contraceptives may be obtained at private hospitals and dispensaries and through commercial outlets.

International migration: The Government is promoting the reduction of the significant non-national labour force, which had been estimated to be about two thirds of the total labour force. A substantial outflow of foreigners took place in 1986 and 1987, as a consequence of the general slow-down in the economy. To promote Omanization, since 1987 the employment of non-nationals in certain occupations has been restricted. In January 1989, the State Consultative Council organized a seminar on Omanization.

Spatial distribution/urbanization: The country's development goals include supporting the maintenance of existing population centres and communities, safeguarding those communities from potential migration to densely populated urban centres and protecting the environment. Concerning urbanization, the Second Five-Year Plan aimed to make available land suitable for urban extension and to conduct town planning, in order to improve the prospects of towns and villages and provide extra land to meet the requirements of population growth. In the area of spatial distribution of the population, the Government wishes to maintain and develop the existing area of population concentration, while reducing immigration and rural-to-urban migration. The Government aims to bring about a wider geographic distribution of investment so that the benefits may be shared by the various regions of the country and to narrow the gaps in the standard of living between different regions, with special emphasis on the least developed regions. The policy for the development of secondary urban centres has been supported by the creation of effective local administrative offices.

Status of women and population: Information on the status of women in Oman is not readily available.

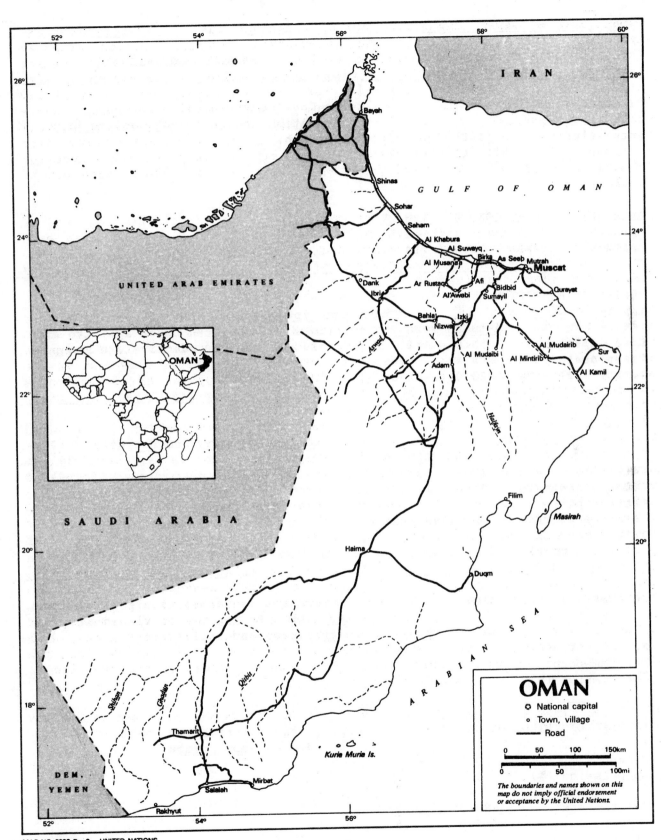

PAKISTAN

DEMOGRAPHIC INDICATORS	CURRENT PERCEPTION
SIZE/AGE STRUCTURE/GROWTH	The Government perceives rates of population growth as <u>not satisfactory</u> and <u>too high</u>.

Population:	1985	2025
(thousands)	103 241	267 089
0-14 years (%)	44.6	28.4
60+ years (%)	4.4	8.0

Rate of:	1980-85	2020-25
growth	3.8	1.5
natural increase	36.0	14.7

MORTALITY/MORBIDITY

Mortality levels are regarded as <u>unacceptable</u>. Of special concern are infants and children under age five and females in the reproductive age group.

	1980-85	2020-25
Life expectancy	54.0	70.7
Crude death rate	14.4	5.4
Infant mortality	120.0	43.0

FERTILITY/NUPTIALITY/FAMILY

Current fertility rates are considered to be <u>not satisfactory</u> and <u>too high</u>.

	1980-85	2020-25
Fertility rate	7.0	2.3
Crude birth rate	50.3	20.1
Contraceptive prevalence rate	7.6 (1984/85)	
Female mean age at first marriage	19.8 (1981)	

INTERNATIONAL MIGRATION

Immigration is viewed as <u>significant</u> and <u>too high</u>. Emigration is viewed as <u>significant</u> and <u>satisfactory</u>.

	1980-85	2020-25
Net migration rate	0.0	0.0
Foreign-born population (%)	...	...

SPATIAL DISTRIBUTION/URBANIZATION

The spatial distribution pattern is regarded as <u>appropriate</u>.

Urban	1985	2025
population (%)	29.8	56.7

Growth rate:	1980-85	2020-25
urban	5.0	2.8
rural	3.3	-0.1

GENERAL POLICY FRAMEWORK

Overall approach to population problems: A reduction in the population growth rate is felt to be essential for improving the country's social and economic conditions; efforts are under way to reduce illiteracy and unemployment, improve health conditions and lower fertility through family planning programmes.

Importance of population policy in achieving development objectives: Population policies are considered to be an integral component of economic and social planning. Developmental strategies and priorities to attain social and economic goals are being pursued within the country's economic development, in which inadequate physical and social infrastructure in rural areas, high fertility and the low literacy rate are considered to be major obstacles to achieving economic progress.

INSTITUTIONAL FRAMEWORK

Population data systems and development planning: Censuses were conducted in 1972 and 1981 and are the responsibility of the Federal Bureau of Statistics. The next census had been provisionally scheduled for 1991. Development plans are prepared by the Planning Commission. The draft Seventh Five-Year Plan for the period 1988/89-1992/93 was issued in early 1988.

Integration of population within development planning: Since 1965 the Population Welfare Division in the Ministry of Planning and Development has been responsible for the formulation and co-ordination of population policies. Together with the Population and Social Planning Section it is responsible for integration of population variables into development planning. To strengthen the multi-sectoral approach of the Population Welfare Programme, a National Institute of Population Studies (NIPS) has been established. The objective of the Institute is to conduct development and population-related studies and serve as a technical arm to the Population Welfare Division. Similarly, one Population Study Centre has been established at the University of Karachi and another at the University of Faisalabad for undertaking research and studies on the interrelationships between demographic variables and community development.

POLICIES AND MEASURES

Changes in population size and age structure: The Government has indicated that the high rate of population growth and the high dependency burden, both youth dependants and old-age dependants, have had an adverse impact on social, economic and political conditions in Pakistan. The Government's objective is to lower population growth to achieve a balance among population growth, the age structure and economic resources. The Sixth Five-Year Plan placed emphasis on policies to expand family planning services, reduce mortality and improve educational opportunities for women. The Plan specified a target growth rate of 2.6 per cent per year by 1988. Under the social security scheme, employees in firms with at least 10 employees are covered, while certain categories of workers, such as family labour and the self-employed, are excluded.

Mortality and morbidity: Under the Prime Minister's Five-Point Programme for the period 1985-1989, the Government was committed to improving health care for all, but especially among the population segments with the highest mortality and morbidity levels. Measures adopted by the Government include the expansion of primary health-care services in rural areas, an expanded immunization programme, family planning and the training of 50,000 traditional birth attendants to ensure one attendant for each of the country's villages and less developed urban areas. Other measures include expanding the provision of potable water supplies, initiating community-based sanitation activities and the addition of 1,180 Basic Health Council Areas. The Sixth Five-Year Plan specified a target crude death rate of 10 per thousand and an infant mortality rate of 100 per thousand by 1988.

Fertility and the family: The Government hopes to promote the small family norm through programmes aimed at socio-economic transformation, rural development, reducing infant and child mortality, and the training of traditional birth attendants. The Population Welfare Programme which was incorporated into the Sixth Five-Year Plan sought to devise programmes based on local needs and to seek the involvement of target groups and non-governmental organizations (NGO)s. The Plan specified quantitative targets for individual contraceptive methods, as well as an overall goal of a contraceptive use rate of 19 per cent by 1988. The Government gives direct support for the provision of contraception. Abortion is permitted only to save the life of the mother, while sterilization is available with the husband's consent to married women having at least two to three children. The target is a total fertility rate of 5.4 by 1988.

International migration: With an estimated 3.3 million refugees at the end of 1988, Pakistan is home to the world's largest single refugee population. As the accuracy of this figure has been questioned, the Government conducts periodic re-enumeration exercises to obtain as accurate a count of the number of Afghan refugees as possible. In April 1988, a Bilateral Agreement signed by the Governments of Afghanistan and Pakistan offered the prospect for the repatriation of Afghan refugees. In 1989, the assistance programme of the Office of the United Nations High Commissioner for Refugees was maintained both in the form of direct subsistence allowances and project support. The programme of repatriation and reintegration will be implemented within the framework of the United Nations Humanitarian and Economic Assistance Programmes relating to Afghanistan. In order to increase the level of emigration, the Government is attempting to extend or re-establish agreements with Middle Eastern countries on the employment of Pakistani labour.

Spatial distribution/urbanization: As 70 per cent of the country's population resided in rural areas as of 1985, rural development is seen as a major tool in readjusting the pattern of internal migration. Under the Prime Minister's Five-Point Programme, a number of targets have been formulated including the electrification of all villages by 1990; the improvement and development of Katchi Abadis (urban squatter settlements) and the conferring of proprietary rights to their residents; the creation of 2.2 million plots to be allocated to landless rural families; the provision of clean water supplies, sanitation, rural electrification and health-care centres in rural areas; and the construction of rural roads and farm-to-market roads. The Seventh Five-Year Plan continues many of the programmes. These initiatives are being supplemented by local development schemes to enhance the role of people's participation in the development of local areas. The Government is also receiving international assistance to promote economic growth in a number of smaller towns in the southern province of Sind.

<u>Status of women and population</u>: Created in 1979, the Women's Division within the Cabinet Secretariat is charged with the formulation of policies and laws to meet the special needs of women. The Sixth Five-Year Plan stressed an integrated approach to improving the status of women and targeted areas that were hindering women such as illiteracy, constant motherhood and the primitive organization of work. In 1989, it was announced that the Women's Division would soon establish centres of excellence at various universities in Pakistan to keep students informed of women's development programmes.

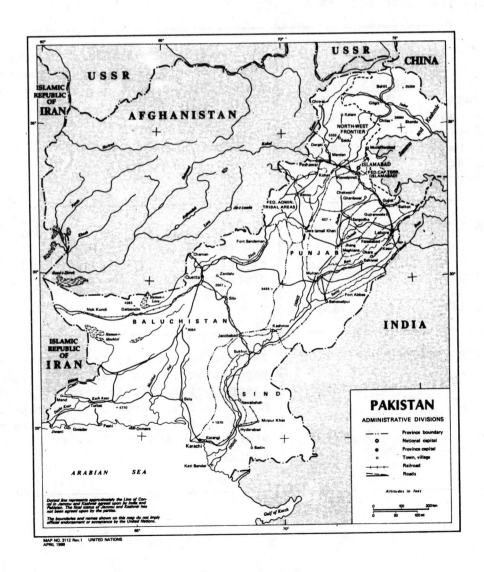

MAP NO. 3112 Rev.1 UNITED NATIONS
APRIL 1989

PANAMA

DEMOGRAPHIC INDICATORS	CURRENT PERCEPTION
SIZE/AGE STRUCTURE/GROWTH	The Government perceives growth rates as <u>satisfactory</u>. A concentration of population in the productive ages, 15-59, has become a cause for concern in the context of job creation.

Population:	1985	2025
(thousands)	2 180	3 862
0-14 years (%)	37.6	23.2
60+ years (%)	6.6	14.2

Rate of:	1980-85	2020-25
growth	2.2	0.9
natural increase	22.6	9.1

DEMOGRAPHIC INDICATORS	CURRENT PERCEPTION
MORTALITY/MORBIDITY	The Government views mortality and morbidity as <u>acceptable</u>. However, levels of mortality among infants, indigenous, marginal urban and isolated populations are seen as a special concern.

	1980-85	2020-25
Life expectancy	71.0	74.3
Crude death rate	5.4	7.1
Infant mortality	26.0	17.0

DEMOGRAPHIC INDICATORS	CURRENT PERCEPTION
FERTILITY/NUPTIALITY/FAMILY	The Government considers the fertility level to be <u>satisfactory</u>. Adolescent fertility is, however, a major concern.

	1980-85	2020-25
Fertility rate	3.5	2.1
Crude birth rate	28.0	16.1
Contraceptive prevalence rate	58.2 (1984)	
Female mean age at first marriage	21.3 (1980)	

DEMOGRAPHIC INDICATORS	CURRENT PERCEPTION
INTERNATIONAL MIGRATION	The <u>insignificant</u> levels of immigration and emigration are viewed as <u>satisfactory</u>. The loss of trained professionals through emigration is a concern.

	1980-85	2020-25
Net migration rate	0.0	-0.5
Foreign-born population (%)	2.6 (1980)	

DEMOGRAPHIC INDICATORS	CURRENT PERCEPTION
SPATIAL DISTRIBUTION/URBANIZATION	The spatial distribution pattern of population in the country is seen as <u>inappropriate</u> and in need of substantial modification. Growth in metropolitan areas is seen as <u>too high</u>, while that in other urban and rural areas is seen as <u>too low</u>.

Urban	1985	2025
population (%)	52.4	74.3

Growth rate:	1980-85	2020-25
urban	2.9	1.5
rural	1.4	-0.9

GENERAL POLICY FRAMEWORK

<u>Overall approach to population problems</u>: Panama does not have an explicit population policy. The marginality of certain groups within the population is a major concern rather than population size. Population policy concerns include, among other things, integrating marginal groups into the development process, the excessive dispersion of rural population, substantial concentration of urban population and the reduction of infant mortality. The Government has formulated various socio-economic policies with demographic implications in successive national development plans as well as demographic policies in rural and urban development projects and government working documents.

<u>Importance of population policy in achieving development objectives</u>: The Government has recognized the complex interrelationship between development and demographic factors, as well as the problems due to an imbalance between demographic and socio-economic forces. Since 1969 development plans have included explicit demographic policies and have recognized that population policy is essential in articulating socio-economic policies. In 1983 a constitutional amendment mandated the formulation of a national population policy conforming to the country's socio-economic development. The National Programme on Population and Development for the period 1989-1993 proposed that a population policy be defined to reflect the interrelationship between socio-economic and demographic variables.

INSTITUTIONAL FRAMEWORK

<u>Population data systems and development planning</u>: Panama has a long tradition of census-taking, with the first census conducted in 1911 and the most recent in 1980. The next census had been provisionally scheduled for 1990. Birth registration is considered to be complete, while death registration is incomplete. National development strategies are incorporated into the 1986 Plan on Guidelines, Objectives and Activities for the Development of Panama.

<u>Integration of population within development planning</u>: In 1981 the Technical Committee on Population (COTEPO) was created in the Ministry of Planning and Economic Policy to serve as the technical secretariat and advisory body to the National Commission on Demographic Policy. Legally institutionalized in 1987, the principal function of COTEPO is to assure the integration of demographic factors in development planning at the national, regional and local levels and to formulate population policy. The Division of Population in the Ministry of Planning and Economic Policy is responsible for disseminating information on population and development. In 1986 a parliamentary group on population and development was incorporated in the President's team of advisors. A lack of adequate personnel and methodologies directed at population and development has been cited as an impediment to integrating demographic factors in planning.

PANAMA

POLICIES AND MEASURES

<u>Changes in population size and age structure</u>: Although the Government reports that no policies have been formulated to modify the rate of population growth, it is concerned about the age structure of its population, particularly the necessity of providing employment as a consequence of the large proportion of people in the working-age population. Emphasis is placed on economic policies to stimulate employment generation. Policies with consequences for population growth include those to lower infant mortality, to adjust the pattern of spatial distribution and to strengthen programmes dealing with women's issues. A pension scheme covers most workers, while excluding family labour and agricultural workers employed less than six months a year.

<u>Mortality and morbidity</u>: The Government's health policy stresses the provision of health-care coverage to all Panamanians, especially remote rural, marginal urban and adolescent groups. In 1987 a study was carried out by the Ministry of Planning and Economic Policy to identify such groups geographically. Infant and child mortality has also been addressed through efforts to increase immunization and decrease malnutrition. General health measures have included goals to improve access to water, sanitation and health services. Policies also aim to rationalize resources as a result of the Government's austerity campaign. Control of blood banks and venereal diseases has been initiated as a means of limiting the transmission of the AIDS virus.

<u>Fertility and the family</u>: The Government has no official policy to influence fertility trends, but has sought to evaluate continually the requirements and instruments of programmes which may result in reducing fertility. Family planning is an integral part of both the primary health care and the maternal and child health services at all health facilities. The Government promotes and distributes natural and modern methods of family planning through the Ministry of Health and the country's private family planning organization. Adolescent fertility is viewed with concern and a programme of sex education in schools has been instituted. Sex education is also being pursued through the promotion of parental participation and dissemination of sex education through the press. The Government provides family benefits. Sterilization is legal, while abortion is permitted to save the mother's life.

<u>International migration</u>: The Government reports that it has no policies aimed at adjusting the insignificant levels of immigration or emigration. In 1988 an evaluation of the country's refugee population, some of which comes from El Salvador, was begun with the aim of revising objectives in order to develop possibilities of insertion. There were an estimated 1,600 refugees in Panama as of January 1989.

<u>Internal migration/spatial distribution</u>: The Government has actively undertaken strategies to reduce migration to metropolitan areas and increase migration to small- and medium-sized urban and rural areas. Strategies involve establishing and developing other growth centres in less populated and developed areas, the decentralization of public services, financial incentives to new industries, adjustment of transport tariffs, investments in human resources and salary incentives in the health sector in areas of difficult access.

<u>Status of women</u>: The Government, recognizing the economic and demographic impact of women, has actively sought to adopt measures to enhance their status. Social security programmes have been broadened and day-care centres created. Policies encouraging the sharing of parental and family planning responsibilities have also been adopted and the National Work Code has established equal remuneration for equal work. The National Programme on Population and Development (1988-1993) underlines the need to promote the participation of women in development. The population programme, however, considers that for the proposed programmes on women to be effective, there is a need for evaluation, research and reflection on the explicit and implicit policies dealing with women. The Office for Women's Affairs in the Ministry of Labour and Social Welfare and the Programme for the Promotion of Action in Marginal Areas (COPRAM) have received international assistance to strengthen their activities in promoting the participation of Panamanian women in the development process. The minimum legal age at marriage is 18 years for women.

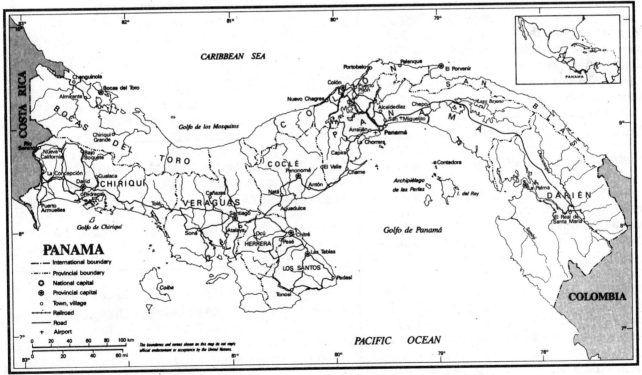

MAP NO.3313   UNITED NATIONS
JANUARY 1985

PAPUA NEW GUINEA

DEMOGRAPHIC INDICATORS	CURRENT PERCEPTION

SIZE/AGE STRUCTURE/GROWTH
 	
Population: 1985   2025
  (thousands) 3 511 8 601
  0-14 years (%) 41.6   32.2
  60+ years (%)   4.6   5.7
 	
Rate of: 1980-85 2020-25
  growth   2.6   1.7
  natural increase 25.8   17.1
	The Government considers the growth rate to be <u>too high</u>.

MORTALITY/MORBIDITY 1980-85 2020-25 Life expectancy 51.9 68.1 Crude death rate 13.1 5.7 Infant mortality 74.0 22.0	Present conditions of health and levels of mortality are regarded as <u>not acceptable</u>.

FERTILITY/NUPTIALITY/FAMILY
 	
             1980-85 2020-25
Fertility rate   5.7   2.7
Crude birth rate 38.8   22.7
Contraceptive
  prevalence rate ...   ...
Female mean age
  at first marriage ...   ...
	The Government considers current fertility levels to be <u>too high</u>.

INTERNATIONAL MIGRATION
 	
             1980-85 2020-25
Net migration rate 0.0   0.0
Foreign-born
  population (%) 0.04 (1980)
	Levels and trends of both immigration and emigration are <u>not significant</u> and <u>satisfactory</u>.

SPATIAL DISTRIBUTION/URBANIZATION
 	
Urban   1985   2025
  population (%) 14.3   38.3
 	
Growth rate: 1980-85 2020-25
  urban   4.3   3.9
  rural   2.3   0.5
	The Government views patterns of spatial distribution as <u>partially appropriate</u>.

GENERAL POLICY FRAMEWORK

Overall approach to population problems: The Government has recognized the need to examine the longer-term implications of population growth. In 1988, guidelines for a future population policy were drafted. Comprehensive policies exist to lower general and infant mortality and to reduce mortality differentials. Various sectoral population distribution strategies have been established such as rural development programmes and programmes for less developed areas.

Importance of population policy in achieving development objectives: In its development plans the Government pays attention to population factors stemming from its conviction that a balance between population and available resources must be found in order to ensure sustained economic and social development. The Government feels that overall development policy is incomplete without a comprehensive population policy. In 1978, a draft population policy submitted to the Government was not approved. In 1988, guidelines for a population policy were submitted to the Government.

INSTITUTIONAL FRAMEWORK

Population data systems and development planning: The country conducted its first complete national census in 1980, as previous censuses in 1966 and 1971 provided only partial coverage. The next census had been provisionally scheduled for 1990. The Manpower and Education Section of the National Planning Office collects demographic data, while the National Statistical Office, also within the National Planning Office prepares population projections and conducts demographic surveys. Since 1975, the Institute for Applied Social and Economic Research (IASER) has reported on the relationship between population and development. Birth and death statistics are considered to be incomplete. In 1976, a National Development Plan was issued as the initial step towards implementing the National Goals and Directive Principles embodied in the Constitution. The 19 new provinces established development strategies but have not yet formulated specific development programmes. A National Public Expenditure Plan was issued for the period 1983-1986.

Integration of population within development planning: In 1987, the Department of Finance and Planning established the National Advisory Committee on Population Policy (NACPP) as the first step in the eventual formulation of a population policy. The Committee, in addition to being charged with the formulation of policy, will oversee and co-ordinate policy implementation once a policy has been approved. The Committee comprises ministerial planning personnel and representatives of major population-related non-governmental organizations. The National Statistical Office prepares population projections.

PAPUA NEW GUINEA

POLICIES AND MEASURES

Changes in population size and age structure: Although the Government is aware that high population growth places burdens on the lives of individuals and on the country, no policy to influence population growth had been formulated as of 1989. However, various policies have been implemented with demographic implications such as those aiming to improve maternal and child health and nutrition, disease control programmes, housing and sanitation. Concerning the social security system, coverage is limited to public employees and persons employed in certain types of firms, with at least 25 employees.

Mortality and morbidity: The National Health Plan for the period 1986-1990 considers primary health care to be the major function of the health system. The Government's major objective has been to achieve an equitable distribution of health-care facilities and to provide comprehensive services by decentralizing health care to the provinces and extending primary health care. Despite budgetary constraints, increased funding was allocated in 1983 for rural health services, community education and provision of village water supplies and to a programme designed to improve primary and preventive health care in the six least developed provinces. Projects are under way to provide adequate maternal and child health, as well as family planning, particularly through proper timing and spacing of births, in order to improve the health of women and children. While overall mortality targets have not been specified, targets for malaria control and environmental sanitation have been identified. The targets generally have been expressed in terms of services provided.

Fertility and the family: The Government has no policy of direct intervention with respect to fertility, even though fertility is viewed as being too high, mainly in relation to family well-being. The Government provides both direct and indirect support to family planning programmes, mostly to improve family health and welfare. Family planning centres have been established throughout the country. Various private organizations also provide family planning services, such as contraceptives, health education, and maternal and child health. Breast-feeding is actively promoted in order to reduce the incidence of diarrhoeal disease. Abortion is available only if the mother's health is at risk. Regulations surrounding sterilization were tightened in 1980 to permit only physicians to perform the procedure. Previously, paramedical personnel could perform sterilizations.

International migration: While the Government has a policy to maintain the level of immigration, there is some fear of job competition from highly skilled immigrants. Immigration ceilings have been established in terms of specific skills, rather than numbers of admissions. As of December 1988, an estimated 5,000 refugees from Irian Jaya, most of whom crossed the border in early 1984, were still accommodated in refugee camps straddling the border. Because of the inaccessibility of the camps, the Government had moved refugees farther inland to a more accessible location in East Awin, on land leased by the Government. Resettlement had been tentatively scheduled for March 1987. While the Office of the United Nations High Commissioner for Refugees continues to facilitate repatriation to Irian Jaya by providing assistance with food, clothes and transportation, it also supports the longer-term installation of those refugees who do not wish to move to East Awin. Concerning emigration, the Government has not formulated a specific policy beyond the usual visa and passport controls.

Spatial distribution/urbanization: While the Government does not report an overall policy to adjust patterns of spatial distribution explicitly, there is concern over the concentration of population and economic activity in Port Moresby, the metropolitan centre, and over wide urban-rural differences (e.g., urban-rural wage differentials, lack of public services and income-earning activities in rural areas). The Department of Urban Development had been making preparations in 1983 to formulate a national urbanization policy, which would be carried out in two stages: the first would deal with the role of Port Moresby in the national urban system and the second would deal with broader national urban policy issues. To retain potential rural-urban migrants, resettlement schemes have been implemented, although there has been some difficulty in reconciling the scheme's dual objectives of assisting residents of disadvantaged areas, while simultaneously attempting to boost export production. The Public Investment Programme for 1988-1992 includes agricultural projects for less developed areas.

Status of women and population: In 1983 the Government established the Office of Youth, Women, Religion and Recreation within the Department of the Prime Minister to strengthen programme development. The Community Women's Organization Programme is an innovative government pilot programme, the core of which is the identification of volunteer female workers recruited from their home villages to work in their villages after an initial training period. The minimum legal age at marriage for women is 16 years.

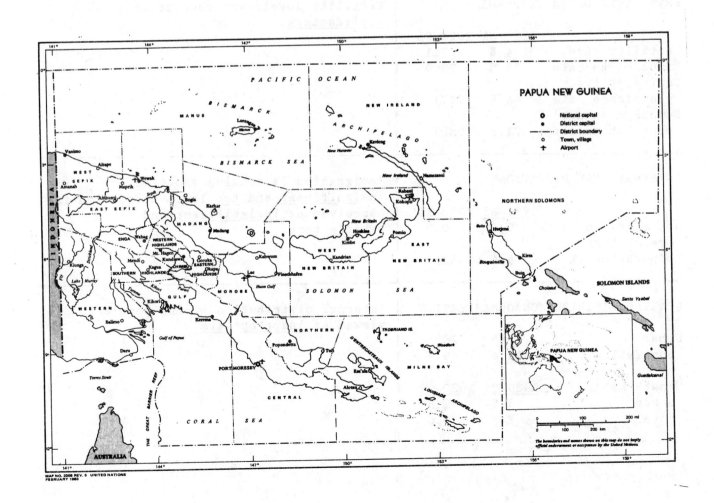

PARAGUAY

DEMOGRAPHIC INDICATORS	CURRENT PERCEPTION
SIZE/AGE STRUCTURE/GROWTH	Current growth rates are seen as <u>satisfactory</u>.

Population: 1985   2025
  (thousands)   3 693   9 182
   0-14 years (%)   41.0   31.3
   60+ years (%)   5.4   9.3
 	
 Rate of: 1980-85   2020-25
  growth   3.2   1.7
  natural increase 29.0 17.2	

MORTALITY/MORBIDITY	Mortality and morbidity levels are perceived as <u>acceptable</u>.
1980-85 2020-25 Life expectancy 66.4 69.6 Crude death rate 6.7 6.6 Infant mortality 45.0 24.0	
FERTILITY/NUPTIALITY/FAMILY	Fertility levels are considered to be <u>satisfactory</u>.

1980-85   2020-25
 Fertility rate   4.8   3.1
 Crude birth rate   35.8   23.9
 Contraceptive
  prevalence rate   44.8 (1987)
 Female mean age
  at first marriage 21.8 (1982)	

INTERNATIONAL MIGRATION	Immigration is considered to be <u>insignificant</u> and <u>too low</u>. Emigration is perceived as <u>insignificant</u> and <u>satisfactory</u>.
1980-85 2020-25 Net migration rate 0.0 0.0 Foreign-born population (%) 5.6 (1982)	
SPATIAL DISTRIBUTION/URBANIZATION	Internal distribution of the population is viewed as <u>inappropriate</u>.

Urban   1985   2025
  population (%)   44.4   69.7
 	
 Growth rate: 1980-85   2020-25
  urban   4.5   2.5
  rural 2.2 0.0	

GENERAL POLICY FRAMEWORK

<u>Overall approach to population problems</u>: Population growth is seen as contributing positively to the country's development. The Government's policy with respect to fertility has focused largely on health-related issues, with policies aiming to improve welfare through better health, especially of mothers and children, education, redistribution of income and increased employment. Health policy consists of developing a hierarchical network by giving priority to the basic and intermediate levels, in order to extend physical accessibility and coverage of services to the entire population. Other policies are in place to modify population distribution and internal migration.

<u>Importance of population policy in achieving development objectives</u>: The Government has indicated that mortality and morbidity and the spatial distribution pattern are its most important population concerns. Population growth is perceived as contributing to the expansion of the domestic market, which is expected to promote the country's development. Programmes are under way to integrate population and socio-economic variables and thus provide the basis for eventually formulating a population policy.

INSTITUTIONAL FRAMEWORK

<u>Population data systems and development planning</u>: Censuses were conducted in 1950, 1962, 1972 and 1982 and are the responsibility of the Directorate-General of Statistics and Census. Owing to problems of cartography and inadequate training of interviewers and field personnel, the 1982 census suffered from significant underenumeration. The next census was provisionally scheduled for 1992. Because of substantial underreporting of births and deaths, a project was launched in 1985 to improve the civil registration system under the Directorate-General of Civil Registry. A civil registration law was passed in 1987 to restructure the organization and simplify and modernize procedures. Personnel have been trained, files microfilmed and the public made aware of the importance of registering vital events. The Five-Year National Development Plan for the period 1984-1989 was prepared by the Technical Secretariat of Planning (STP).

<u>Integration of population within development planning</u>: STP has been responsible for co-ordinating and integrating demographic variables in the planning process since 1977, while the Paraguayan Centre for Population Studies evaluates programmes dealing with the family, the rural sector and marginal populations. A computing centre has been created and integrated demographic and socio-economic projections have been made resulting in the training of STP personnel in computer skills. Demographic statistics were used in formulating the 1984-1989 Development Plan but were not based on the 1982 census, as the data were available too late. The Division of Population and Human Resources is responsible for demographic analysis, population projections and research on socio-economic and demographic relationships.

PARAGUAY

POLICIES AND MEASURES

<u>Changes in population size and age structure</u>: The Government pursues a policy of non-intervention with respect to the rate of population growth. However, sectoral policies are in place to improve population welfare through improved health conditions and family planning activities, redistribution of income and increased employment. Policies have also been created to encourage the settlement of unpopulated areas. A pension scheme covers employed persons while railroad, banking and public employees are covered under a special system.

<u>Mortality and morbidity</u>: The Government intervenes to lower levels of morbidity and mortality. An immunization programme for children and pregnant women has been enacted, as has the extension of safe drinking water through a national health strategy that aims at developing primary health care with community participation. Priority is being given to children, mothers and rural and low-income groups and areas. Objectives include expanding coverage, developing a system of pre-natal and post-natal care, informing and educating women on child-spacing, expanding rural outreach through health promoters and training medical, paramedical and community personnel. Programmes have also been implemented to improve sanitation, drinking water supplies and immunization programmes.

<u>Fertility and the family</u>: While there is no intervention to modify rates of fertility, the Government has programmes to promote positive attitudes, knowledge and practice of responsible parenthood and to improve the provision of family planning services as an integral part of maternal and child health care. Family planning is supported to promote child-spacing and the health of the mother. Health sector policies have been complemented by an education policy that includes family life education in the school system's curricula. Information, education and communication programmes have also been implemented. The public sector has provided natural family planning services as a health measure and as part of maternal and child care, while the private sector has provided other modern methods of contraception that are available on the commercial market. Owing to a rising concern with the welfare of the family and health of the mother, the Government decided in 1988 to expand the provision of family planning to include other methods. Abortion is allowed only to save the life of the mother. There are no specific legal provisions for sterilization, but the law prohibiting corporal injury may apply.

<u>International migration</u>: The Government would like to increase the insignificant level of immigration to the country for the purpose of either residency or work. The country was estimated to have only 50 refugees at the end of 1988. Immigration is viewed as making a positive contribution to the country's economic development. A reduction in emigration in the future is desired.

<u>Spatial distribution/urbanization</u>: The Constitution of Paraguay encourages the settlement of unpopulated areas, and a policy of resettlement has been institutionalized through an agricultural statute law, the creation of the Institute of Rural Welfare and the implementation of numerous land settlement schemes. A decrease in migration towards the major metropolitan area is

encouraged, while greater migration towards other urban and rural areas is desired. The Division of Regional Planning of STP had received international assistance in order to strengthen regional planning at the national level.

<u>Status of women and population</u>: Equal political and civil rights for women are affirmed in Paraguay's Constitution. Women's concerns have representation through established groups such as the Paraguayan League for Women's Rights, the Inter-American Commission of Women and the Department of the Woman Worker. Special programmes on women's health, child-spacing and responsible parenthood have also aimed at improving the status of women. In 1986 a project involving education, training and production activities was begun to enhance the welfare of women, their families and communities through better nutrition and health within a general strategy to increase income-generating options for women and involve them in family decision-making. Information on the minimum legal age at marriage for women is not readily available.

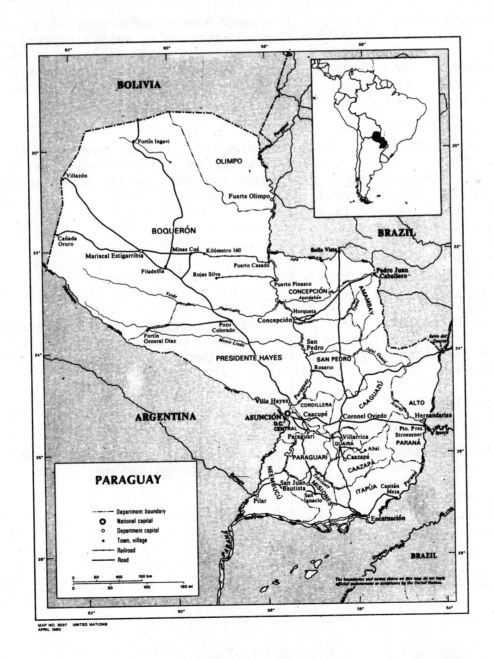

MAP NO. 3097 UNITED NATIONS
APRIL 1980

PERU

DEMOGRAPHIC INDICATORS	CURRENT PERCEPTION
SIZE/AGE STRUCTURE/GROWTH	The Government perceives the current rate of growth as <u>unsatisfactory</u> and <u>too high</u>.

Population: 1985 2025
 (thousands) 19 698 41 006
  0-14 years (%) 40.5 25.2
  60+ years (%) 5.6 11.5

Rate of: 1980-85 2020-25
 growth 2.6 1.2
 natural increase 26.0 11.8

| **MORTALITY/MORBIDITY** | Current levels and trends of mortality are considered to be <u>unacceptable</u>, particularly with reference to infants, pregnant women, Andean and marginal urban areas population. |

  1980-85 2020-25
Life expectancy 58.6 72.0
Crude death rate 10.7 6.4
Infant mortality 99.0 47.0

| **FERTILITY/NUPTIALITY/FAMILY** | The Government views levels of fertility as <u>unsatisfactory</u> and <u>too high</u>. There is major concern over the level of induced abortions. |

  1980-85 2020-25
Fertility rate 5.0 2.3
Crude birth rate 36.7 18.2
Contraceptive
 prevalence rate 45.8 (1986)
Female mean age
 at first marriage 22.7 (1981)

| **INTERNATIONAL MIGRATION** | Levels of immigration and emigration are considered to be <u>not significant</u> and <u>satisfactory</u>. |

  1980-85 2020-25
Net migration rate 0.0 0.0
Foreign-born
 population (%) 0.4 (1981)

| **SPATIAL DISTRIBUTION/URBANIZATION** | Patterns of spatial distribution are viewed as <u>inappropriate</u>. |

Urban 1985 2025
 population (%) 67.4 84.0

Growth rate: 1980-85 2020-25
 urban 3.5 1.5
 rural 0.9 -0.6

GENERAL POLICY FRAMEWORK

<u>Overall approach to population problems</u>: The 1985 National Population Policy Law establishes principles of Government action concerning population which are: to promote a balanced relationship between population and socio-economic development, to enhance responsible parenthood, to attain a significant reduction in morbidity and mortality, and to promote a better territorial distribution of the population. Since 1986, the Government has intensified its efforts towards reducing the fertility rate.

<u>Importance of population policy in achieving development objectives</u>: The Government considers that population and development are closely linked. The goal of the country's population policy, within the context of the development planning process, is to achieve a rate of population growth, a pattern of spatial distribution and an age structure of the population that conform to Peru's socio-economic development.

INSTITUTIONAL FRAMEWORK

<u>Population data systems and development planning</u>: Censuses were conducted in 1961, 1972 and 1981 and are the responsibility of the Instituto Nacional de Estadística. A census had been provisionally scheduled for 1992. Registration of births and deaths is considered incomplete. A new law on civil registration was being considered by the Parliament in 1987. The National Development Plan (1986-1990), prepared by the Instituto Nacional de Planificación, is currently in effect.

<u>Integration of population within development planning</u>: The National Population Council is responsbile for formulating and co-ordinating population policies, while the Population Department, created in 1986 within the Instituto Nacional de Planificación, is charged with taking into account demographic variables in planning. Appointed in 1987 to advise the President, the Presidential Commission on Population will assist in the integration of population within development planning. The Instituto Nacional de Planificación serves as the secretariat for the Commission.

POLICIES AND MEASURES

<u>Changes in population size and age structure</u>: There is an official policy to decrease the rates of growth and natural increase. The Government has established a target rate of growth of around 2 per cent and a population size of 26.9 million by the year 2000. Under the social security scheme, employed persons are covered. Voluntary coverage exists for the self-employed and economically active no longer in covered employment.

PERU

Mortality and morbidity: From the standpoint of mortality policy, the major concerns are: diarrhoeal and gastro-intestinal diseases, measles, malaria, respiratory infections and complications of induced abortion. Malnutrition, unsafe drinking water, defective sanitation and sewage disposal, lack of adequate family planning services and inability to obtain medical supplies are considered the main underlying causes of morbidity and mortality. The principal objectives of the national health policy are to extend coverage to reach the goal of Health for All by the Year 2000 and to reduce the differences in levels of health care received by different segments of the population. Since 1985, the Government has conducted a large campaign of immunization aimed at achieving 100 per cent coverage for all children under one year of age with poliomyelitis, measles, diptheria, whooping cough and tetanus and BCG vaccines by the year 1990, and at obtaining sufficient coverage of pregnant women with tetanus toxoid so that tetanus will cease to be a serious health problem. In 1986, 40 per cent of the population still did not have access to permanent health services. The target is a life expectancy of 63 years for males and 65 years for females by the year 2000.

Fertility and the family: Since the formulation of Peru's 1985 population policy, the Government has increasingly stressed the crucial role of family planning within the development process. To promote the constitutional concept of responsible parenthood, the official policy aims to provide people with the means to decide freely and responsibly the number of children they wish to have. The Government has fixed a target fertility rate of 3.0 for the period 1995-2000. The newly formed Directorate-General of Family Planning, within the Ministry of Health, took charge of the national programme and co-ordination of all activities in the public and private sectors. The main targets of family planning services are the poor living in the suburbs of Lima and in other urban areas. While fertility among adolescents is considered to be a major concern, access to contraception, although generally permitted, is forbidden to unmarried adolescents. In addition, abortion and female sterilization are not considered to be family planning methods. Both are permitted only for health reasons.

International migration: There is no official policy concerning immigration. However, the Government is worried about the number of illegal immigrants entering the country. In order to limit the emigration of professionals, which is a major concern, the State promotes the repatriation, through financial incentives, of Peruvians who, because of their training and experience, are necessary for national, cultural, scientific and technological development.

Spatial distribution/urbanization: No explicit policy exists to alter spatial distribution. The Government has, however, taken several measures to decrease migration into metropolitan areas and has undertaken a development plan in the poor rural regions. Zero interest loans have been granted to small farmers, aimed at encouraging people to remain in, or return to, rural areas. Moreover, the Ministry of Housing has set up a Territorial Development and Rural Housing Programme to provide infrastructure and housing in these areas. In addition, the 1985 National Population Policy Law considers economic and administrative decentralization based on the generation of productive employment and better income distribution as a means of redirecting migratory flows to areas of agricultural and industrial development and limiting the excessive growth of metropolitan areas. The law also prohibits urban expansion into areas of potential or actual agriculture use.

Status of women and population: The Constitution of 1979 eliminated sex discrimination. In 1983, the Government created the Office for Women and in 1986 the Special Commission for Women's Rights. The Government intends to improve the relationship between the sexes through information and education programmes and modification of laws. The minimum legal age at marriage for women is 14 years.

Other issues: The 1985 National Population Policy Law emphasizes the importance of educational programmes in the field of population, including socio-demographic and environmental aspects, family life and sex education. Such programmes are taught at the primary and secondary school levels.

MAP NO.2953 Rev.1 UNITED NATIONS
JANUARY 1986

PHILIPPINES

DEMOGRAPHIC INDICATORS	CURRENT PERCEPTION

SIZE/AGE STRUCTURE/GROWTH
 	
Population: 1985 2025
 (thousands) 55 120 111 393
  0-14 years (%) 41.1 24.9
  60+ years (%) 5.2 10.6
 	
Rate of: 1980-85 2020-25
 growth 2.6 1.1
 natural increase 27.1 11.3
	The Government considers the rate of population growth to be <u>unsatisfactory</u> because it is <u>too high</u>.

MORTALITY/MORBIDITY 1980-85 2020-25 Life expectancy 61.9 72.7 Crude death rate 8.5 6.1 Infant mortality 51.0 17.0	Levels and trends are viewed as <u>unacceptable</u>. Areas of particular concern are infant, child and maternal mortality.
FERTILITY/NUPTIALITY/FAMILY 1980-85 2020-25 Fertility rate 4.7 2.1 Crude birth rate 35.6 17.4 Contraceptive prevalence rate 45.3 (1986) Female mean age at first marriage 22.4 (1980)	Fertility levels and trends are considered to be <u>unsatisfactory</u> because they are <u>too high</u>.
INTERNATIONAL MIGRATION 1980-85 2020-25 Net migration rate 0.0 0.0 Foreign-born population (%) 0.1 (1980)	Immigration levels are perceived as <u>significant</u> and <u>satisfactory</u>, while emigration is felt to be <u>not significant</u> and <u>too high</u>. The brain drain is a cause of particular concern.
SPATIAL DISTRIBUTION/URBANIZATION Urban 1985 2025 population (%) 39.6 66.1 Growth rate: 1980-85 2020-25 urban 3.8 2.1 rural 1.9 -0.6	The pattern of spatial distribution is considered to be <u>inappropriate</u>. There is particular concern about the primacy and high growth rate of Metro Manila.

GENERAL POLICY FRAMEWORK

Overall approach to population problems: Together with economic and social policies, the Government intervenes to modify demographic variables. In 1986 the new administration adopted a cautious approach to population problems and, following a national dialogue, revised the population programme in 1988, largely decentralizing it. The new policy reiterates the importance of the family, stresses responsible parenthood, family welfare and the reduction of fertility, and promotes the integration of population factors within development planning. The ultimate goal is to improve the quality of life for all. Other major objectives are improving the health situation, the provision of primary health care and adjusting patterns of spatial distribution.

Importance of population policy in achieving development objectives: The Government seeks to revitalize the national population programme in support of development objectives. The Population Programme Five-Year Plan for 1989-1993 is intended to expand family planning and service delivery coverage and further to integrate population concerns into national and regional development plans. The National Medium-Term Development Plan for 1987-1992 states that development objectives can be realized only if economic growth is sustained along with the reduction of population growth.

INSTITUTIONAL FRAMEWORK

Population data systems and development planning: Censuses are held decennially, with the most recent in 1980 and the next scheduled for 1990. Vital registration is incomplete. The Population Research Unit, National Census and Statistics Office (NCSO), evaluates census results. The Population Institute, University of the Philippines (UPPI), conducts research, assesses the impact of development policies and programmes on population variables and evaluates the population programme in the context of other development programmes. The National Economic Development Authority (NEDA) prepares national development plans. The 1983-1987 Development Plan, updated in 1984, was made redundant owing to the political and economic crisis. In 1986, the new Government issued a replacement plan, the National Medium-Term Development Plan for the period 1987-1992.

Integration of population within development planning: The Government is aware of the interrelationship between population and development, as shown by the Medium-Term Development Plan. NEDA integrates population factors into development planning, while UPPI provides information on population-development interrelationships and with NCSO takes into account population variables in planning. Responsibility for the national population programme was transferred from the Commission on Population, formerly the overall co-ordinating body, to individual departments, particularly the Department of Health. The Population Programme Five-Year Plan promotes the integration of population in development planning and ensures that national well-being is addressed in development programmes.

POLICIES AND MEASURES

Changes in population size and age structure: Policies seek to modify population growth by reducing fertility, improving well-being and stressing responsible parenthood. The attainment of small family size on a voluntary basis is promoted. Family planning activities are regarded as part of the primary health-care approach. Efforts to improve education, health and socio-economic conditions are pursued to promote the welfare of women, and measures have been adopted to deal with morbidity, mortality, spatial distribution and urbanization. Quantitative targets for fertility levels, population growth, provision of contraceptives and use-effectiveness have been set. A target population of 65.5 million, with an annual growth rate of 2.22 per cent by 1993, has been specified. Social security covers employees, government workers and the self-employed with annual incomes above 1,800 pesos.

Mortality and morbidity: The Medium-Term Development Plan promotes effective, efficient and accessible health services focusing on poor, underserved, unserved and high-risk groups (mothers, children, the aged and workers). Further improvements in a regionally equitable, community-based system of primary health care have been specified. Policies include emphasizing nutrition and family planning programmes as a component of maternal and child health. Information, education and communication campaigns dealing with hygiene, sanitation, oral rehydration, immunization, alcoholism and drug addiction will be strengthened. A greater reliance is to be placed on indigenous technology. Targets include universal child immunization by 1990 and a crude death rate of 7.0 per thousand by 1993.

Fertility and the family: Policy principles include respecting the right of couples to determine family size and voluntarily choose the contraceptive method and promoting family welfare and responsible parenthood. An integrated approach has been adopted to the delivery of health, nutrition and family planning services at the community level. The population programme is characterized by multi-agency participation, the partnership of public and private sectors and stress on population welfare. In 1988, a new mandate was given to the Department of Health as the lead agency in implementing the population programme. Education, information, communication and motivation activities are being intensified and family planning is being promoted to reduce infant and maternal morbidity and mortality. Improvements being made in the communication skills of personnel, outreach activities and overall quality of care are expected to reduce the high contraceptive dropout rate. Targets for 1993 are to extend family planning coverage to an additional 1.5 million couples, to achieve a contraceptive prevalence rate of over 50 per cent and to lower total fertility to 3.7. Sterilization is permitted only for married women over 20 years of age, with at least three living children and the husband's consent. Abortion is viewed as an unacceptable method of contraception and is prohibited by law.

International migration: The Government aims to stem the influx of refugees and asylum-seekers. At the end of 1988, there were 5,030 Vietnamese asylum-seekers in a camp at Palawan, while the Philippine Refugee Processing Centre in Bataan had 9,461 Indo-Chinese, all of whom had been accepted for resettlement. To reduce the exodus of professional and skilled workers and encourage return migration, salaries and opportunities are being improved. The Overseas Employment Program is viewed as a temporary policy to alleviate domestic unemployment, pending the country's full economic recovery. In 1989,

the Philippine Overseas Employment Administration announced that it would
promulgate a new set of rules on overseas employment. There is concern over
the unfavourable working conditions of many single woman migrants.

<u>Spatial distribution/urbanization</u>: Policies encourage more balanced regional
development, population distribution and city-size distribution. To promote
regional development, the 1987-1992 Development Plan includes a land reform
scheme that gives priority to labour-intensive, rural-based small- and medium-
scale enterprises; assistance to low-income communities; population
distribution by industrial dispersion and rural-based development; reinforcing
decentralization efforts; and developing urban systems. Because the Metro
Manila Regional Development Framework Plan which was finalized in 1986, had
not been formally endorsed by local governments and the various agencies,
there was no approved plan overseeing public or private development in Manila.

<u>Status of women and population</u>: The National Commission on Women was created
to integrate women in the development process. The Government recognizes that
female status has a significant impact on demographic trends, and it has
instituted a new family code to eliminate statutory inequities in family
relationships. A major strategy of population, health and nutrition
programmes has been to enhance female status. In 1989, the Philippine
Development Plan for Women was launched to outline measures that address the
poor and disadvantaged not only on the basis of class, ethnicity or region,
but also gender. The legal minimum age at marriage for females is 18 years.

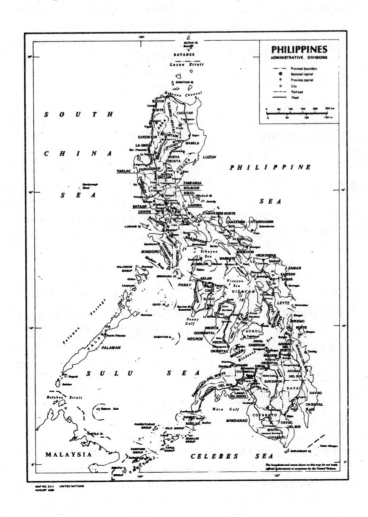

POLAND

DEMOGRAPHIC INDICATORS	CURRENT PERCEPTION

SIZE/AGE STRUCTURE/GROWTH

Population:	1985	2025
(thousands)	37 203	45 066
0-14 years (%)	25.5	19.6
60+ years (%)	13.8	22.2

Rate of:	1980-85	2020-25
growth	0.9	0.3
natural increase	9.6	3.3

The Government perceives the size and growth rate of the population as satisfactory. However, concern is voiced over the present age structure of the population, which is classified as unsatisfactory.

MORTALITY/MORBIDITY

	1980-85	2020-25
Life expectancy	70.9	77.3
Crude death rate	9.6	9.8
Infant mortality	20.0	7.0

Current levels of mortality and morbidity are considered to be unacceptable. Major concerns are excess male mortality in the working-age population due to cardio-vascular diseases, cancer and accidents.

FERTILITY/NUPTIALITY/FAMILY

	1980-85	2020-25
Fertility rate	2.3	2.1
Crude birth rate	19.2	13.1
Contraceptive prevalence rate	75.0 (1977)	
Female mean age at first marriage	22.8 (1984)	

Current fertility levels are perceived as satisfactory. However, the Government is concerned by the high level of induced abortions.

INTERNATIONAL MIGRATION

	1980-85	2020-25
Net migration rate	0.0	0.0
Foreign-born population (%)	...	...

Immigration is felt to be insignificant and satisfactory. Emigration is viewed as significant and too high because of problems associated with the brain drain.

SPATIAL DISTRIBUTION/URBANIZATION

Urban	1985	2025
population (%)	61.0	71.0

Growth rate:	1980-85	2020-25
urban	1.9	0.5
rural	-0.5	0.0

Spatial distribution is considered to be partially appropriate. A major Government concern is the unsatisfactory age distribution in rural areas.

GENERAL POLICY FRAMEWORK

<u>Overall approach to population problems</u>: Government policies are based on the need to establish a stable population. Policies are in place to control internal migration, thus preventing distortions in the age-sex structure of the population and avoiding the depopulation of certain agricultural areas, as well as improving mortality and living conditions.

<u>Importance of population policy in achieving development objectives</u>: Population policy in Poland constitutes an integral part of socio-economic and family policies. The analysis of demographic trends and their consequences for socio-economic policies provides the foundation for formulating development plans and programmes.

INSTITUTIONAL FRAMEWORK

<u>Population data systems and development planning</u>: Censuses were conducted in 1960, 1970, 1978 and 1988 under the direction of the Central Statistical Office. Registration of births and deaths is considered to be complete. Development planning is the responsibility of the Planning Commission of the Council of Ministers. The most recent development plan is the National Socio-Economic Plan for the period 1986-1990.

<u>Integration of population within development planning</u>: The three government agencies charged with the responsbility of formulating and co-ordinating population policy are the National Population Commission, the Council for Family Affairs and the Council for the Aged and Handicapped. Since 1950, the Planning Commission of the Council of Ministers is responsible for taking population variables into account in the planning process. Information on population-development relationships has been provided by the Institute of Statistics and Demography, Central School of Planning and Statistics, since 1975.

POLICIES AND MEASURES

<u>Changes in population size and age structure</u>: The country's demographic processes have been adversely influenced by irregularities in the age structure of the population, as a consequence of alternating periods of baby "booms" and baby "busts". Consequently, the Government seeks to achieve stable population growth. To this end, policies have been implemented to encourage family well-being, improve health and socio-economic conditions, reduce migration from rural areas and reverse the negative immigration balance. Government policies take into consideration the growing number of the aged and its economic implications. Polish society is responsible for protecting the standards of living of the aged and this is reflected in appropriate budget allocations.

POLAND

<u>Mortality and morbidity</u>: The right to health care is guaranteed by the Polish Constitution. Free medical care is provided to all workers and their families. Health-care development is promoted through five-year plans at the central and provincial levels adopted by the Sejm and the relevant national provincial councils, respectively. In addition, the Ministry of Health and Social Welfare has prepared detailed programmes on specific issues such as diseases of the circulatory system, cancer, maternal and child health and worker's health. The policy is to undertake improvements in health care and mortality and morbidity rates by expanding and modernizing the health-care infrastructure, improving health education and promoting healthy life-styles. Efforts are under way to alleviate a severe shortage of pharmaceuticals by increasing their production and supply. Poland has established a Council for AIDS, has created training programmes for medical personnel in AIDS-related problems and is testing persons belonging to high-risk groups. Targets include an infant mortality rate of 10 per thousand by the year 2000.

<u>Fertility and the family</u>: The State's current policy is to encourage the well-being of the family as a whole. An extensive system of social benefits is in existence and includes paid maternity leave, a three-year leave for child-rearing, annual leave for taking care of sick children of up to 60 days annually, birth grants, family allowances to low-income families and loans and scholarships to assist student marriages until the couple is financially independent. Family life education courses have been established in schools. With the aim of strengthening the family, the Government announced in 1987 that it was creating a Council for the Family to identify government activities that could affect family life. An alimony fund ensures a minimum income to divorced mothers not receiving alimony. The Government has voiced its concern over the high number of induced abortions and the lack of popularity of contraceptive methods. Abortion is legal in Poland and is free in government health facilities. As of September 1981, abortions in public health facilities must be authorized by a physician and the woman must be informed about contraceptive methods by her doctor. Sterilization is prohibited for both men and women.

<u>International migration</u>: The insignificant level of immigration is not an active policy concern. In recent years, several thousand foreigners, mainly from the Middle East seeking asylum in Western Europe, have transited through Poland. Emigration, however, is viewed as being too high. Emigration is permitted only on family, economic and humanitarian grounds. The Government's policy to encourage the return of citizens who have emigrated is based on the key objective of maintaining and using all citizens for the improvement of society. The Government has been concerned over the consequences of the emigration of professionals and skilled workers. An economic reform, designed to improve living and working conditions in Poland, has been introduced. In 1987, the Government asked all Polish emigrants to return to Poland.

<u>Spatial distribution/urbanization</u>: Policies are in place to stem the flow of rural-to-urban migration, which has brought about distortions in the age-sex distribution of population and the depopulation of certain agricultural areas. Strategies include reducing metropolitan growth, promoting small town growth, the development of lagging and border regions, and rural development. Among the various measures are State investment in new industries,

restrictions on industrial location, decentralization of administrative functions and human resources investment. The Planning Commission of the Council of Ministers has issued a number of documents on this issue such as the "Foundations of a National Town and Country Development Plan until 1995" in 1986 and an evaluation of town and country development in 1987.

<u>Status of women and population</u>: Equal rights of men and women are guaranteed by the Constitution of the Polish People's Republic. The Family Code calls for the joint sharing of family responsibilities between husband and wife and for the legal adjudication of disputes. There is an attempt, by establishing maternity, paternity and educational leave, to create conditions that permit women to combine labour market activities with family responsibilities. The Government has stated that while all institutional barriers that barred women from education, vocational training, professional work and health care have been abolished, some traditions as well as cultural and economic barriers still hinder the achievement of complete equality between men and women. The minimum legal age at marriage for women is 16 years.

EUROPE

The boundaries shown on this map do not imply official endorsement or acceptance by the United Nations.

MAP NO. 2771.13   UNITED NATIONS
SEPTEMBER 1990

PORTUGAL

DEMOGRAPHIC INDICATORS	CURRENT PERCEPTION

SIZE/AGE STRUCTURE/GROWTH
 	
Population: <u>1985</u>   <u>2025</u>
 (thousands)   10 157   10 935
  0-14 years (%)   23.5   17.1
  60+ years (%)   17.0   24.8
 	
Rate of: <u>1980-85</u> <u>2020-25</u>
 growth   0.8   0.0
 natural increase   5.1   0.8
	The rate of population growth is viewed as <u>satisfactory</u>.

MORTALITY/MORBIDITY <u>1980-85</u> <u>2020-25</u> Life expectancy 72.2 78.8 Crude death rate 9.6 10.6 Infant mortality 20.0 6.0	The Government considers the present level of mortality to be <u>unacceptable</u>. Infant mortality and differential mortality are particular concerns.
FERTILITY/NUPTIALITY/FAMILY <u>1980-85</u> <u>2020-25</u> Fertility rate 2.0 1.9 Crude birth rate 14.7 11.4 Contraceptive prevalence rate 66.3 (1979/80) Female mean age at first marriage 22.1 (1981)	The level of fertility is considered to be <u>satisfactory</u>.
INTERNATIONAL MIGRATION <u>1980-85</u> <u>2020-25</u> Net migration rate 0.0 -0.4 Foreign-born population (%) 2.9 (1981)	Both immigration and emigration are considered to be <u>insignificant</u> and <u>satisfactory</u>.
SPATIAL DISTRIBUTION/URBANIZATION Urban <u>1985</u> <u>2025</u> population (%) 31.2 57.8 Growth rate: <u>1980-85</u> <u>2020-25</u> urban 1.5 1.3 rural 0.3 -1.6	The spatial distribution is viewed as <u>inappropriate</u>.

GENERAL POLICY FRAMEWORK

Overall approach to population problems: The Government has implemented various socio-economic measures that deal with spatial distribution of the population, support of emigration, support for emigrants' return, educational and social security policy, and health and family planning policy.

Importance of population policy in achieving development objectives: The Government has indicated that while it has not formulated an integrated overall population policy, there are sectoral programmes and policies that have an impact on population. The Government intends to integrate population variables in the planning process through development plans. One of the major objectives of such development plans is the realization of the human potential.

INSTITUTIONAL FRAMEWORK

Population data systems and development planning: The most recent census was conducted by the National Statistical Institute in 1981. The next census is scheduled for 1991. Vital registration is considered to be complete. The annual development plan for 1988 prepared by the Secretária de Estado do Planeamento e do Desenvolvimento Regional aims to develop and modernize the country.

Integration of population within development planning: The Centre for Population Studies, part of the National Statistical Institute, is the agency responsible for analysing population variables and for the formulation and co-ordination of population policies. The Central Planning Department is charged with including population variables in planning.

POLICIES AND MEASURES

Changes in population size and age structure: The Government has indicated that it has not formulated any population policies intended to influence the size or growth of the population. However, many socio-economic measures have been implemented to deal with health conditions, family planning services, family benefits, the spatial distribution of the population and support for emigration and returning emigrants.

Mortality and morbidity: The Government accords high priority to the primary health-care approach, based on the active involvement of communities. Specific attention has focused on environmental sanitation, which is a problem in rural areas, and the National Vaccination Plan. Vaccination against rubella was made mandatory in 1984 and against mumps in 1987. To reduce infant mortality to the levels prevailing in the rest of Europe, programmes of maternal and child health have been implemented. In addition, information

PORTUGAL

campaigns have been undertaken against drug, alcohol and tobacco abuse and centres have been built for the treatment of drug addiction. In 1984, a new Directorate-General of Primary Health Care was created. To reallocate human and financial resources more efficiently, a decentralization process was established, such as the creation of regional health boards with administrative autonomy. In 1985, a Working Group on AIDS was created for the purpose of co-ordinating government efforts to combat the disease.

Fertility and the family: The Government does not intervene with respect to the level of fertility, although various indirect measures have been implemented within the sphere of family policy and without any demographic objectives. The family is viewed as an essential element of Portuguese society and policies have as their aim the protection of maternity and paternity, as well as strengthening the family unit. Among the measures are a maternity benefit of 100 per cent of earnings payable during 30 days before and 60 days after confinement, and as of 1987, a marriage grant of 10,000 escudos (Esc 146 = $US 1 as of 1986), a birth grant of 12,000 escudos for each birth, a nursing allowance of 2,200 escudos per month for up to 10 months, a family allowance of 1,120 escudos a month for the first two children and 1,680 escudos for each subsequent child. Provision of contraceptives is directly supported by the Government. Abortion in the first 12 weeks of pregnancy is permitted only when the mother's physical or mental health is in danger, when there is irreversible malformation of the foetus or if the pregnancy results from rape. Sterilization is permitted for women over the age of 25 years. A target had been specified of providing contraceptives to 30 per cent of women in the child-bearing years by 1989.

International migration: The insignificant level of immigration is not an active policy concern. Concerning emigration, article 44 of the Constitution of the Portuguese Republic establishes the right to free emigration and also guarantees the right of return to Portugal. The Government has sought to create favourable conditions for the reintegration of Portuguese emigrants who decide to resettle permanently in Portugal. In 1985, the first centre was opened in Portugal to provide information and assistance to returning Portuguese migrants. To protect the rights of Portuguese emigrants, the Council of Portuguese Communities, a governmental consultative body composed of emigrant representatives from around the world, was created in 1982.

Spatial distribution/urbanization: To readjust the inappropriate pattern of spatial distribution, various measures have been implemented and include public infrastructure subsidies, grants, loan and tax incentives to new industries, decentralization of administrative functions, migration assistance and investments in human resources. Territorial policy is carried out through regional plans for comprehensive territorial development, specific sectoral policies and integrated regional development. Preparation of these plans is the responsibility of the Ministry of Planning and Territorial Administration. International assistance has been received for training to support the development of rural zones suffering from the effects of depopulation.

Status of women and population: Although there is not yet a specific policy related to the status of women and aimed at influencing demographic trends, the Portuguese Civil Code describes responsibilities shared between married couples concerning family life and children's education. It foresees in a concrete way that marriage is based on the equal rights and duties of husband and wife. In 1988, the Government reported its intention to increase female participation in the modernization of Portuguese society through various measures. Discriminatory employment practices will be eliminated and programmes of professional training for women will be developed to raise female labour force participation. The minimum legal age at marriage for women is 16 years.

QATAR

DEMOGRAPHIC INDICATORS	CURRENT PERCEPTION
SIZE/AGE STRUCTURE/GROWTH	Population growth among the national population of Qatar is seen as <u>unsatisfactory</u> and <u>too low</u>. A rapidly growing native-born population is considered to be a means of reducing future dependence on expatriate labour.

Population:	1985	2025
(thousands)	299	863
0-14 years (%)	33.9	33.5
60+ years (%)	2.6	11.7

Rate of:	1980-85	2020-25
growth	5.3	2.0
natural increase	30.0	19.6

MORTALITY/MORBIDITY	Mortality and morbidity levels are seen as <u>acceptable</u>.

	1980-85	2020-25
Life expectancy	67.6	76.8
Crude death rate	4.6	5.7
Infant mortality	38.0	9.0

FERTILITY/NUPTIALITY/FAMILY	Fertility rates are seen as <u>satisfactory</u>.

	1980-85	2020-25
Fertility rate	5.9	3.6
Crude birth rate	34.6	25.3
Contraceptive prevalence rate	...	...
Female mean age at first marriage	...	...

INTERNATIONAL MIGRATION	Immigration is viewed as <u>significant</u> and <u>satisfactory</u>. Emigration is seen as <u>insignificant</u> and <u>satisfactory</u>.

	1980-85	2020-25
Net migration rate	0.0	0.0
Foreign-born population (%)	...	...

SPATIAL DISTRIBUTION/URBANIZATION	Spatial distribution pattern of the population is viewed as <u>appropriate</u>.

Urban	1985	2025
population (%)	88.0	94.3

Growth rate:	1980-85	2020-25
urban	5.7	2.1
rural	2.3	0.3

GENERAL POLICY FRAMEWORK

Overall approach to population problems: The Government sees the purpose of all efforts in the population field as improving the quality of life through the provision of social and economic security, the protection and welfare of the individual and family, the provision of adequate housing and nutrition, the exploitation of natural resources and wealth, and the protection of the environment.

Importance of population policy in achieving development objectives: The general population policy of Qatar aims at promoting development in all of its facets. The Government seeks a balanced policy of development in the context of the large resident foreign-born population upon which it depends to meet its labour needs.

INSTITUTIONAL FRAMEWORK

Population data systems and development planning: Qatar's first census was conducted in 1970 but was affected by age misreporting, underenumeration of females and misreporting of nationality by older immigrants. Data from the census were never officially published. The second census was conducted in 1986 by the Central Statistical Organization (CSO). The collection and publication of vital statistics was begun by CSO in the early 1980s. CSO also has responsibility for conducting special demographic surveys to meet specific needs of planning. In 1987 a programme for training in basic demographic methods was begun.

Integration of population within development planning: There is no single government agency that is responsible for the formulation or co-ordination of population policies. Since 1980 CSO has been chiefly responsible for providing information on population-development interrelationships.

POLICIES AND MEASURES

Changes in population size and age structure: The Government has expressed interest in reducing its labour dependence on the foreign-born segment of the population, which comprises over 50 per cent of the total population. It recognizes, however, that the demand for immigrant labour is unlikely to diminish in the near future and therefore balances this recognition with a desire to increase the native-born population. The provision of free schooling and health services to all residents is consistent with this balanced approach. Qatar has one of the most advanced and extensive welfare systems in the Gulf and is committed to ensuring that oil wealth benefits all citizens of Qatar. There is no information readily available on the status of social security schemes.

QATAR

Mortality and morbidity: The national health system requires that comprehensive primary health-care services constitute the basis for supporting hospital services.   Health centres established in Doha, the capital, and other areas provide preventive, as well as curative and rehabilitative, services in addition to maternal and child care, and family and individual health registration.   Provision of health services is free to the entire population. The State covers the expenses of treating its nationals abroad in the event that the necessary medical treatment cannot be provided locally.   The Government hopes that eventually the provision of health services will be undertaken by nationals of Qatar.   Co-operation with members of the Gulf Co-operation Council exists in a number of fields such as drugs, health manpower development, information regarding treatment abroad and the specialized curative services available in each country.

Fertility and the family: The Government's policy is one of intervention to maintain the rate of fertility.   Family allowances for each child are granted to male heads of households employed in the government sector.   There are no major limits on access to contraception and there is no government support of contraceptive use or distribution.   There is no information readily available on the legal status of abortion or sterilization in Qatar, but the criminal code is assumed to apply in both contexts.

International migration: Issues of active policy concern for the Government are the immigration of foreign workers and their dependants, who compose over one half of the total population, and the number of undocumented immigrants. The policy is to reduce eventually immigration and dependency on foreign labour by the replacement of expatriate workers with nationals.   However, the necessity of immigrant labour is recognized.   All of Qatar's residents are entitled to free public health care and schooling.   Security is an important basis for the country's strict entry and immigration rules and the administration of its foreign manpower programmes has been tightened.   In 1985 laws were introduced limiting the activities of non-nationals in trade and industry.   In 1986, territorial conflict between Qatar and Bahrain resulted in the deportation of some Bahrainis living in the country.

Spatial distribution/urbanization: The Government has enacted a development programme with all the necessary facilities such as health centres, educational institutions, social services and youth welfare aiming to encourage settlement in urban areas outside of Doha.   Through the establishment of various industrial complexes in Qatar, new urban settlements have been developed.   The industrial centre of Umm Said, south of Doha, is being extensively developed, while as of 1987 a new town was being planned for Ras Laffan in the north-east, near the site of a huge offshore gas development.   In addition, the Government has also encouraged agricultural development as a means of promoting new settlements.

Status of women and population: Considerable attention has been given to equality of education for girls.   There is no information readily available on the minimum legal age of marriage for women.

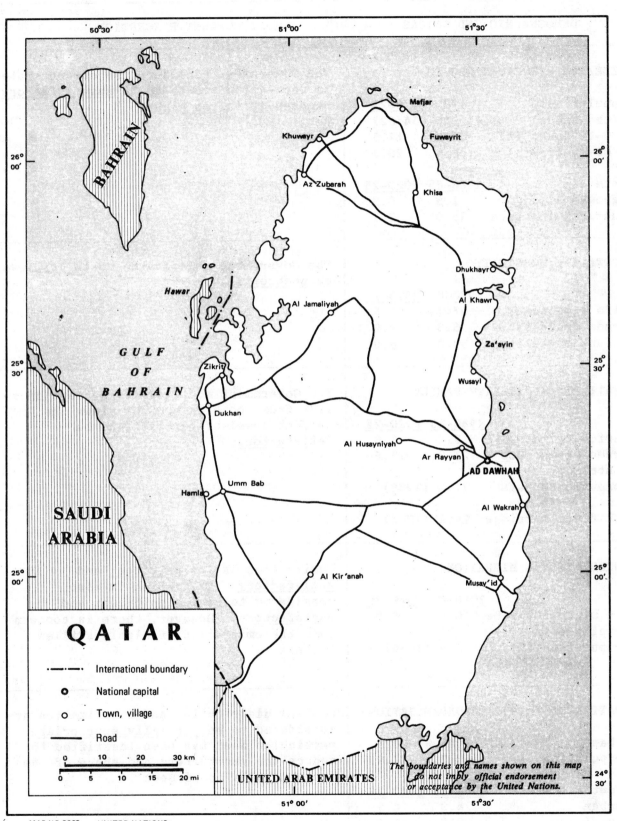

QATAR

---·--- International boundary

◎ National capital

○ Town, village

——— Road

REPUBLIC OF KOREA

DEMOGRAPHIC INDICATORS	CURRENT PERCEPTION

SIZE/AGE STRUCTURE/GROWTH
 	
Population: <u>1985</u>   <u>2025</u>
 (thousands)   41 056   54 627
  0-14 years (%)   30.0   17.5
  60+ years (%)   6.8   20.7
 	
Rate of: <u>1980-85</u>   <u>2020-25</u>
 growth   1.5   0.3
 natural increase   15.0   2.7
	The Government considers the current rate of population growth to be <u>unsatisfactory</u> because it is <u>too high</u>.

MORTALITY/MORBIDITY <u>1980-85</u> <u>2020-25</u> Life expectancy 67.7 76.6 Crude death rate 6.3 8.9 Infant mortality 30.0 8.0	The Government regards the mortality level as <u>unacceptable</u>.
FERTILITY/NUPTIALITY/FAMILY <u>1980-85</u> <u>2020-25</u> Fertility rate 2.4 1.8 Crude birth rate 21.3 11.6 Contraceptive prevalence rate 77.0 (1988) Female mean age at first marriage 24.1 (1980)	The Government modified its perception in 1988 from too high and now views the current level of fertility to be <u>satisfactory</u>.
INTERNATIONAL MIGRATION <u>1980-85</u> <u>2020-25</u> Net migration rate 0.0 0.0 Foreign-born population (%) 1.5 (1980)	Immigration is <u>insignificant</u> and <u>satisfactory</u>. Emigration is also considered to be <u>insignificant</u> and <u>satisfactory</u>. However, there is concern over the emigration of highly skilled workers.
SPATIAL DISTRIBUTION/URBANIZATION Urban <u>1985</u> <u>2025</u> population (%) 65.3 87.9 Growth rate: <u>1980-85</u> <u>2020-25</u> urban 4.3 0.5 rural -2.9 -1.4	Spatial distribution and urbanization are considered to be <u>partially appropriate</u>. A particular need has been identified to reduce the growth rate and share of the urban population of Seoul.

GENERAL POLICY FRAMEWORK

Overall approach to population problems: The Government has formulated a comprehensive population policy directed primarily at reducing population growth. Considerable success has been achieved in modifying both fertility and mortality, although the need to lower fertility further has led to strengthening family planning efforts. The scope of population policy now extends to broader welfare-oriented policies. The Government's attempts to decentralize population away from Seoul began in the late 1960s. Since then, increasing attention has been given to adjusting the spatial distribution pattern, improving social equity and the status of women and securing the welfare of the aged.

Importance of population policy in achieving development objectives: The Government has consistently accorded major importance to its population policy in order to achieve development objectives. The national family planning programme, instituted in 1962, has been promoted as a major policy objective. Rapid population growth continues to be considered a hindrance to socio-economic progress and income growth, and also adds to the already high population density. The implications of population growth for education, employment, social security and other sectors and programmes are recognized, as is the importance of more balanced regional development.

INSTITUTIONAL FRAMEWORK

Population data systems and development planning: Censuses are held every five years, with the last census conducted in 1985 by the National Bureau of Statistics. A census had been provisionally scheduled for 1990. Vital registration is considered to be virtually complete. The institutional bases for both economic planning and population research have become increasingly sophisticated. Various agencies collect and research demographic data. Ongoing monitoring and evaluation of population processes and policies are chiefly conducted by the Korean Institute for Population and Health (KIPH). The Fifth Five-Year Economic and Social Development Plan (1982-1986) placed greater emphasis on social development than previous plans, which were mostly concerned with fostering economic growth. The Sixth Five-Year Economic and Social Development Plan for the period 1987-1991 is currently in effect.

Integration of population within development planning: The major population research centre, KIPH, provides information for policy-making to the Ministry of Health and Social Welfare and other ministries. The Manpower Development Division of the Economic Planning Board also takes into account population variables in development planning and is largely responsible for formulating population policy. The national family planning programme has always been an integral part of the five-year development plans. In the 1980s demographic parameters became more widely incorporated into development planning. The Fifth Five-Year Plan attempted to integrate more fully population and development policies and the Sixth Five-Year Plan further emphasized the importance of population variables.

POLICIES AND MEASURES

Changes in population size and age structure: The Government has adopted various measures to lower population growth. The most far reaching has been the family planning programme, which together with rapid socio-economic changes, has contributed to a substantial reduction of fertility. Fertility policy measures were strengthened in the 1980s to account for the post-Korean War baby boom generation entering the reproductive ages. For the Sixth Five-Year Economic and Social Development Plan, a target rate of 1.0 per cent growth by 1993 was set so as to attain zero population growth by 2025. Measures are also in place to assure the long-term care of the aged. The national pension system implemented in 1988 covers all those aged 18 to 60 years not otherwise covered.

Mortality and morbidity: Rapid gains in health status have been achieved owing to progress in public health, medical technology and socio-economic development. Major strategies have included extending primary health care to rural areas, improving the accessibility and quality of medical care, and improving nutritional status and environmental and sanitary conditions, especially the provision of clean water. Recent efforts have been directed at strengthening and improving maternal and child health care and family planning services, which have become increasingly integrated. Target groups include the urban poor and those in remote rural areas. The medical insurance scheme has been extended and universal coverage was expected to be achieved by 1989. Specified targets include a life expectancy of 70 years for males and 74 years for females and an infant mortality rate of 15 per thousand by the year 2000.

Fertility and the family: A host of new measures have been implemented to lower fertility, such as monetary incentives to encourage both the one-child family and sterilization after the first delivery, improved contraceptive record-keeping, a greater focus on women aged 20 to 30 years and the use of mobile family planning clinics targeted at high-risk groups, i.e., young persons with limited education, the urban poor and remote rural residents. Exemptions from the education allowance tax are available only for the first two children. The Government promotes information, education and communication activities and public awareness on population matters. Measures are also in effect to enhance female status and reduce preference for sons. The national family planning programme employs both field workers and physicians, uses public and private sector channels and provides all contraceptives free of charge. Population and family planning education are included in the school curriculum. Menstrual regulation is subsidized and abortion and sterilization are permitted. Welfare assistance and housing loan priorities are provided to women with one child who accept sterilization and subsidies are available to low-income acceptors to compensate for lost wages. The target is a total fertility rate of 1.86 by 1991.

International migration: The insignificant immigration level is not an active policy concern. Although the Government reported in 1988 that it did not have an emigration policy, an annual emigration target of 40,000 had been incorporated into the country's population projections. The substantial outflow of temporary workers, largely employed by national construction and business companies in the Middle East, has been regulated and managed by an array of laws. The Ministry of Labour establishes overseas employment policy, licenses worker recruitment and regulates the management of overseas workers.

The Government is concerned over the brain drain and has taken steps to reduce it, as for example by requiring that some overseas trainees return to the country.

<u>Spatial distribution/urbanization</u>: The Government has sought to reduce urban primacy, curb the metropolitan growth of Seoul and Pusan and stabilize city size distribution. Policies seek to redress spatial imbalances between rural and urban areas, different regions and cities of varying size. Strategies include tax incentives for industries to relocate from Seoul, the creation of satellite cities and, as part of the National Land Development Plan, 1982–1991, new growth poles, the improvement of educational facilities in non–urban areas and services in smaller cities, zoning restrictions and the relocation of government offices away from Seoul. Resettlement allowances for the urban poor and greater employment opportunities in regional growth centres have been provided. In 1988, it was reported that two satellite cities would be built in Pundang and Ilsang, villages on the outskirts of Seoul.

<u>Status of women and population</u>: The Government feels that improved female status is needed to meet demographic targets and enhance women's well–being. In 1983, the Labour Standard Law was revised to provide job opportunities in areas traditionally reserved for men, while the Korean Women's Development Institute and the National Committee on Women's Policies were created to study women's issues and reflect findings in national policies. The Sixth Five–Year Plan included provisions for maternity leave, more nurseries and the gradual revision of family law to enable women to become the head of the family and to eliminate sexual discrimination in property inheritance. The minimum legal age at marriage for women is 20 years.

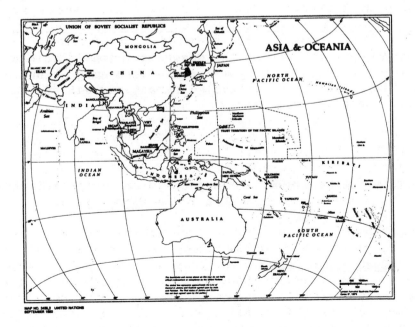

ROMANIA

DEMOGRAPHIC INDICATORS	CURRENT PERCEPTION
SIZE/AGE STRUCTURE/GROWTH	Although population growth rates are considered to be <u>satisfactory</u>, the Government is very concerned by the age structure as a consequence of the two world wars and population aging.

Population: 1985 2025
(thousands) 22 725 25 745
  0-14 years (%) 24.7 18.4
  60+ years (%) 14.4 20.9
 	
Rate of: 1980-85 2020-25
 growth 0.5 0.2
 natural increase 5.6 1.7	

MORTALITY/MORBIDITY	Mortality levels are viewed as <u>acceptable</u>. There is concern, however, for infants and young children and the aged.
1980-85 2020-25 Life expectancy 69.6 77.1 Crude death rate 10.2 10.4 Infant mortality 26.0 7.0	
FERTILITY/NUPTIALITY/FAMILY	The Government considers the level of fertility to be <u>unsatisfactory</u> and <u>too low</u>. It is felt to be undesirable from the demographic, political, economic and social point of view.
1980-85 2020-25 Fertility rate 2.2 1.9 Crude birth rate 15.8 12.2 Contraceptive prevalence rate 58.0 (1978) Female mean age at first marriage 21.1 (1977)	
INTERNATIONAL MIGRATION	The Government considers the levels of immigration and emigration to be <u>insignificant</u> and <u>satisfactory</u>.
1980-85 2020-25 Net migration rate 0.0 0.0 Foreign-born population (%)	
SPATIAL DISTRIBUTION/URBANIZATION	The perception of spatial distribution is that it is <u>appropriate</u>.
Urban 1985 2025 population (%) 49.0 60.9 Growth rate: 1980-85 2020-25 urban 0.8 0.7 rural 0.1 -0.6	

GENERAL POLICY FRAMEWORK

<u>Overall approach to population problems</u>: The Government aims to raise growth rates by encouraging higher fertility rates, consolidating the role of the family, adjusting the age structure, reducing mortality, and affirming the role of women as active participants in societal development. Population policy is fully integrated in socio-economic policy, and the achievement of a sufficient level of growth is considered to be necessary to ensure an optimal population age distribution.

<u>Importance of population policy in achieving development objectives</u>: Demographic policy is organically integrated with the country's general policy towards economic and social development. The achievement of a sufficient level of growth is viewed as necessary to ensure an optimal distribution of the population by age.

INSTITUTIONAL FRAMEWORK

<u>Population data systems and development planning</u>: Population censuses were conducted in 1948, 1956, 1966 and 1977 by the Central Statistical Office, which also prepares population estimates. The next census was provisionally scheduled for 1991. Development plans are prepared by the State Planning Commission. The Seventh Five-Year Plan for the period 1986-1990 is currently in effect.

<u>Integration of population within development planning</u>: Since 1971, the National Commission for Demography has been responsible for the formulation and co-ordination of population policies. The Commission is also responsible for co-ordinating demographic research at the national level and for undertaking special demographic surveys. Since 1949 the State Committee for Planning has been responsible for taking into account population variables in planning. The Central Statistical Office, in collaboration with the State Committee for Planning and the National Commission for Demography, has since 1950 prepared population projections used in development and programme planning. Information on population-development interrelationships has been provided, since 1953, by the Institute of the Socialist Economy.

POLICIES AND MEASURES

<u>Changes in population size and age structure</u>: The Government has a policy of intervention to raise rates of population growth. The target is a total population of 25 million by 1990 and 30 million by the year 2000. Government objectives include increasing fertility, lowering the death rate and infant mortality, boosting the rate of natural increase and ensuring a balanced age distribution of the population.

ROMANIA

Mortality and morbidity: The Romanian Constitution guarantees the right of health protection to all citizens. Health care is an integral part of socio-economic development plans, and health objectives are included in the Government's long-term, medium-term and annual programmes. At the district level, plans are adapted to local circumstances. The Government seeks to improve levels of morbidity and mortality further, including infant mortality. Medical care is free and health services are equally accessible to all citizens. The Government also seeks to integrate preventive, curative and recuperative care at the level of the collectives. An increase in medical personnel, hospitals, dispensaries and health centres is also being promoted.

Fertility and the family: The Government's pro-natalist policy sought to boost fertility to 19-20 births per thousand population. Measures included those for the improvement of the status of women, for the care and protection of the aged, child welfare allowances, and maternity, paternity and other family benefits. Women were eligible for maternity leave payable for up to 52 days before and 60 days after confinement up to a maximum of 94 per cent of earnings for the third child and subsequent children, a reduction in working hours with no loss of salary, and special paid leave to look after sick children. Lump sum birth grants, monthly child allowances which increase with higher birth order and allowances to families with low income are also provided. The legal marrying age for girls was reduced from 18 to 15 years of age. Special classes for pregnant students were organized to permit them to resume their secondary level schooling after giving birth. Those not married by age 25 paid an additional surtax on wages. One of the first acts of the new Government in December 1989 was to repeal the law that strictly limited abortions. Abortion is now permitted on demand up to 12 weeks of pregnancy. Contraception has also been legalized.

International migration: International migration is not a major policy concern of the Government. Romania, which in recent years has sent specialists to the Union of Soviet Socialist Republics, Bulgaria and Hungary to work on various projects of the Council for Mutual Economic Assistance (CMEA), has received similar manpower from the German Democratic Republic, Czechoslovakia and the Soviet Union.

Spatial distribution/urbanization: The specific objectives are to continue to assure a national distribution of the population within various territories and zones; to assure a "socio-professional structure" corresponding to a modern economy, by increasing the proportion of the population engaged in industry; to increase the productivity of the labour force; and to establish a new equilibrium between the urban and rural population. Strategies were aimed at slowing metropolitan growth, promoting small towns and intermediate cities, and rural and regional development for lagging regions. Policy instruments include: public infrastructure subsidies and development, direct restrictions and controls on industrial location, direct state investment, transport rate and interregional cost adjustments, housing and social services, human resource investments and job training and residential controls. Regional development policies were included in the National Programme for Territorial Systematization of all regions until 1990 and were officially adopted in one-year and five-year plans. Special attention is given to the development in rural areas and small cities of small-scale industry, communal administration as well as various socio-cultural services. To stabilize the size of the rural population, 556 local community centres were to be consolidated into agro-industrial centres and a number of rural centres were to receive the status of new towns.

<u>Status of women and population</u>: The Government reported in 1987 that all institutional discrimination against women had been eliminated. The National Commission on Women is responsible for the elimination of discrimination against women. The minimum legal age at marriage for women is 15 years.

<u>Other issues</u>: At the time of the preparation of this publication, little information was readily available as to the extent to which the Government that assumed power in December 1989 maintains the same perceptions or policies regarding population phenomena as the previous Government. Consequently, the description presented above is based largely on the perceptions and policies of the previous administration.

MAP NO. 2771.15   UNITED NATIONS
SEPTEMBER 1990

RWANDA

DEMOGRAPHIC INDICATORS	CURRENT PERCEPTION

SIZE/AGE STRUCTURE/GROWTH
 	
Population: 1985   2025
 (thousands) 6 102 18 079
  0–14 years (%) 49.0   32.5
  60+ years (%)   3.9   5.2
 	
Rate of: 1980–85 2020–25
 growth   3.3   1.7
 natural increase 33.3   16.7
	Growth rates are felt to be <u>unsatisfactory</u> and <u>too high</u>.

MORTALITY/MORBIDITY 1980–85 2020–25 Life expectancy 46.5 62.5 Crude death rate 18.8 7.6 Infant mortality 132.0 61.0	Current levels and trends are considered to be <u>unacceptable</u>.
FERTILITY/NUPTIALITY/FAMILY 1980–85 2020–25 Fertility rate 8.5 3.0 Crude birth rate 52.2 24.2 Contraceptive prevalence rate 10.1 (1983) Female mean age at first marriage 21.2 (1983)	Rates are considered to be <u>unsatisfactory</u> and <u>too high</u>.
INTERNATIONAL MIGRATION 1980–85 2020–25 Net migration rate 0.0 0.0 Foreign–born population (%) 0.9 (1978)	Levels and trends of immigration are viewed as <u>insignificant</u> and <u>satisfactory</u>, although refugees and asylum seekers are an active policy concern. Emigration is felt to be <u>insignificant</u> and <u>too low</u>.
SPATIAL DISTRIBUTION/URBANIZATION Urban 1985 2025 population (%) 6.2 25.6 Growth rate: 1980–85 2020–25 urban 7.7 4.6 rural 3.1 0.8	The spatial distribution pattern is viewed as being <u>inappropriate</u>. Rates of growth and resulting high density are perceived as a problem in relation to declining agricultural production, overcultivation and land degradation.

GENERAL POLICY FRAMEWORK

<u>Overall approach to population problems</u>: The Government's policies intervene to reduce rates of population growth, fertility and morbidity and to adjust the spatial distribution pattern of the population.

<u>Importance of population policy in achieving development objectives</u>: It is felt that high rates of population growth are an obstacle to the achievement of economic development objectives; they will outstrip food supplies and other natural resources, as well as place strains on the labour market and educational system. Consequently, there is increased attention to integrating population variables more thoroughly into the development process and to formulating population policies more vigorously.

INSTITUTIONAL FRAMEWORK

<u>Population data systems and development planning</u>: The first national census, undertaken in 1978 by the National Census Office, was followed by a post-census survey in 1980-1981 that was not fully completed. Vital registration is considered to be incomplete. A national fertility survey was held in 1983, and in 1985 a national inquiry was conducted on Rwandese attitudes towards family size. A second national census planned for 1988 had been rescheduled for 1991. The Fourth Development Plan (1987-1991), prepared by the Ministry of Planning, is currently in effect.

<u>Integration of population within development planning</u>: The National Office of Population (ONAPO) was created in 1981 as an autonomous body within the Ministry of Health to be responsible for the drafting and co-ordination of population policy and the preparation of demographic surveys and projections. The General Committee on Planning (1962), located in the Division of Human Resources, is responsible for the integration of demographic variables into planning.

POLICIES AND MEASURES

<u>Changes in population size and age structure</u>: To cope with problems posed by declines in agricultural productivity, the limited supply of land, unemployment and other economic and environmental problems, policies are in place to reduce the rate of population growth. This is implemented by intervening to reduce fertility, morbidity and mortality and adjust the pattern of spatial distribution. Within policy interventions aimed at fertility, morbidity and mortality reduction, women and children are target groups. The target is a population of 9.3 million by the turn of the century. The social security scheme covers employed persons, while voluntary insurance is available for non-salaried persons.

RWANDA

Mortality and morbidity: The Government's policy is to raise life expectancy. Infant and child mortality is also to be reduced through nutrition programmes for mothers and children, programmes to protect women during pregnancy and birth, and the training of traditional birth attendants, as well as through efforts to reduce transmittable diseases. Additional programmes aimed at reducing mortality and morbidity have been enacted in the areas of expanded immunization coverage, improved nutrition, essential drugs, housing improvements and environmental hygiene. The Government has also adopted five- and 10-year national strategies to control the spread of the AIDS virus. All these measures have taken place in the context of a primary health-care approach with emphasis on preventive health care and the expansion of services to rural areas, where 94 per cent of the country's population resided in 1985. A target has been specified to raise life expectancy at birth to 53.5 years by the year 2000.

Fertility and the family: There is an official policy of intervention to lower fertility. The Government has stated, however, that any fertility-related efforts to curb natural increase must be accompanied by measures to improve health, nutrition, housing and education. A strategy exists to integrate maternal and child health with family planning, and subsequently family planning has become one of the eight elements of primary health care as defined by the Government. The Central Committee of the Government's ruling party in 1986 called for a maximum of four children per family and has included this goal within the Fourth Development Plan (1987-1991). The Government supports the delivery of family planning services and contraceptives through established clinics and other outlets, birth-spacing and raising the age at marriage. Sterilization is allowed only on medical grounds and not for contraceptive purposes. Abortion is illegal except to save the life of the pregnant woman. The country aims to achieve a total fertility rate of 6.5 children by the year 2000.

International migration: There are no known policy statements concerning what the Government considers an insignificant level of immigration. As a consequence of disturbances in neighbouring Burundi, Rwanda's refugee population jumped from 20,000 to 80,000 in the second half of 1988. Emergency assistance in the form of health care, emergency food supplies and other essential items was being provided to the refugees who had not returned to Burundi. By the end of 1988 many of the refugees from Burundi had been voluntarily repatriated. The Government has viewed emigration as one means of relieving population density. In July 1986, the country's President announced that demographic pressures prevented his Government from permitting the return home of any Rwandese refugees in neighbouring countries.

Spatial distribution/urbanization: Since the 1960s, a population resettlement programme, "paysannat", has been in effect, with the purpose of directing settlements to other areas. Other major policies include rural development, regional development and the promotion of small towns. The objective is to control the expansion of existing urban districts by reducing rural-to-urban migration. Rural development strategy has included the creation of administrative structures at the village level. The Government restricts the right of residence in cities to those born there or with recognized employment.

<u>Status of women and population</u>: The Government has indicated its commitment to integrating women into development. Under projects dealing with population and family life education, provision has been made to assist women to improve their living conditions by providing them with educational skills as well as health, nutrition and child-care programmes. The programmes are under way to improve the legal, economic and social status of women, The minimum legal age at marriage for women has been raised to 21 years.

<u>Other issues</u>: The Government feels that to deal effectively with its population concerns, continued international assistance will be necessary. The country's human and financial resources remain inadequate to cope with the problems posed by high population growth.

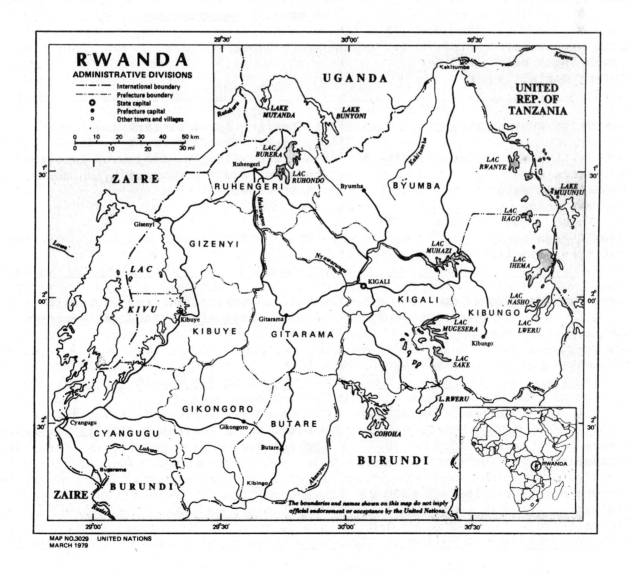

MAP NO.3029   UNITED NATIONS
MARCH 1979

SAINT KITTS AND NEVIS

DEMOGRAPHIC INDICATORS	CURRENT PERCEPTION
SIZE/AGE STRUCTURE/GROWTH	The Government views population growth as <u>too high</u>, given the high population density.

Population: <u>1985</u>   <u>2025</u>
  (thousands) 46   72
  0-14 years (%) ...   ...
  60+ years (%)	

Rate of: <u>1980-85</u> <u>2020-25</u>
  growth   0.7   0.7
  natural increase	

MORTALITY/MORBIDITY	The current expectation of life at birth is seen as <u>unacceptable</u>.
<u>1980-85</u> <u>2020-25</u> Life expectancy ... ... Crude death rate ... ... Infant mortality	
FERTILITY/NUPTIALITY/FAMILY	The current level of fertility is seen as <u>too high</u>. The Government is deeply concerned with the problem of teen-age pregnancy and its resultant social consequences.

<u>1980-85</u> <u>2020-25</u>
Fertility rate ...   ...
Crude birth rate ...   ...
Contraceptive
  prevalence rate 40.6 (1984)
Female mean age
  at first marriage	

INTERNATIONAL MIGRATION <u>1980-85</u> <u>2020-25</u> Net migration rate ... ... Foreign-born population (%) 6.0 (1980)	Levels of immigration and emigration are seen as <u>insignificant</u> and <u>satisfactory</u>.
SPATIAL DISTRIBUTION/URBANIZATION	The country's current distribution of population is seen as <u>partially appropriate</u>.
Urban <u>1985</u> <u>2025</u> population (%) 45.0 71.4	

Growth rate: <u>1980-85</u> <u>2020-25</u>
  urban   2.5   1.4
  rural -0.6 -1.0	

GENERAL POLICY FRAMEWORK

Overall approach to population problems: The Government intervenes to improve morbidity and mortality and lower population growth and fertility. Adequate health care is recognized as a human right irrespective of economic status. Emphasis is given to population and health issues that have an important social, educational or economic impact and involve priority groups, mothers and children, adolescents and the elderly.

Importance of population policy in achieving development objectives: The Government, concerned with the large number of young adults entering the labour market and remaining unemployed for long periods of time, has implemented programmes of adolescent family planning, family life and job-training programmes. The Government sees improvement in the health situation of the country's population as contingent on the correction of imbalances and social disparities in the health delivery system. The health policy has contributed to the further development of water-quality control and supply, adequate solid waste disposal, sanitary housing and monitoring of adverse impacts on the environment.

INSTITUTIONAL FRAMEWORK

Population data systems and development planning: Population censuses exist for Saint Kitts and Nevis beginning in 1844 with the most recent census held in 1980. The results of the 1980 census were published in 1985 by the Caribbean Community (CARICOM), of which Saint Kitts and Nevis is a member. The next census had been scheduled to be conducted in 1990. Registration of births and deaths is considered to be virtually complete. All deaths are medically certified and classified according to international standards. Hospital and health centre records, including information on child health, family planning, pre-natal and post-natal care and immunization, are collected by the Central Statistical Unit.

Integration of population within development planning: As with all States members of CARICOM, the Government recognizes the importance of population variables in development planning and has created a population task force to undertake further studies and make recommendations. In addition, a ministerial committee has been established with the aim of promoting intersectoral co-ordination in the formulation of a national health plan. At present the Ministry of Education, Health and Community Affairs is responsible for health sector policy. The Central Statistical Unit collaborates with the country's Planning Unit to facilitate national planning.

SAINT KITTS AND NEVIS

POLICIES AND MEASURES

Changes in population size and age structure: The Government intervenes to lower population growth through its National Family Planning Programme, which provides family planning services by physicians and specially trained nurses at 13 public health centres on the two islands. Specialized adolescent programmes for family life education and family planning have been implemented. Saint Kitts and Nevis appears to have had one of the few stable population sizes in the world which has historically not varied by more than 10 to 15 per cent. Under the National Pension System, employed persons are covered, while voluntary coverage is available to those not compulsorily covered.

Mortality and morbidity: The Government has a policy of direct intervention to improve mortality and morbidity levels. The National Health Policy emphasizes primary health care as the major strategy for achieving national health goals, and seeks to correct imbalances and social disparities in health delivery and improve the managerial process. All public health services in the country are free. Among the services provided by the Government are clinical services for maternal and child health care, dental services for children, and hospitalization for the needy. Through co-operative agreements the Government has enacted measures to train medical personnel, maintain medical equipment, develop a national laboratory service, expand delivery of personal health care and improve environmental health and water supply. Other specific measures enacted through international co-operative agreements address diarrhoeal diseases, adolescent health, perinatal care, acute respiratory infection and school health. Programmes have also been undertaken in the surveillance of child nutrition and zoonosis, vector control, immunization, diabetes, hypertension and heart disease.

Fertility and the family: The Government has a policy of direct intervention to reduce fertility. Through the National Family Planning Programme, family planning services have been fully integrated within health-care services as a means of reducing the overall level of fertility and natural increase, as well as resolving health and social problems. In 1971 a strategy was begun for the introduction of family planning into government health services. In 1976 the project was extended to include a health and family life education component aimed at the country's youth. A project was initiated in 1986 with international assistance to strengthen family life education and family planning for adolescents. Through co-operative agreements the Government has modernized clinics, trained nurses and physicians in family planning and augmented the provision of contraceptive supplies. Provision is made for a maternity grant and maternity benefits. Sterilization is legal and abortion is allowed only to save the life of the mother.

International migration: The Government's policy is to maintain the levels of emigration and immigration. A history of net emigration has contributed to the country's stable population size. In light of current fertility levels the country may have to rely on continued net emigration for the population size to stabilize.

Spatial distribution/urbanization: The Government has reported a policy of non-intervention to modify the pattern of spatial distribution, which it views as partially appropriate. Community health centres and major primary health-care centres are established with reference to population distribution so that the entire population of Nevis is within three to four miles of a health centre while in Saint Kitts the distance is less.

Status of women and population: The country's Strategy for the Extension of Family Planning in Health Services has included the strengthening of female health services through the establishment of a national cytology service and the extension of post-natal services. Through the country's National Child Care Committee, day-care services have been established. Information on the minimum legal age at marriage for women is not readily available.

SAINT LUCIA

DEMOGRAPHIC INDICATORS	CURRENT PERCEPTION
SIZE/AGE STRUCTURE/GROWTH Population: 1985 2025 (thousands) 128 211 0-14 years (%) ... ... 60+ years (%) ... ... Rate of: 1980-85 2020-25 growth 1.6 1.0 natural increase	The Government perceives the current growth rate as <u>unsatisfactory</u> and <u>too high</u> and is concerned by the large proportion of the population under 15 years of age.
MORTALITY/MORBIDITY 1980-85 2020-25 Life expectancy ... ... Crude death rate ... ... Infant mortality	Levels and trends are seen as <u>unacceptable</u>. Priority groups include the disabled, mothers and children.
FERTILITY/NUPTIALITY/FAMILY 1980-85 2020-25 Fertility rate ... ... Crude birth rate ... ... Contraceptive prevalence rate 42.7 (1981) Female mean age at first marriage	Current fertility levels are perceived as <u>unsatisfactory</u> and <u>too high</u>. Adolescent fertility is a major concern.
INTERNATIONAL MIGRATION 1980-85 2020-25 Net migration rate ... ... Foreign-born population (%) 3.1 (1980)	Current levels of immigration are perceived as <u>significant</u> and <u>satisfactory</u>. Current levels of emigration are perceived as <u>insignificant</u> and <u>satisfactory</u>.
SPATIAL DISTRIBUTION/URBANIZATION Urban 1985 2025 population (%) 43.8 69.3 Growth rate: 1980-85 2020-25 urban 2.5 1.8 rural 0.9 -0.8	The current distribution of population is seen as <u>appropriate</u>, although there is concern over increasing population density. Population growth in the major metropolitan area is seen as <u>too high</u>, while in other urban areas it is <u>satisfactory</u>. Growth in rural areas is felt to be <u>too low</u>.

GENERAL POLICY FRAMEWORK

<u>Overall approach to population problems</u>: The Government does not have an explicit population policy. Measures aimed at addressing population occur within the context of health policy or family planning programmes. To date special concern has focused on malnutrition, maternal and child health, sanitation, sewage and medical supplies. Health programmes aim to reduce mortality and morbidity, while family planning programmes involve education and delivery of services with special emphasis on adolescents.

<u>Importance of population policy in achieving development objectives</u>: The present rate of population growth is seen as having a major negative impact on social and economic development objectives. The Government has observed that the current growth rate is too high for a small island State with an agricultural economy, and that modernization of the economy must take place in order to provide the growing population with employment, school places and housing.

INSTITUTIONAL FRAMEWORK

<u>Population data systems and development planning</u>: Saint Lucia has a long history of reliable census-taking, thus permitting the analysis of the island's population trends. Decennial censuses exist for the periods 1851-1921 and for 1946. Since 1960 a decennial census has been conducted, with the most recent in 1980. The next one had been provisionally scheduled for 1990. In addition, several fertility surveys have been conducted in the country. The Government has cited a lack of data on population-development interrelationships, a lack of adequate methodologies and the unpredictable migration of skilled personnel as hindering both the development of an adequate data base and demographic analysis. The National Development Strategy for the period 1987-1991 has as its major objective carrying out a structural adjustment of the economy.

<u>Integration of population within development planning</u>: The Ministry of Health, Housing and Labour is responsible for the formulation and co-ordination of population policy, while the Ministry of Planning and Personnel is charged with the responsibility of integrating population variables into planning. The Health Sector Plan containing measures aimed at expanding primary health care, addressing maternal and child health and implementing family planning services was integrated in the National Development Plan for the period 1981-1985.

POLICIES AND MEASURES

<u>Changes in population size and age structure</u>: The Government has stated its aim to reduce population growth, although no specific quantitative target has been set. High fertility combined with constant net emigration has given

SAINT LUCIA

Saint Lucia one of the youngest populations in the eastern Caribbean. The adolescent segment of this population has become a cause for concern and policy action has taken the form of school educational programmes on family life. Efforts to lower population growth have been directed towards family planning programmes. The social security scheme covers employed persons and apprentices, while excluding civil servants.

Mortality and morbidity: The Government is actively committed to continued improvement in mortality and morbidity although no quantitative targets have been set. Within the country's National Development Plan for 1981-1985 a Health Sector Plan was formulated based on the goal of Health for All by the Year 2000. Health programmes are delivered free of charge at health centres, or at general practitioners' private offices on payment of a fee. Preventive services include pregnancy care; child care; immunization of children against poliomyelitis, diphtheria, tetanus, tuberculosis, measles and whooping cough; free food supplements to pregnant and nursing mothers and malnourished children; as well as family planning services. Curative services are provided by district nurses at all health centres and by medical doctors at weekly clinics. An intensive information campaign has been undertaken to combat AIDS.

Fertility and the family: Although the Government views the level of fertility as being high, it has not formulated an explicit policy of modifying fertility. Various measures, however, have been implemented in the area of family planning programmes, establishment of day-care centres and tax incentives. Specific measures have been the training of district nurses in general family planning and natural contraceptive methods since 1980, and beginning in 1984 the delivery of services through health clinics and centres. In addition, education on population issues and promotion of family life has been undertaken, particularly for adolescents. Adolescent fertilty is a major concern which has been addressed primarily through educational programmes. In 1983 a project was begun by the Ministry of Health to develop a national policy on family life education through mass media and community involvement, the expansion of services and education to adolescents and improved training in the maternal and child health sector. The Government directly supports the provision of contraceptive methods. Abortion is allowed only to save the life of the mother. There are no restrictions on male or female sterilization.

International migration: Concerning the significant level of immigration, the Government has a policy to reduce the flow into the country of persons on non-permanent work permits and that of their dependants. The Government has a specific policy of publicizing investment incentives to encourage the return of Saint Lucians who have emigrated, yet are in a position to make an intellectual or financial contribution to the country's development.

Spatial distribution/urbanization: Current strategies are to slow primate city growth, promote the growth of existing small towns and intermediate cities and develop industrial growth centres, lagging regions and rural areas in order to attract or retain rural population. Measures enacted with respect to these strategies have been public infrastructure subsidies and development grants, loans, and tax incentives to new industries and relocatees, administrative and educational research decentralization, the provision of housing and social services to retain households, and investment in human resources.

<u>Status of women and population</u>: The Government has no specific measures with regard to the status of women and its influence on demographic trends. Nevertheless, the Government views the status of women as having a significant impact on demographic trends. Since 1975 programmes in health centres and clinics and the training of district nurses in family planning in general and specifically in natural contraceptive methods have been undertaken. The Government also reports that day-care and nursery centres have been created. The minimum legal age at marriage for women is 18 years.

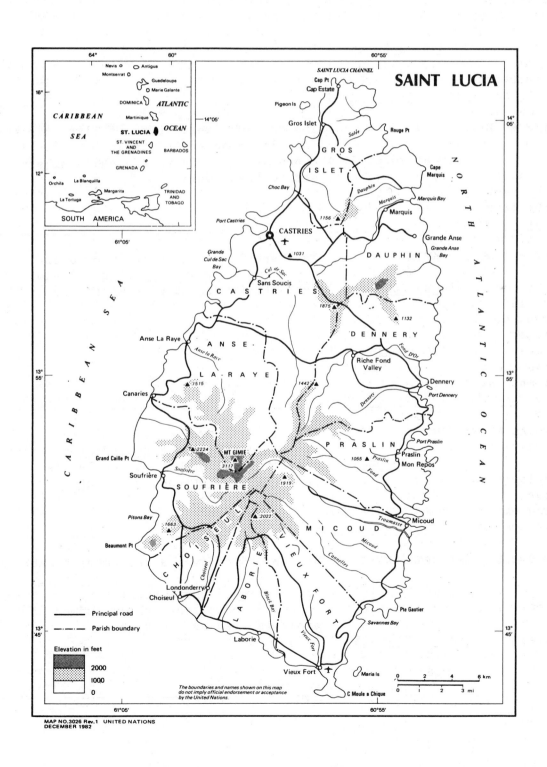

SAINT VINCENT AND THE GRENADINES

DEMOGRAPHIC INDICATORS	CURRENT PERCEPTION
SIZE/AGE STRUCTURE/GROWTH	The present rate of population growth is seen as <u>unsatisfactory</u> and <u>too high</u>.

Population:	1985	2025
(thousands)	104	171
0-14 years (%)	...	...
60+ years (%)	...	...

Rate of:	1980-85	2020-25
growth	0.9	1.0
natural increase	...	...

MORTALITY/MORBIDITY

The current expectation of life at birth is felt to be <u>unacceptable</u>. Particular concerns are infants and children aged one to five years.

	1980-85	2020-25
Life expectancy	...	...
Crude death rate	...	...
Infant mortality	...	...

FERTILITY/NUPTIALITY/FAMILY

The fertility levels are viewed as <u>unsatisfactory</u> and <u>too high</u>. Adolescent fertilty is viewed as a major concern.

	1980-85	2020-25
Fertility rate	...	...
Crude birth rate	...	...
Contraceptive prevalence rate	41.5 (1981)	
Female mean age at first marriage	...	...

INTERNATIONAL MIGRATION

The present level of immigration is seen as <u>insignificant</u> and <u>satisfactory</u>. The current level of emigration is also seen as <u>insignificant</u> and <u>satisfactory</u>.

	1980-85	2020-25
Net migration rate	...	....
Foreign-born population (%)	2.2 (1980)	

SPATIAL DISTRIBUTION/URBANIZATION

The Government views the current pattern of spatial distribution as <u>partially appropriate</u>. The current rate of growth in the metropolitan, urban and rural areas is seen as <u>too high</u>.

Urban	1985	2025
population (%)	18.4	46.6

Growth rate:	1980-85	2020-25
urban	2.8	2.8
rural	0.6	-0.5

GENERAL POLICY FRAMEWORK

Overall approach to population problems: The Government has a population policy that aims to improve the quality of life and standard of living. The Government intervenes to lower population growth, mortality and fertility and to change the pattern of spatial distribution. A project was initiated in 1986 to integrate family life education and family planning fully into primary health care and the school system.

Importance of population policy in achieving development objectives: The Government has emphasized that in the existing international climate, real socio-economic progress will be possible only within the context of an integrated population policy. The purpose of the Government's policy is to improve the quality of life and raise the standard of living.

INSTITUTIONAL FRAMEWORK

Population data systems and development planning: Vital statistics registration is considered to be complete. Decennial censuses were conducted in 1960, 1970 and 1980. The next census had been provisionally scheduled for 1990. No census data exist for the period 1946-1960. In 1986 the Government adopted a rolling two-year national development plan strategy. The latest available plan is the Development Plan for the period 1986-1988 and its first update for 1987-1989, prepared by the Central Planning Division within the Ministry of Finance, Planning and Development.

Integration of population within development planning: Representatives of the Ministries of Agriculture, Industry and Labour, Education, Youth and Women's Affairs, and Communications and Works, as well as from non-governmental agencies, participate in all aspects of programme planning in health. The Government reported in 1987 that a population task force had formulated a national population policy which was adopted by the Cabinet. Future policy will be directed by a ministerial National Population Council to be chaired by the Director of Planning. A policy exists of integrating population variables in the development planning process, and the Central Planning Division is responsible for this activity. The Government has cited the lack of trained personnel, methodologies, adequate data and research as hindering the integration of population factors into planning.

POLICIES AND MEASURES

Changes in population size and age structure: The Government views population size, growth and structure as major influences on the country's development. It is felt that the current growth rate will severely strain the country's limited natural resources. Policies are in effect to reduce growth by lowering fertility and mortality and readjusting the pattern of spatial

SAINT VINCENT AND THE GRENADINES

distribution. The target is to reduce the rate of population growth to 0.7 per cent by the year 2030 in order to achieve a total population of 150,000 by that year. Under the social security scheme as of 1987 coverage included all employed persons aged 16-59. Coverage was to be extended to the self-employed at a future date.

Mortality and morbidity: The Government intervenes to lower mortality and morbidity through a national health plan delivering primary health care with emphasis on community involvement, a team approach to health problems, the maximum use of human resources and free medical services to the indigent. The plan also stresses appropriate training of all staff, use of appropriate technology, health promotion, risk reduction, the integration of preventive and curative services at the community level and competent management of health services. In 1985 the Ministry of Health was in the process of developing a resource centre within the Health Education and Planning Unit to act as a source of health information for health professionals. Representatives from the Ministries of Agriculture, Industry and Labour, Education, Youth and Women's Affairs, and Communications and Works, as well as from non-governmental agencies, participate in all aspects of health programme planning. Maternal and child health programmes are being strengthened, as is the community health outreach programme and the National Food and Nutrition Council. Targets have been set to reduce malnutrition in children and pregnant and nursing mothers; nutrition supplements are provided in primary schools. Legislation has been enacted to ensure that all children under the age of three entering school are immunized. A council has been set up to establish policies and procedures for the control of AIDS.

Fertility and the family: The Government has actively sought to lower fertility through a national family planning programme by which the Ministry of Health provides free family planning services in all health centres. Special emphasis is placed on adolescents, for whom outreach programmes exist. Family planning has been a priority in the training of health-care personnel and in health education. A wide range of modern contraceptives is available to men and women, as well as adolescents, regardless of marital status. The Ministry of Health has begun a parent-education programme to train 50 professionals as a core team to create parent workshops on sexuality, family planning, parent-child relationships and communication skills. Other measures include improving the status of women, nurseries and day-care centres and tax exemptions. The Government directly supports the provision of modern methods of contraception. Abortion is prohibited without exception. Female sterilization is permitted upon the assurance that the woman will not want more children, the consent of the spouse and consideration of her age and marital status.

International migration: Government policies towards immigration seek to maintain the flow of immigrants on non-permanent work permits, their dependants and those seeking permanent settlement, while aiming to halt the flow of undocumented immigrants. A constant level of emigration is to be maintained. The return of expatriates whose skills and training can enhance the nation's development is encouraged through moral suasion. To reduce the emigration of skilled professionals, the Government has sought a pay review in the public sector, as well as international assistance.

Spatial distribution/urbanization: The Government has adopted a policy to alter population distribution by slowing primate city growth, by developing growth centres and lagging regions, and by rural development to attract and retain rural population. Specific measures enacted have been public infrastructure subsidies and development, financial incentives for those relocating, decentralization of administrative and education/research functions, and investments in human resources.

Status of women and population: The Government has adopted measures relating to the status of women that it sees as an influence on demographic trends. It has established a Women's Division in the Ministry of Tourism, Aviation and Culture to promote the image of women as equal members of society and educate the population on issues such as sexual harassment. The sharing of responsibilities between men and women in family planning is promoted and day-care centres and nurseries have been established. Measures with respect to the status of women have mainly taken the form of information, education and institutional supports such as the free and equal availability of contraception to both men and women. The minimum legal age at marriage for females is 16 years.

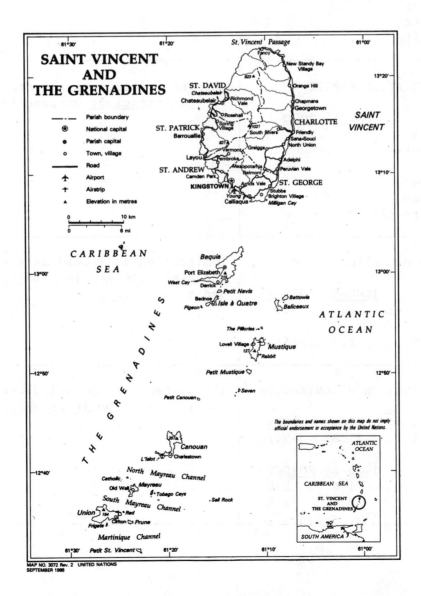

MAP NO. 3072 Rev. 2   UNITED NATIONS
SEPTEMBER 1986

SAMOA

DEMOGRAPHIC INDICATORS	CURRENT PERCEPTION
SIZE/AGE STRUCTURE/GROWTH Population:　　　　1985　　2025 　(thousands)　　163　　203 　0-14 years (%)　...　　... 　60+ years (%)　　...　　... Rate of:　　1980-85　2020-25 　growth　　　1.0　　0.2 　natural increase　...　　...	The Government perceives current growth rates as <u>unsatisfactory</u> because they are <u>too high</u>. The large proportion of the population under age 15 is viewed as creating an unfavourable dependency ratio.
MORTALITY/MORBIDITY 　　　　　1980-85　2020-25 Life expectancy　　...　　... Crude death rate　　...　　... Infant mortality　　...　　...	Current levels of mortality are regarded as <u>unacceptable</u>.
FERTILITY/NUPTIALITY/FAMILY 　　　　　1980-85　2020-25 Fertility rate　　...　　... Crude birth rate　　....　　... Contraceptive 　prevalence rate　...　　... Female mean age 　at first marriage　...　　...	Current fertility rates are considered to be <u>unsatisfactory</u> because they are <u>too high</u>.
INTERNATIONAL MIGRATION 　　　　　1980-85　2020-25 Net migration rate　...　　... Foreign-born 　population (%)　1.3 (1976)	Immigration is viewed as <u>significant</u> and <u>too high</u>. Emigration is <u>insignificant</u> and <u>satisfactory</u>.
SPATIAL DISTRIBUTION/URBANIZATION Urban　　　　1985　　2025 　population (%)　21.8　45.7 Growth rate:　1980-85　2020-25 　urban　　　1.4　　2.0 　rural　　　0.9　　-1.2	The pattern of spatial distribution is considered to be <u>inappropriate</u>.

GENERAL POLICY FRAMEWORK

Overall approach to population problems: Although the Government has no explicit population policy, national objectives are to promote and protect the health and well-being of mothers, children and the family. Population-related goals include conserving the environment, creating a more equitable distribution of economic benefits and controlling population growth through emigration and planned family growth.

Importance of population policy in achieving development objectives: Population factors are viewed as of fundamental importance to development. Reducing population growth is seen as necessary in order to make it more compatible with the development of other potential resources. Family planning integrated with maternal and child health and population education is believed fundamental to the attainment of economic development.

INSTITUTIONAL FRAMEWORK

Population data systems and development planning: The most recent population census was conducted in 1986 and the next had been provisionally scheduled for 1991. Vital registration is considered to be incomplete. The Department of Statistics under the Ministry of Economic Affairs is responsible for conducting censuses and population projections. Efforts have been made to improve the capability of the Department of Statistics to conduct censuses and surveys and to institutionalize the process of statistical production, in order to provide a continuous flow of consistent, timely and accurate data relevant to the needs of development planning and programme monitoring evaluation. The Government has had national development plans since the mid-1960s. The Fifth Development Plan for the period 1985-1987 made specific provision to upgrade standards of health, educational and family planning services. The Sixth Development Plan (1988-1990) is currently in effect.

Integration of population within development planning: The Ministry of Economic Affairs is responsible for co-ordinating the preparation of national development plans which integrate policies affecting population. The Government is interested in improving development planning by implementing a monitoring scheme. An Inter-ministerial Committee on Population was formed with the objective of formulating a population policy.

POLICIES AND MEASURES

Changes in population size and age structure: The Government has directly intervened to reduce population growth by promoting family planning and encouraging emigration to control population growth. A Council of Youth has

SAMOA

been created as a youth-co-ordinating mechanism at the national level to prepare future programmes and formulate youth policy. The capacity of the Ministry of Youth is being enhanced to improve the economic welfare and social well-being of young workers and their families by strengthening training activities. There is no information readily available on the status of pension schemes.

Mortality and morbidity: The Government has intervened to expand access to primary health care to achieve coverage at the village level. Planned family growth is also encouraged as a means of reducing mortality and morbidity among mothers and children. Samoa's health development strategy has been formulated according to several phases which coincide with the country's national development plans, and task forces have been created for specific objectives such as safe water and disease prevention. The task forces have specified national targets with respect to increasing life expectancy, improving nutritional status, providing clean water, reducing the incidence of communicable and chronic diseases, and achieving better family health in general. The Fifth National Development Plan for 1985-1987 aimed to strengthen basic health services at the village level, increase health manpower, control communicable diseases and improve family planning services and dental care.

Fertility and the family: The Government has actively intervened to improve access to family planning information and services. It is committed to integrating family planning services with mother and child health programmes and intends to integrate population and family education into the educational system. A Family Welfare Section was established in the Public Health Division of the Department of Health in 1971 to facilitate the delivery of antenatal, post-natal and family planning services in the metropolitan area with nurses operating sub-centres at the district level. Projects to introduce population education into the primary and secondary school system through the training of teachers and curriculum development have been undertaken. The Family Health Association, established in 1984, collaborates with the Government in providing information, education, training and services in family planning in which birth-spacing rather than limiting family size is emphasized. The Government directly supports the provision of modern methods of contraception. Sterilization is available in family planning clinics and abortion is permitted for medical reasons only.

International migration: The Government actively intervenes to reduce immigration and encourage emigration. Immigration is permitted only on a temporary basis for workers and their families until the positions can be filled by trained Samoans. In the Fourth National Development Plan, the Government expressed its intention to rely on emigration to control total population growth.

Spatial distribution/urbanization: The Government has a policy to decelerate the flow of migrants from rural to urban areas. The rapid rate of rural migration into towns and the problems associated with urbanization are viewed as major factors to be taken into consideration in population development planning. Measures aimed at improving rural and lagging areas include general and regional development strategies. To improve the efficiency of land use, the Government has undertaken efforts to introduce commercial plantation norms and practices and to implant freeholders by bringing virgin land into cultivation.

Status of women and population: In 1979 the Government instituted a Women's Advisory Committee (WAC) whose task was to formulate and monitor plans, policies and programmes for the advancement of women as well as disseminate research and promote grass-roots organization. Major programmes undertaken by WAC have been to foster women's participation through agricultural production, project administration, and the promotion of health through maternal and child care, family planning and health and nutrition education. Each village has a women's committee that works in conjunction with the Government through the National Council of Women, whose efforts are concentrated on health. Information on the minimum legal age at marriage for women is not readily available.

Other issues: At the third round-table meeting for Samoa in October 1988, donors identified priority areas for future assistance, such as agriculture, manpower development, strengthening of public services and improvement of the institutional infrastructure.

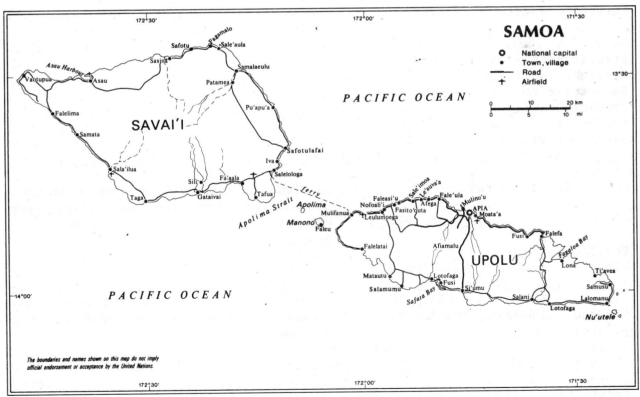

MAP NO.3210 UNITED NATIONS
NOVEMBER 1982

SAN MARINO

DEMOGRAPHIC INDICATORS	CURRENT PERCEPTION
SIZE/AGE STRUCTURE/GROWTH	The Government considers the rate of population growth to be <u>satisfactory</u>.

	1985	2025
Population: (thousands)	22	25
0-14 years (%)	...	...
60+ years (%)	...	...

Rate of:	1980-85	2020-25
growth	0.9	0.0
natural increase	...	...

MORTALITY/MORBIDITY

The Government views mortality levels as <u>acceptable</u>.

	1980-85	2020-25
Life expectancy	...	...
Crude death rate	...	...
Infant mortality	...	...

FERTILITY/NUPTIALITY/FAMILY

The level of fertility is viewed as <u>satisfactory</u>.

	1980-85	2020-25
Fertility rate	...	...
Crude birth rate	...	...
Contraceptive prevalence rate	...	...
Female mean age at first marriage	...	...

INTERNATIONAL MIGRATION

The immigration level is considered to be <u>unsatisfactory</u> because it is <u>too high</u>, while emigration is <u>insignificant</u> and <u>satisfactory</u>.

	1980-85	2020-25
Net migration rate	...	...
Foreign-born population (%)	42.7 (1976)	

SPATIAL DISTRIBUTION/URBANIZATION

Spatial distribution is felt to be <u>appropriate</u>.

Urban	1985	2025
population (%)	...	...

Growth rate:	1980-85	2020-25
urban	...	...
rural	...	...

GENERAL POLICY FRAMEWORK

<u>Overall approach to population problems</u>: The Government aims to maintain the population growth rate. Measures concerning health policies include the provision of preventive, curative and rehabilitative services.

<u>Importance of population policy in achieving development objectives</u>: The Government considers that the country's population growth rate is suitable for economic and social development. It is aware of the interrelationship between population and development and is concerned with the environment, child health, housing and the aged. Present trends are considered to be adequate for providing demographic dynamism sufficient to maintain the national innovative capacity and to achieve the desired levels of replacement of population. However, there is no formulated comprehensive policy concerning population variables.

INSTITUTIONAL FRAMEWORK

<u>Population data systems and development planning</u>: Censuses were conducted in 1970 and 1976. The National Statistical Office is charged with collecting and processing population data. The Social Security Institute undertakes epidemiological surveys.

<u>Integration of population within development planning</u>: There is no reported agency responsible for integrating population variables into development planning. The Government receives data related to population and development directly from the National Statistical Office.

POLICIES AND MEASURES

<u>Changes in population size and age structure</u>: While there are no known policy statements, it appears that the Government intervenes to maintain the rate of population growth. Since 1956, the Government has maintained a comprehensive social insurance programme, including disability, family supplement payments and old-age pensions.

<u>Mortality and morbidity</u>: The Government guarantees to all its citizens, regardless of income, the right to health services and temporary or long-term economic assistance. Basic medical services are provided by three health centres, which are co-ordinated by a single management board. The health services focus on preventive, diagnostic, curative and rehabilitative services, in order to meet the needs of public health and social integration. A 1977 law calls for popular involvement in planning and management to ensure that the demand for services equals the supply and that social and public

SAN MARINO

assistance services are integrated with health services. The Environmental Hygiene Department examines the impact of development and town planning schemes, new construction projects and the sanitary conditions of dwellings and their health and ecological impact.

Fertility and the family: There is no official policy aiming to modify the level of fertility. It is felt that the present fertility rate contributes positively to family well-being, making possible the achievement of the desired number of children and ensuring continuity of the family. Divorce was first allowed in 1986.

International migration: In the early 1960s, the number of citizens resident abroad exceeded the number of citizens within the country. There are no known policy statements concerning the significant level of immigration. In 1982 San Marino women who married foreign citizens were allowed to retain their citizenship. A 1984 law permitted foreigners who had been resident in San Marino for 30 years to become naturalized citizens.

Spatial distribution/urbanization: The present spatial distribution is viewed as appropriate from the point of view of protecting the environment, full employment and the well-being of the population in general. However, slight adjustments are felt to be necessary in the distribution of economic and social activities, favouring the implementation of industrial activities in rural areas. In addition to promoting tourism, the Government has encouraged the establishment of small-scale industries and service-oriented enterprises (40-60 employees) by offering tax exemptions for five to 10 years.

Status of women and population: Although women obtained the right to vote in 1960, they were only given the right to hold public office in 1973.

EUROPE

ICELAND

ATLANTIC OCEAN

SWEDEN

FINLAND

NORWAY

UNION OF
SOVIET SOCIALIST REPUBLICS

UNITED KINGDOM

DENMARK

IRELAND

NETHERLANDS

BYELORUSSIAN
SSR

POLAND

GERMANY

UKRAINIAN SSR

BELGIUM

CZECHOSLOVAKIA

LUXEMBOURG

LIECHTENSTEIN

FRANCE

AUSTRIA HUNGARY

SWITZERLAND

ROMANIA

BLACK SEA

SAN
MARINO

YUGOSLAVIA

MONACO

BULGARIA

ANDORRA

TURKEY

ITALY

ALBANIA

SPAIN

GREECE

PORTUGAL

CYPRUS

Gibraltar

MEDITERRANEAN   SEA

MALTA

The boundaries shown on this map do not imply official
endorsement or acceptance by the United Nations.

0   200   400   600 mi

0   200   400   600 km

MAP NO. 2771.16   UNITED NATIONS
SEPTEMBER 1990

SAO TOME AND PRINCIPE

DEMOGRAPHIC INDICATORS	CURRENT PERCEPTION

SIZE/AGE STRUCTURE/GROWTH
 	
Population: 1985 2025
 (thousands) 97 284
  0-14 years (%) ... ...
  60+ years (%) ... ...
 	
Rate of: 1980-85 2020-25
 growth 2.7 2.1
 natural increase ... ...
	The Government views population growth as <u>satisfactory</u>.

MORTALITY/MORBIDITY 1980-85 2020-25 Life expectancy ... ... Crude death rate ... ... Infant mortality	The level of mortality and morbidity is seen as <u>unacceptable</u>. Mortality among children 0-5 years of age is seen as a particular concern.
FERTILITY/NUPTIALITY/FAMILY 1980-85 2020-25 Fertility rate ... ... Crude birth rate ... ... Contraceptive prevalence rate ... ... Female mean age at first marriage	Fertility is viewed as <u>satisfactory</u>.
INTERNATIONAL MIGRATION 1980-85 2020-25 Net migration rate ... ... Foreign-born population (%) 6.9 (1981)	Immigration is considered to be <u>insignificant</u> and <u>satisfactory</u>. Emigration is also seen as <u>insignificant</u> and <u>satisfactory</u>.
SPATIAL DISTRIBUTION/URBANIZATION Urban 1985 2025 population (%) 37.6 67.2 Growth rate: 1980-85 2020-25 urban 5.4 3.0 rural 1.2 0.4	The pattern of spatial distribution of the population is seen as <u>inappropriate</u>.

GENERAL POLICY FRAMEWORK

Overall approach to population problems: The Government's general policy towards population is to provide integrated family planning and maternal and child health services, which it sees as a prerequisite to economic development and improved productivity. With respect to health programmes, the approach is a functional integration of preventive and curative services and the adoption of intersectoral solutions to problems.

Importance of population policy in achieving development objectives: The Government recognizes the relationship between demographic and socio-economic factors and seeks to formulate population policies in line with economic policies that will promote development and improvements in the standard of living.

INSTITUTIONAL FRAMEWORK

Population data systems and development planning: Censuses were conducted in 1960, 1970 and 1981, with the next census provisionally scheduled for 1991. The Government actively seeks to use census data to create a demographic data base upon which to establish a population policy and socio-economic decision-making. The registration of births and deaths is estimated to be virtually complete. Responsibility for demographic data collection rests with the Ministry of Health. The Government prepared a national development plan for the period 1986-1990 that includes health objectives affecting population.

Integration of population within development planning: A project was initiated in 1982 to integrate demographic variables into social and economic development plans and to ensure coherent planning to satisfy the needs of the country. The Department of Statistics is responsible for the collection of demographic data to meet planning needs. Since 1978 the Ministry of Health has been responsible for the elaboration of short- and long-term health plans, and for co-ordination and monitoring.

POLICIES AND MEASURES

Changes in population size and age structure: In the absence of a comprehensive population policy, it appears that no policies have been formulated aimed at influencing the rate of population growth. The Government does, however, report programmes to improve the health-care system and to promote child-spacing activities. The country's national pension scheme established in 1979 covers employed persons, while excluding the self-employed and domestics.

Mortality and morbidity: One of the objectives of the country's National Socio-economic Development Plan for the period 1982-1985 was to improve the

SAO TOME AND PRINCIPE

health status of the population in order to increase productivity and, consequently, economic growth. The Plan called for a more effective health-care system and enhanced integration of preventive and curative services. The Government actively seeks to reduce mortality and morbidity by extending health services and coverage in rural areas and focusing on children aged 0 to 5 years. The intensification of maternal and child services, the eradication of malaria, expanded immunization, health education, and nutrition and community health agent programmes are also seen as priorities. In 1983 a programme was launched to train volunteers in all villages and districts to provide basic health care. It was hoped that this programme would contribute to achieving greater community participation. The Government has cited a shortage of funds, an inadequate mobilization of the population and the loss of trained health workers as hindering the achievement of its health objectives. Quantitative targets had been set in the past with respect to reducing infant and child mortality. Outbreaks of malaria in 1986 and cholera in 1989 necessitated medical assistance from abroad.

Fertility and the family: The Government has not reported any intervention intended to influence the level of fertility. However, it promotes programmes of child-spacing among the population as a means of improving the health of mothers and children and the welfare of the family. The second phase of a project on training activities for a national integrated maternal and child health and family planning programme was initiated in 1985 for the purpose of strengthening the ongoing activities of personnel, providing contraceptives and preparing for a Government takeover of the project. Integration of sex education into the school curricula at the upper primary and lower secondary levels was initiated in 1985. The Government directly supports the provision of modern methods of contraception. Information on the status of abortion and sterilization is not readily available.

International migration: The Government has not expressed an explicit policy concerning the insignificant levels of immigration and emigration. Because of the substantial increase in the population of secondary school pupils, increasing numbers of students have been sent to universities abroad.

Spatial distribution/urbanization: The Government reported that it has undertaken policies to promote a more balanced development between regions. The Government is enhancing access to services in various regions. International assistance has been provided for economic, social and industrial developments, and especially for balanced agricultural development. Land distribution from the State to private individuals and co-operatives has been initiated outside the 15 large Government-owned estates. A matter of concern has been the growing concentration of the population in the district of Agua Grande, comprising the capital and its outskirts, which in 1983 contained almost one third of the country's population.

Status of women and population: The Government seeks to integrate women in the process of development and to promote their active participation in the country's social, economic and political life. Information on the minimum legal age at marriage for women is not readily available.

<u>Other issues</u>: Sao Tome and Principe has participated along with the other Portuguese-speaking African countries in co-operative programmes in health research, education, training and information systems development. A comprehensive assessment of population needs and population assistance required by the Government in future years was undertaken in 1988. In 1989 the Government received international assistance to lessen the social impact of structural adjustment programmes. An autonomous agency will finance employment-generating activities and will rehabilitate infrastructure such as urban facilities, schools and health centres. Social and preventive health services will also be expanded.

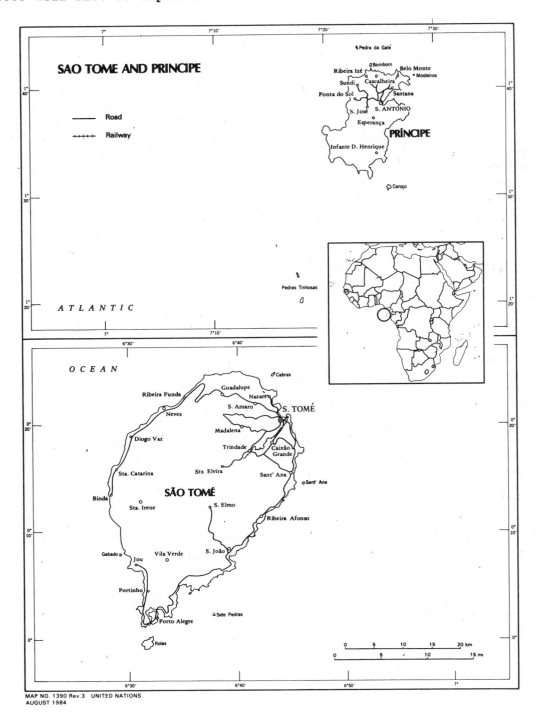

MAP NO. 1390 Rev.3   UNITED NATIONS
AUGUST 1984

SAUDI ARABIA

DEMOGRAPHIC INDICATORS	CURRENT PERCEPTION
SIZE/AGE STRUCTURE/GROWTH	The Government perceives the current growth rate as <u>unsatisfactory</u> and <u>too low</u>.

SIZE/AGE STRUCTURE/GROWTH

Population:	1985	2025
(thousands)	11 595	44 780
0-14 years (%)	44.9	38.0
60+ years (%)	4.2	6.0

Rate of:	1980-85	2020-25
growth	4.3	2.4
natural increase	34.3	24.2

The Government perceives the current growth rate as unsatisfactory and too low.

MORTALITY/MORBIDITY

	1980-85	2020-25
Life expectancy	60.9	74.3
Crude death rate	8.9	3.7
Infant mortality	85.0	21.0

The present conditions of morbidity and mortality are viewed as unacceptable.

FERTILITY/NUPTIALITY/FAMILY

	1980-85	2020-25
Fertility rate	7.3	3.6
Crude birth rate	43.2	27.9
Contraceptive prevalence rate	...	...
Female mean age at first marriage	...	...

Current fertility rates are considered to be satisfactory.

INTERNATIONAL MIGRATION

	1980-85	2020-25
Net migration rate	...	...
Foreign-born population (%)	...	...

The significant immigration levels are viewed as too high. Emigration is insignificant and satisfactory.

SPATIAL DISTRIBUTION/URBANIZATION

Urban	1985	2025
population (%)	73.0	88.2

Growth rate:	1980-85	2020-25
urban	6.0	2.7
rural	0.2	0.7

The spatial distribution is felt to be partially appropriate.

GENERAL POLICY FRAMEWORK

Overall approach to population problems: The Government does not have a comprehensive policy dealing specifically with population. Population problems are viewed in the context of protecting the national identity and in terms of meeting the labour requirements of the economy. Consequently, an increase of the population is desired. Measures have been implemented to reduce mortality, maintain the high level of fertility and reduce dependency on the expatriate labour force.

Importance of population policy in achieving development objectives: Although the Government has not formulated an explicit population policy, successive development plans have cited the necessity of improving the quantity and quality of the Saudi Arabian labour force in order to achieve development objectives. The Fourth Five-Year Development Plan (1986-1990) has, as a major objective, raising the cultural standards of the population, as well as upgrading human resources to ensure a constant supply of labour. The strategy for developing Saudi Arabian labour is based on educational and training programmes, provision of social welfare and health care, and greater participation in the development process.

INSTITUTIONAL FRAMEWORK

Population data systems and development planning: The most recent population census was taken in 1974 and as of 1989 no other census had been scheduled. Vital registration is considered to be incomplete. The absence of reliable data on the size and distribution of the indigenous population is acknowledged as a major obstacle to accurate planning in all areas of the economy and social services. As of 1984 plans were underway to introduce medical certification of the cause of death. The Fourth Five-Year Plan (1986-1990), prepared by the Ministry of Planning, is currently in effect. In October 1988 the Cabinet endorsed the guidelines for the country's Fifth Five-Year Plan for the period 1990-1994.

Integration of population within development planning: The Central Committee for the Population Census Programme was created in 1973 as the first step in the strengthening of institutional arrangements for the eventual formulation of a national population policy. The Ministry of Planning, the Central Department of Statistics, various ministries and the university were also represented on the Committee. Recommendations had been made for the creation of a national population committee to act as a permanent advisory board.

POLICIES AND MEASURES

Changes in population size and age structure: The Government would like to increase population size so that it would be commensurate with development objectives. Measures concerning the welfare of the population have been

SAUDI ARABIA

implemented, aiming to improve the health status and housing of the elderly, the disabled, orphans and those unable to support themselves. An important objective is developing and upgrading national human resources to ensure a constant supply of native-born labour. The national pension scheme is limited to employees of firms with at least 20 workers and public employees, while excluding agricultural workers, domestic servants and family labour. As of March 1987, foreign workers were no longer covered.

Mortality and morbidity: Health policy is embodied in five-year health plans, which are included in national development plans. Although a ministerial decree in 1980 integrated preventive services offered by the health bureau and maternal and child health centres with curative services delivered by dispensaries which now function as primary health-care centres, the Government reports that the major problem facing health management is the persistence of the division between preventive and curative services. One measure being pursued to implement primary health care is to extend the use of a "family health record" to all health centres. Emphasis is being placed on promoting community involvement, improving data collection and analysis, training nationals in health-care management and increasing the number of native-born physicians. Through the Secretariat-General of Health for the Arab Countries of the Gulf Area, joint activities have been undertaken in health legislation, health planning, malaria control, maternal and child health and anti-smoking campaigns.

Fertility and the family: It is believed that the Government views intervention to maintain fertility rates as appropriate. In 1982, new measures were announced to encourage Saudi Arabian men to marry in Saudi Arabia, despite the high dowries that they are required to pay their brides. A grant of up to $US 7,000 was provided to men about to marry who can prove that they both adhere to the practices of Islam and have insufficient funds. It was hoped that this would encourage marriage between Saudi Arabians and halt the trend of Saudi Arabian men marrying abroad. The policy also aims to encourage marriage at an earlier age and to increase the rate of population growth. Other Government measures that were in effect as of 1980 include a child allowance for low-income families and maternity benefits. Elective abortion is not allowed, while female sterilization is not prohibited.

International migration: The Government is determined to develop the nation's indigenous labour resources in order to reduce its dependence on foreign-born labour. The Five-Year Plan for 1986-1990 aimed to reduce the expatriate population by 600,000 by 1990. To ensure an adequate labour supply, priority is being given to the development of human resources through improved educational and vocational training. One of the aims of the Fifth Five-Year Development Plan for 1990-1994 will be the adoption of measures for the replacement of foreign-born manpower by Saudi Arabian personnel. A number of regulations have already been issued to promote Saudization such as requiring that all vacancy advertisements be sent to the Ministry of Labour for examination and the stipulation in article 45 of the Saudi Arabian Labour Code that the proportion of Saudi Arabian workers on a company's payroll be at least 75 per cent of the total work force, except in special circumstances. A plan to impose income taxes on all foreign businesses and foreign workers was rescinded in January 1989.

Spatial distribution/urbanization: Measures aim at organizing regional development in metropolitan centres and rural areas, making the nomadic population sedentary through agricultural development and establishing industrial zones in different regions. Under the Regional Development Planning Project begun in 1980, which aims to integrate urban and rural development, planning studies were undertaken in Hail, Qassim, Makkah, Baha, Tabuk, Jizan, Qatif and Ihsa. The objective is to provide urban-level services to rural settlements that involve as little displacement as possible. The Government has completed the construction of Jubail, a planned industrial city on the Gulf at a cost of $US 20 billion, and of Yambu, a smaller sister development across the country on the Red Sea. Guidelines for the Fifth Five-Year Plan (1990-1994) place emphasis on achieving balanced development between various regions by linking development to the actual needs of the population, selecting growth centres to make full use of available facilities and checking the trend towards dispersing services and resources.

<u>Status of women and population</u>: The advancement and development of Saudi Arabian women is taking place within the framework of Islamic values and social practices. Women's progress is parallel to, but separate from, that of men. In 1980, the Government announced that a special inter-ministerial committee would be set up to study the issue of suitable female employment within an Islamic framework. A Special Department for Women in the Civil Service has been established. Women in Government employment are guaranteed equal pay for equal work. The Development Plan for 1990-1994 aims to increase female labour force participation. Information on the minimum legal age at marriage for women is not readily available .

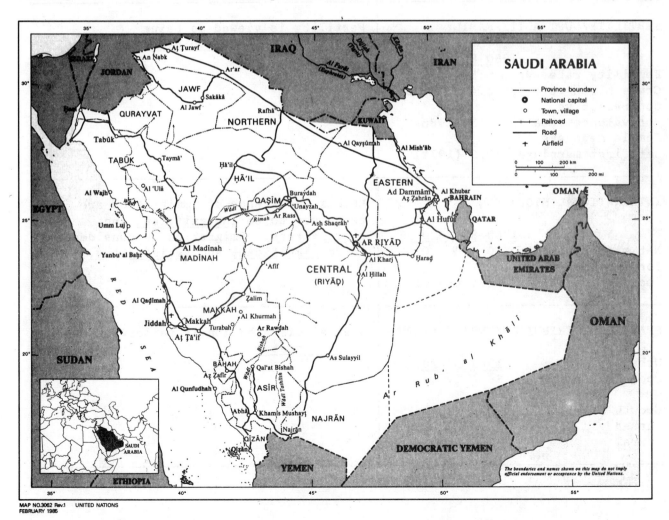

MAP NO.3062 Rev.1   UNITED NATIONS
FEBRUARY 1985

SENEGAL

DEMOGRAPHIC INDICATORS	CURRENT PERCEPTION
SIZE/AGE STRUCTURE/GROWTH	The growth rate of the population is considered to be <u>unsatisfactory</u> because it is <u>too high</u>.

Population:	1985	2025
(thousands)	6 444	16 364
0-14 years (%)	44.4	33.2
60+ years (%)	4.8	6.3

Rate of:	1980-85	2020-25
growth	2.6	1.5
natural increase	25.5	15.4

MORTALITY/MORBIDITY

Levels are felt to be <u>unacceptable</u>. The Government has expressed concern over high rates of infant and maternal mortality.

	1980-85	2020-25
Life expectancy	43.3	59.8
Crude death rate	20.9	9.3
Infant mortality	142.0	66.0

FERTILITY/NUPTIALITY/FAMILY

Fertility is viewed as being <u>unsatisfactory</u> and <u>too high</u>.

	1980-85	2020-25
Fertility rate	6.5	3.0
Crude birth rate	46.4	24.6
Contraceptive prevalence rate	11.3 (1986)	
Female mean age at first marriage	18.3 (1978)	

INTERNATIONAL MIGRATION

Levels and trends of immigration are perceived to be <u>insignificant</u> and <u>satisfactory</u>. Emigration is considered to be <u>significant</u> and <u>satisfactory</u>.

	1980-85	2020-25
Net migration rate	0.0	0.0
Foreign-born population (%)	2.4 (1976)	

SPATIAL DISTRIBUTION/URBANIZATION

Spatial distribution is perceived to be <u>inappropriate</u>.

Urban	1985	2025
population (%)	36.4	62.6

Growth rate:	1980-85	2020-25
urban	3.3	2.6
rural	2.1	-0.1

GENERAL POLICY FRAMEWORK

<u>Overall approach to population problems</u>: The Government considers
population problems to be very important in relation to development. It
maintains a policy of direct intervention to lower fertility and places
great emphasis on reducing infant/child mortality and encouraging
migration to rural areas of the country.

<u>Importance of population policy in achieving development objectives</u>: The
Government views population as a factor in economic and social development
and considers population research to be an essential basis for
socio-economic planning. The Government reports that it adopted a
population policy in April 1988 and that it has issued clear instructions
on ministerial responsibilities with regard to the implementation and
evaluation of population policy; these include fertility and
child-spacing, immigration, urbanization, employment, legal measures and
measures to strengthen the Commission Nationale de la Population and the
Division of Human Resources.

INSTITUTIONAL FRAMEWORK

<u>Population data systems and development planning</u>: Census-taking is the
responsibility of the Bureau National du Recensement under the Direction
de la Statistique. The country's first complete census was conducted in
1976 and a subsequent census in 1988. A project was initiated in 1984
with the objective of improving civil registration in terms of
geographical coverage and the quality of birth, death and marriage
statistics. The Seventh Five-Year Economic and Social Development Plan
(1985-1989), prepared by the Ministère du Plan et de la Coopération, is
currently in effect.

<u>Integration of population within development planning</u>: The Commission
Nationale de la Population, established in 1979, is charged with
formulating and co-ordinating population policy. The Population Unit was
established with international assistance to serve as the secretariat to
the Commission and to assist in defining a national population policy.
The Direction de la Planification of the Ministère du Plan et de la
Coopération has responsibility for taking population variables into
consideration in planning.

POLICIES AND MEASURES

<u>Changes in population size and age structure</u>: The Government, concerned by
the impact that the country's demographic dynamics is having on employment,
education and health, would like to achieve a greater harmony between
population growth and economic development. The population policy adopted in
1988 seeks to lower fertility, limit rural-to-urban migration, promote
population education and create employment opportunities, and calls upon the

SENEGAL

Commission Nationale de la Population to evaluate current legislation, taxation and the social security system. The social security scheme covers employed persons, including domestic, seasonal and day workers, while a special system exists for public employees.

Mortality and morbidity: The general objective of the Seventh Development Plan (1985-1989) reiterates the Government's two major principles: the right to health of all citizens and access to all levels of the national health system. The policy is based on the integration and decentralization of services and on comprehensive, preventative, curative, educational and social activities. Primary health care for all is now an integral part of the health system. The Government is creating and expanding health clinics so as to improve the hygiene and well-being of infants and children. In order to implement a family health policy, whose objective was to improve maternal and child health, a project was initiated in 1982 to strengthen the service delivery infrastructure by provision of medical equipment and the training of health personnel in community health. In 1988 the country received international assistance to establish an anti-AIDS campaign.

Fertility and the family: The family is viewed as a sacred institution which requires assistance and protection. The Government has a policy of reducing the rate of fertility through the integration of family planning programmes into maternal and child health services, the development of information and training programmes to promote child-spacing, the encouragement of breast-feeding and the provision of contraceptives. Adolescent pregnancies are a major concern to the Government. The Government also seeks to lower the incidence of infertility and sterility in order to permit families to achieve their desired family size. Abortion is allowed only in cases where the mother's health is in danger, and it is carried out by a qualified medical practitioner. Sterilization is not permitted.

International migration: Immigration has not been an active policy concern of the Government. However, in April 1989 a border incident between Senegal and Mauritania led to the simultaneous exodus of nationals of each of the two countries living in the other country. The Government of Senegal reported that as of June 1989 there were 57,000 refugees in Senegal. In addition, 14,000 Senegalese nationals formerly resident in Mauritania had returned to Senegal. To avoid creating a situation of dependence, it has been decided to assist the refugees in becoming self-sufficient as soon as possible while waiting for a lasting solution instead of establishing camps. The Ministry of Emigration has implemented policies to encourage the return of Senegalese who have emigrated and to help them readjust to the economic and social conditions in Senegal.

Spatial distribution/urbanization: The Government is implementing policies to reduce the major imbalances in the pattern of population distribution. The Government has undertaken a project to formulate a National Spatial Distribution Plan. The Plan seeks to reduce migration from rural to urban and metropolitan areas in the western part of the country by promoting the growth of existing towns, decentralizing education and research functions, and implementing measures for human resource investments such as job training and educational facilities.

Status of women and population: One of the Government's main concerns is to improve the status of women by emphasizing education and women's integration into the social, economic and cultural life of Senegal.   Measures are currently being implemented to facilitate women's access to education and employment through the adoption of a Plan of Action for Women, through the Family Code and the creation of centres for the protection of mothers and children.   The minimum legal age at marriage for women is 16 years.

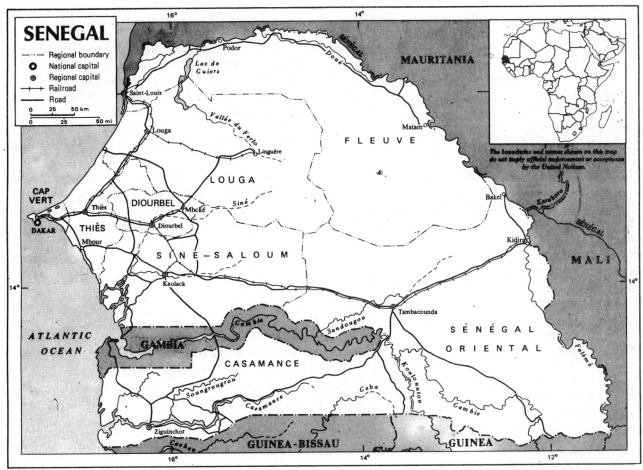

MAP NO. 3016 Rev.2   UNITED NATIONS
SEPTEMBER 1985

SEYCHELLES

DEMOGRAPHIC INDICATORS	CURRENT PERCEPTION
SIZE/AGE STRUCTURE/GROWTH Population: 1985 2025 (thousands) 65 84 0-14 years (%) ... ... 60+ years (%) ... ... Rate of: 1980-85 2020-25 growth 0.7 0.1 natural increase	The Government considers the rate of population growth to be <u>unsatisfactory</u> because it is too <u>high</u>.
MORTALITY/MORBIDITY 1980-85 2020-25 Life expectancy ... ... Crude death rate ... ... Infant mortality	The Government views mortality levels as <u>acceptable</u>. Considerable progress has been made in reducing health problems, while diseases associated with old age are becoming prominent.
FERTILITY/NUPTIALITY/FAMILY 1980-85 2020-25 Fertility rate ... ... Crude birth rate ... ... Contraceptive prevalence rate ... ... Female mean age at first marriage	Current fertility levels are perceived as <u>unsatisfactory</u> because they are <u>too high</u>. There is particular concern about the high incidence of teen-age pregnancy.
INTERNATIONAL MIGRATION 1980-85 2020-25 Net migration rate ... ... Foreign-born population (%) 3.1 (1977)	Immigration is considered to be <u>insignificant</u> and <u>satisfactory</u>. Emigration is considered to be <u>significant</u> and <u>too high</u>.
SPATIAL DISTRIBUTION/URBANIZATION Urban 1985 2025 population (%) 51.8 80.1 Growth rate: 1980-85 2020-25 urban 4.5 0.6 rural -2.8 -1.6	The Government views spatial distribution as <u>inappropriate</u>.

GENERAL POLICY FRAMEWORK

Overall approach to population problems: The Government's policies aim to decrease population growth by reducing fertility and mortality, as well as to provide for the health of all individuals. Concern about the increasing birth rate in the 1960s led to the implementation of family planning services, which came under the Government's direct supervision in 1978. It has also been anticipated that policies pursued in various social and economic sectors will have an indirect impact on reducing population growth. The Government has consistently placed emphasis on upgrading preventive health services and making them accessible at the community level, within the context of general welfare.

Importance of population policy in achieving development objectives: The Government considers it necessary to consolidate the country's social and economic gains made since independence in 1976. An early objective of development planning was the introduction of family planning. The Government continues to support family planning efforts, which would also improve maternal and child health, and to work towards increasing awareness of the implications of the country's population growth. It is recognized that reducing growth rates would ease pressure on the provision of social services and on the limited amount of land available for development.

INSTITUTIONAL FRAMEWORK

Population data systems and development planning: A census was conducted in 1977 and no new census had been scheduled as of 1989. Vital registration, which is the responsibility of the Civil Status Office of the Statistics Division, has improved considerably in the past 20 years and is now considered to be virtually complete. Until 1984, Seychelles had a rolling plan that was periodically revised. The National Development Plan for the period 1985-1989 continued the emphasis on social services, notably education and health care, but also gave higher priority than previously to sectors such as tourism, which is the dominant industry, as well as agriculture and fisheries. The National Development Plan for the period 1990-1994 was under preparation in early 1989.

Integration of population within development planning: The Statistics Division produces semi-annual reports on population and vital statistics, as well as on employment and other economic indicators. It also prepares information on population and development interrelationships, so that population variables may be taken into account in development planning. However, there does not appear to be a single government agency that is responsible for the formulation and co-ordination of population policies.

SEYCHELLES

POLICIES AND MEASURES

Changes in population size and age structure: The Government has adopted a policy to reduce growth in order to achieve a growth rate and age structure more compatible with the country's economic capabilities. No quantitative targets have been set regarding the rate of population growth. In addition to the provision of integrated family planning and maternal and child health services, the Government aims to reduce fertility levels through adjustment of social, cultural and economic factors and the introduction of population and family welfare into worker education. The Government has made a strong commitment to extending health-care services to the population, so as to reduce mortality and morbidity. The social security scheme extends coverage to employed persons including domestic and casual workers, self-employed, non-employed with unearned income and public employees.

Mortality and morbidity: The Government's policy is to provide adequate health services for all through a tax-financed health service, without charge at the point of use. Considerable resources have been devoted to the health sector, with a network of polyclinics established to provide a range of services from general medical care to dentistry and pre- and post-natal care. The Government continues to expand and upgrade preventive services and the quality of child and maternal care. Significant progress has been achieved in reducing infant mortality and combating both infectious diseases and malnutrition, and almost universal coverage has been attained for maternal and child health services, including immunization. Audio-visual equipment and teaching aids have been used to promote breast-feeding. To combat the problem of malnutrition among children, the Government has launched a child-feeding programme providing midday meals at primary schools, day-care centres and maternal and child health clinics. A Plan of Action for the period 1985-1989 prepared by the Ministry of Health had the following among its goals: to reduce life-style-related health risks associated with hypertension, cardio-vascular diseases, alcoholism, accidents and sexually transmitted diseases through health promotion and disease prevention activities; to improve environmental conditions through the provision of a safe water supply, adequate sanitary conditions and safe disposal of sewage and solid waste; and to promote responsible use of health facilities by encouraging self-reliance and self-care through information and education.

Fertility and the family: The Government intervenes to lower the rate of fertility and aims to improve maternal and child health and family well-being. It has promoted family planning, and since 1978 family planning services have been provided directly within the context of the maternal and child health programme at government clinics and social centres, and by community health nurses in outlying rural areas. A major concern is the high teen-age pregnancy rate, which the Government has actively sought to lower. Family life and sex education now form an integral component of the curriculum in all schools. Sterilization is legal and abortion is permitted to protect the life of the mother, on juridical grounds, and in cases where the child would be seriously handicapped, physically or mentally, if born.

International migration: The insignificant level of immigration is not an active policy concern. As regards emigration, the scarcity of skilled manpower is a recognized constraint on development and the country suffers from problems associated with the brain drain. It has proved difficult to persuade Seychellois with medical training to stay in the country. Consequently, the health service remains heavily dependent on expatriate medical personnel that are subject to frequent turnover.

<u>Spatial distribution/urbanization</u>: To readjust the inappropriate pattern of spatial distribution, whereby around 90 per cent of the population lives on the island of Mahé, where the capital, Victoria, is situated, the Government has undertaken the development of the outer islands, which are underpopulated and unexploited. In 1980 the Islands Development Company, a parastatal, was created to manage some of the outer islands on a commercial basis. It is responsible for 10 islands.

<u>Status of women and population</u>: A National Women's Association exists to promote nutrition, child care, and income-generating activities, including small-scale industries such as tie-dyeing, sewing and crafts. The overall aim is to encourage women to be agents of social change and development in their communities. The Government has taken steps to institute social change and women in the Seychelles now enjoy equal legal rights with men. Information on the minimum legal age at marriage is not readily available.

<u>Other issues</u>: The Government has consistently accorded high priority to education. As a result, literacy and education levels have risen substantially. Nearly all children aged four to six years attend free crèches as part of a pre-school education programme that is thought to have a beneficial effect on the child and family, particularly in light of the fact that a high percentage of children live with only one parent. The Government has also attached major importance to the development of social and day-care centres within the community services programme. Many children aged two to three years attend government day-care centres that aid the disadvantaged sectors of the population, especially employed mothers.

SEYCHELLES

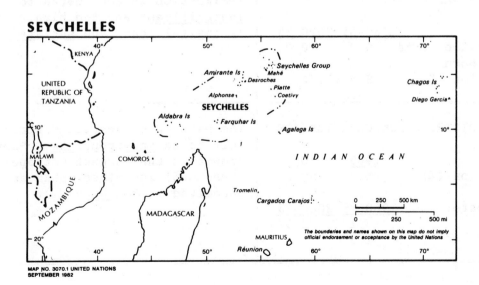

MAP NO. 3070.1 UNITED NATIONS
SEPTEMBER 1982

SIERRA LEONE

DEMOGRAPHIC INDICATORS	CURRENT PERCEPTION
SIZE/AGE STRUCTURE/GROWTH	The Government has recently taken the view that the population growth rate is <u>unsatisfactory</u> because it is <u>too high</u>.

Population: <u>1985</u>   <u>2025</u>
 (thousands)   3 665   9 641
  0-14 years (%)   43.9   37.3
  60+ years (%)   5.2   5.5
 	
Rate of: <u>1980-85</u> <u>2020-25</u>
 growth   2.3   1.8
 natural increase 23.2 18.0	

MORTALITY/MORBIDITY	Current levels and trends are perceived as <u>unacceptable</u>. Particular concerns are infant, child and maternal mortality.
<u>1980-85</u> <u>2020-25</u> Life expectancy 39.0 55.0 Crude death rate 25.2 11.5 Infant mortality 166.0 85.0	
FERTILITY/NUPTIALITY/FAMILY	Current rates are considered to be <u>unsatisfactory</u> because they are <u>too high</u> in relation to maternal and child health and family well-being. Adolescent fertility and illegal abortions are major concerns.
<u>1980-85</u> <u>2020-25</u> Fertility rate 6.5 3.6 Crude birth rate 48.4 29.5 Contraceptive prevalence rate ... ... Female mean age at first marriage	
INTERNATIONAL MIGRATION	Immigration is considered to be <u>insignificant</u> and <u>too high</u>. Emigration is <u>insignificant</u> and <u>satisfactory</u>.
<u>1980-85</u> <u>2020-25</u> Net migration rate 0.0 0.0 Foreign-born population (%) 3.4 (1974)	
SPATIAL DISTRIBUTION/URBANIZATION	The pattern of spatial distribution is felt to be <u>inappropriate</u>. Population growth in the largest metropolitan area (Freetown) and other urban areas is perceived as <u>too high</u>.
Urban <u>1985</u> <u>2025</u> population (%) 28.3 59.1 Growth rate: <u>1980-85</u> <u>2020-25</u> urban 5.1 3.0 rural 1.3 0.2	

GENERAL POLICY FRAMEWORK

<u>Overall approach to population problems</u>: In 1988 the Government was in the process of formulating a national population policy to address high population growth and fertility rates. Current policy aims to lower morbidity and mortality rates and adjust spatial distribution.

<u>Importance of population policy in achieving development objectives</u>: The Government has integrated population variables into socio-economic planning efforts and is now committed to formulating eventually a national population policy so as to improve its development efforts.

INSTITUTIONAL FRAMEWORK

<u>Population data systems and development planning</u>: The country's first two complete censuses were conducted in 1963 and 1974. The most recent census was held in 1985. A project was initiated in 1979 to strengthen the civil registration and vital statistics system. Formal development planning has existed since 1974. The Government's development objectives, strategies and priorities are articulated in the framework for the Economic Recovery Programme and the first and second stages of the Public Investment Programme for 1986/87-1988/89 and 1989/90-1991/92.

<u>Integration of population within development planning</u>: The National Population Commission, in the Ministry of Development and Economic Planning, was established in 1982 to formulate and co-ordinate population policies. In 1988 it was in the process of formulating a national population policy. The Population and Human Resources Section of the Central Planning Unit, located in the same Ministry, was formed in 1978 for the purpose of integrating population into development planning, as well as for preparing population projections and providing information on population and development interrelationships. It also provides assistance to the National Population Commission.

POLICIES AND MEASURES

<u>Changes in population size and age structure</u>: The National Population Commission has been in the process of formulating a national population policy that will directly address the perceived problem of population growth. Between 1982 and 1985 a number of task forces were established to examine various population issues, including fertility, morbidity and mortality, migration and women in development, and their conclusions will form the basis of an eventual national policy. Some of the Government's policies have indirectly affected population size and growth. These include efforts to reduce the high rates of infant, child and maternal morbidity and mortality, and to improve the spatial distribution pattern and the provision of family planning services as part of family health services. A social security scheme exists for public employees only.

SIERRA LEONE

Mortality and morbidity: The Primary Health Care Programme has been implemented to reduce high infant and maternal mortality rates, and the high incidence of malaria and other communicable diseases. Under the National Health Policy, various strategies have been pursued and include the provision of a network of appropriately staffed health facilities accessible to all, especially in rural areas; the control of communicable diseases mainly through an expanded programme of immunization; the provision of safe and adequate drinking water supplies and basic sanitation; prevention and control of locally endemic diseases; the promotion of adequate food supplies and proper nutrition; and the provision of essential drugs. A diarrhoeal diseases control programme has been established and family planning is being integrated into maternal and child health centres. The future national population policy is expected to address the main causes for the generally poor health conditions, including low nutritional and educational levels and poor environmental sanitation, as well as to improve the quality of mortality data. No quantitative targets have been set.

Fertility and the family: As of 1989 the Government did not report any measures intended to influence directly the rate of fertility. Measures have, however, been taken to improve maternal and child health and family well-being. These measures include the integration of family planning services in maternal and child centres, and since 1977 a programme aimed at integrating population education into school curricula and pre-service and in-service teacher education courses. Programmes have also been implemented to introduce population and family welfare education into worker education programmes and to expand family life education into the formal school system as a means of reducing adolescent fertility. Among the task forces created by the National Population Commission are units examining fertility and reproduction, and law and population. Their findings regarding fertility and its consequences will be considered when the Commission formulates a national policy. Since 1988 the Government has been providing direct support for access to contraceptives. Abortion is illegal except to save the life of the mother. There are no legal provisions concerning sterilization.

International migration: The Government would like to limit further the insignificant level of immigration by reducing the flow of permanent migrants, persons with non-permanent work permits and undocumented migrants. The Government is concerned by the impact of immigration on urban growth and employment in the informal sector. Concerning emigration, the Government, as a means of reducing the departure of professional and skilled workers, has attempted to improve working conditions through salary revisions and the creation and upgrading of employment possibilities.

Spatial distribution/urbanization: The Government wants to introduce major changes in the spatial distribution pattern of the population by decreasing migration to urban areas and out-migration from rural areas. Development of growth centres in lagging and border regions is undertaken within a broader policy of regional development. The Government considers regional development as the corner-stone of its development policy. Towards this end there are a number of integrated rural development projects. Sierra Leone has been subdivided into agricultural/rural development regions. The development of growth centres is also being undertaken and industrial growth centres are being established. These programmes will form elements of a population policy that was being formulated in 1988.

<u>Status of women and population</u>: Several projects are being implemented to enhance the status of women and provide them with employment outside the home. These projects involve vocational training for unskilled women, upgrading the management skills of female executives and integrating women in rural development. The minimum legal age at marriage for women is 15 years.

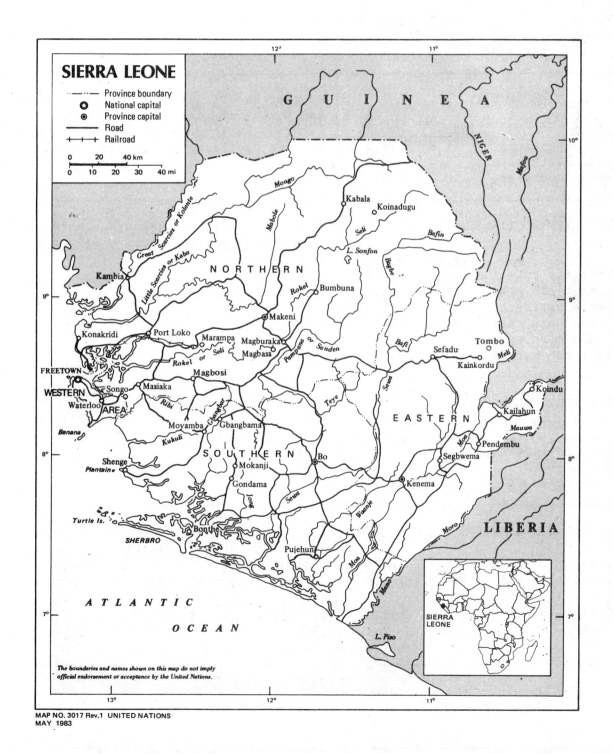

SINGAPORE

DEMOGRAPHIC INDICATORS	CURRENT PERCEPTION

SIZE/AGE STRUCTURE/GROWTH
 	
Population: 1985   2025
 (thousands) 2 559   3 239
  0-14 years (%)   24.5   16.6
  60+ years (%)   7.7   27.0
 	
Rate of: 1980-85 2020-25
 growth   1.2   0.1
 natural increase   11.6   1.2
	The Government perceives current growth rates to be <u>satisfactory</u>. It has indicated concern about population aging and future population size.

MORTALITY/MORBIDITY 1980-85 2020-25 Life expectancy 71.8 78.3 Crude death rate 5.4 9.8 Infant mortality 10.0 5.0	Present conditions of health and levels and trends of mortality and morbidity are regarded as <u>acceptable</u>. Major concerns are now neoplasms and cardio-vascular diseases.
FERTILITY/NUPTIALITY/FAMILY 1980-85 2020-25 Fertility rate 1.7 1.8 Crude birth rate 17.0 11.0 Contraceptive prevalence rate 74.2 (1982) Female mean age at first marriage 26.2 (1980)	Current fertility rates are considered to be <u>unsatisfactory</u> because they are <u>too low</u>.
INTERNATIONAL MIGRATION 1980-85 2020-25 Net migration rate ... ... Foreign-born population (%) 21.8 (1980)	Both immigration and emigration levels and trends are viewed as <u>insignificant</u> and <u>satisfactory</u>.
SPATIAL DISTRIBUTION/URBANIZATION Urban 1985 2025 population (%) 100.0 100.0 Growth rate: 1980-85 2020-25 urban 1.2 0.1 rural 0.0 0.0	The Government considers the present pattern of spatial distribution to be <u>appropriate</u> and not an issue because the country is a small island city state.

GENERAL POLICY FRAMEWORK

<u>Overall approach to population problems</u>: The birth rate continues to be the focus of population concerns. The Government in 1985 reversed its long-standing "stop at two" anti-natalist policy and introduced incentives for couples to have at least three children. The Government is concerned over the low fertility of more educated women resulting in undesirable trends in population quality, and though it remains concerned about fertility differentials, it has modified earlier attempts to stimulate higher fertility among women university graduates in favour of a new programme that encourages fertility among the entire population. Other government programmes promote social and economic advancement.

<u>Importance of population policy in achieving development objectives</u>: The Government has consistenty attached major importance to population policy in achieving development objectives. It now considers that the marked fall in fertility will retard economic growth and is a hindrance to the country's becoming an important international business centre and a high-technology, export-oriented economy. Worries about a lower tax base to support the elderly and a shortage of recruits for the armed forces have also led to the promotion of the new policy, which advocates couples "to have three children, if you can afford it", so as to achieve development objectives.

INSTITUTIONAL FRAMEWORK

<u>Population data systems and development planning</u>: The last census was held in 1980 and the next was scheduled for 1990. Censuses are conducted by the Census Office of the Department of Statistics. Various demographic surveys have also been held, including the National Family Planning Survey in 1982. Vital registration, which is complete, is the responsibility of the Registrar-General of Births and Deaths. National development plans have guided socio-economic development, but as of 1988 there was no plan in effect. The development strategy of the Economic Development Board gives priority to the upgrading of industrial technology and the further development of manpower resources and public sector services.

<u>Integration of population within development planning</u>: An integrated approach has been adopted covering all aspects of development planning. In 1985, the Government abolished the Singapore Family Planning and Population Board, which formulated policy to control population growth and oversaw the population programme, on the grounds that family planning had become a way of life and below-replacement level fertility had been reached. The functions of the Board were transferred to other Government ministries, particularly the Ministry of Health. The Population Planning Unit, formed in 1986 as a part of the Ministry of Health, is the research institution chiefly responsible for providing information on population-development interrelationships. Government ministries take population variables into account in planning. The Inter-Ministerial Population Committee formulates and co-ordinates population policy.

SINGAPORE

POLICIES AND MEASURES

<u>Changes in population size and age structure</u>: Concerned by population aging, as a consequence of the rapid fertility decline and the consequent possibility of severe labour shortages, the Government has implemented measures to maintain the rate of population growth and increase the size of the population. Measures to promote larger families include tax rebates, subsidies and priority in school registration and public housing allocation. An eventual stationary population of 3.5 million people by the year 2050 is the specified target. Under the social security scheme, coverage includes employed persons earning more than $S 50 a month and some self-employed workers, while excluding members of existing private plans. A special pension system has been established for public employees.

<u>Mortality and morbidity</u>: The Government continues to strive for high standards of health care. The main emphasis is the promotion of health through the prevention of disease, health education activities and the upgrading and improvement of primary health care and hospital services. Specific measures are mass immunization, provision of safe water, effective vector control, fluoridation of water and nutritional supplements. A community-based health-care approach is promoted to meet the needs of the elderly more adequately. Under the Government's Medisave scheme, introduced in 1984, assistance is provided to help defray the costs of hospitalization if the need arises. To deal with the AIDS crisis, surveillance, public education, counselling and support services for high-risk individuals have been promoted.

<u>Fertility and the family</u>: Concerns over below-replacement level fertility prompted a dramatic reversal of policy in the 1980s. The Government now encourages large families and hopes that its new campaign will be as effective as its former two-child policy. A host of pro-natalist measures have been implemented, including generous tax rebates for parents with at least three children, child-care subsidies, priority registration for early schooling and in obtaining Government-subsidized housing and subsidized hospital and delivery services. A $S 20,000 tax rebate ($S 2.0 = $US 1 as of 1987) was available to families with a fourth child born after 1 January 1988, which followed a similar rebate for a third child introduced in 1987. The Government continues to support the Social Development Unit (SDU), established to promote marriages among college graduates, reflecting official concern that many women, especially the well educated, are either remaining single or having fewer children. Family planning services are integrated with those of maternal and child health and are also provided through private agencies. Sterilization is legal, but is discouraged for women with fewer than three children. In 1980, more restrictive regulations were placed on the legal performance of abortion, which was made available on demand in 1968, subject to certain conditions; since 1987, pre- and post-abortion counselling was made compulsory to discourage "abortions of convenience".

<u>International migration</u>: Concerning the level of immigration, new measures, which went into effect in 1989, lowered from 50 per cent to 40 per cent the number of expatriate workers a company could employ. Companies having a work force exceeding 40 per cent foreign-born will not be permitted to employ additional expatriates and will have one year to reduce the percentage to 40 per cent. Taxes on foreigners were also substantially increased. To reduce illegal immigration, as of April 1989 anyone found working without proper documentation is subject to three months' imprisonment. In July 1989, the

Government announced that it would permit up to 25,000 residents of Hong Kong and their dependants to immigrate to Singapore over the next five years. Although emigration is not significant, the Government would like to attract back Singaporeans who can contribute to the country's overall development.

Spatial distribution/urbanization: The Planning Department of the Ministry of National Development is responsible for overall physical planning and for ensuring that the scarce land resources are well managed. It co-ordinates all physical development through the Master Plan Committee and the zoning system developed for the totally urbanized city-state. The national housing programme of the Housing and Development Board has provided accommodation for 85 per cent of the population, mostly in new high-rise apartments. The Urban Redevelopment Authority undertakes programmes of urban renewal and a greening programme, including tree planting and park development.

Status of women and population: Under the Constitution, women have equal rights with men and the 1961 Women's Charter further stipulated that women have material, divorce and property rights, equal pay and status, and protection from abuse and exploitation. However, no formal mechanism for integrating or co-ordinating women's affairs with overall national development policy has been created. The Government has promoted the participation of women in the labour force. The minimum legal age at marriage for women is 18 years, except Muslims for whom it is 16 years.

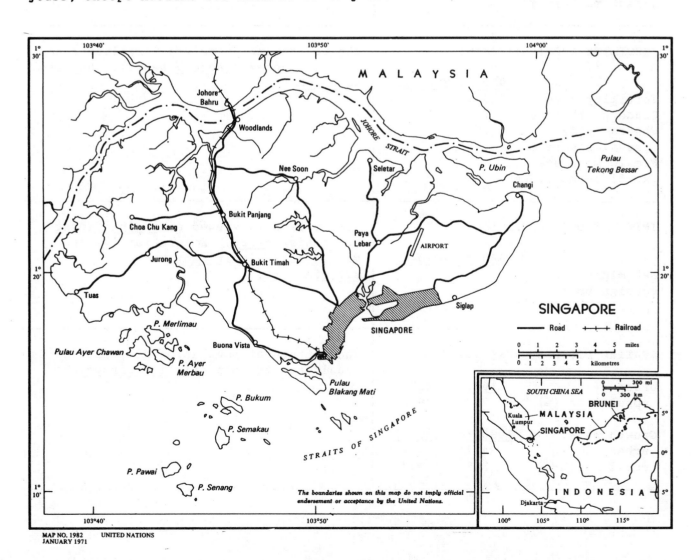

SOLOMON ISLANDS

DEMOGRAPHIC INDICATORS	CURRENT PERCEPTION

SIZE/AGE STRUCTURE/GROWTH
 	
 Population: <u>1985</u>   <u>2025</u>
  (thousands)   269   771
  0-14 years (%)   ...   ...
  60+ years (%)   ...   ...
 	
 Rate of: <u>1980-85</u> <u>2020-25</u>
  growth   3.6   1.7
  natural increase   ...   ...
	The Government considers the growth rate to be <u>unsatisfactory</u> because it is <u>too high</u>.

MORTALITY/MORBIDITY <u>1980-85</u> <u>2020-25</u> Life expectancy ... ... Crude death rate ... ... Infant mortality	Levels and trends of mortality and morbidity are regarded as <u>unacceptable</u>.

FERTILITY/NUPTIALITY/FAMILY
 	
        <u>1980-85</u> <u>2020-25</u>
 Fertility rate   ...   ...
 Crude birth rate   ...   ...
 Contraceptive
  prevalence rate   ...   ...
 Female mean age
  at first marriage   ...   ...
	The Government perceives fertility rates as being <u>unsatisfactory</u> because they are <u>too high</u>.

INTERNATIONAL MIGRATION <u>1980-85</u> <u>2020-25</u> Net migration rate ... ... Foreign-born population (%) 2.5 (1976)	Immigration is viewed as <u>insignificant</u> and <u>satisfactory</u>. Emigration is also viewed as <u>insignificant</u> and <u>satisfactory</u>.

SPATIAL DISTRIBUTION/URBANIZATION
 	
 Urban   <u>1985</u>   <u>2025</u>
  population (%)   9.7   29.6
 	
 Growth rate: <u>1980-85</u> <u>2020-25</u>
  urban   4.7   4.4
  rural   3.5   0.7
	The pattern of population distribution is considered to be <u>partially appropriate</u>.

GENERAL POLICY FRAMEWORK

Overall approach to population problems: There are policies in place to modify population growth by decreasing fertility levels, modifying the pattern of spatial distribution and adjusting social and economic factors. As of 1988, the Government was gradually moving towards adopting a comprehensive national population policy.

Importance of population policy in achieving development objectives: The Government's growing awareness of the importance of population policy as part of development strategy stems from an increasing perception that high rates of population growth are impeding progress in achieving development objectives. Although Solomon Islands has a relatively small population base, a favourable land-to-population ratio and good agricultural potential, the findings of the 1986 census have drawn attention to population issues and, in particular, to rapid population growth. As a result, the Government is considerably more supportive of family planning efforts. A draft population policy outline and strategy for implementation was awaiting Cabinet approval in 1988.

INSTITUTIONAL FRAMEWORK

Population data systems and development planning: National censuses were conducted in 1959, 1970, 1976 and 1986 by the Statistics Office of the Ministry of Finance. Vital registration, especially the registration of deaths, is incomplete and there is very little information on inter-island migration. At present, local capacity for research into population issues is limited, although sample demographic surveys are carried out on a periodic basis by the Statistics Office. The Central Planning Office (CPO) is responsible for overall development planning. The National Development Plan for the period 1980-1984 was essentially a compilation of the sectoral plans developed by the various ministries and provincial governments. The objectives of the Second National Development Plan (1985-1989) are the promotion of physical, mental and social well-being, the advancement of knowledge, the equitable distribution of the benefits of development and greater self-reliance. The Plan places emphasis on rural development, particularly in the areas of community development and adult education.

Integration of population within development planning: The analysis of the 1986 census results and the work of the Solomon Islands Planned Parenthood Association (SIPPA) have indicated the need to integrate further population issues within development planning. Both the 1980-1984 and 1985-1989 national development plans contained implicit population objectives in sectoral plans and considered the implications of demographic trends. However, development planning is hindered by the recognized absence of reliable demographic and other data that would facilitate the integration of population variables into development planning. The Statistics Office and the Ministry of Health and Medical Services have been involved in the development planning process.

SOLOMON ISLANDS

POLICIES AND MEASURES

<u>Changes in population size and age structure</u>: The implications of high population growth rates have been recognized by the Government and policies are in place to lower the growth. The first and second national development plans, while expressing the Government's intention to lower growth, did not indicate specific measures. Prompted by increasing concern over high growth rates, the Government was considering a draft population policy in 1988. The National Development Plan for 1980-1984 specified a population growth rate target of 3.0 per cent by 1984. Under the social security scheme, coverage is available to all employed workers earning more than a certain amount or working at least six days a week, while public employees are included in a special scheme.

<u>Mortality and morbidity</u>: Health policies, which are the responsibility of the Ministry of Health and Medical Services and are administered locally by provincial health committees, are directed towards achieving development objectives and the principles of health for all. An epidemic of malaria in 1984 led to a mass drug administration programme to supplement insecticide spraying, which was carried out in the most affected areas. The Government has been concerned by the persistence of leprosy and scheduled a campaign to decrease its incidence in certain areas. The provision of safe water supply and sanitation facilities is being extended. The Government reported in 1985 that a reorientation of health workers towards primary health care was needed, as well as more native-born physicians to reduce dependence on expatriate medical personnel. In 1985, a review of the entire Ministry of Health was undertaken and a comprehensive health plan based on health for all was drafted.

<u>Fertility and the family</u>: The Government has reinforced its commitment to family planning as a consequence of the 1986 census results, indicating the persistence of extremely high population growth. Government policy is to reduce fertility in order to lower population growth rates. Efforts focus on improving women's health and encouraging the use of family planning services, giving particular stress to the importance of child-spacing. Emphasis is placed on health education, which includes family planning education. Family planning services are provided through government health clinics and hospitals, as well as by private organizations. In 1987, a community-based distribution project was established in 10 villages to increase the number of family planning acceptors. Messages about health and family life are regularly broadcast on radio. Information on the status of abortion and sterilization is not readily available.

<u>International migration</u>: The insignificant levels of immigration and emigration do not appear to be major policy concerns of the Government. The Government suffers from an acute shortage of skilled manpower, and a large proportion of the professional and technical labour force is recruited from abroad. There is some concern over the brain drain, particularly as it relates to medical professionals.

<u>Spatial distribution/urbanization</u>: The Government's policy is to adjust the pattern of spatial distribution through intervention in various areas including agriculture and rural development, industrialization, development of tourism

and expansion of social and economic infrastructure. Policies in effect to reduce the drift to urban areas include the devolution of government services to the countryside and the creation of provincial centres. These centres are expected to develop into small urban centres and to serve as alternative migration destinations to Honiara, thereby easing congestion in the capital.

Status of women and population: The Women's Interest Section is responsible for formulating women's programmes and activities, but there is no mechanism for integration with overall national development planning and policy-making. The Government seeks to ensure equality and increase the active participation of women in all forms of socio-economic activities and to strengthen women's organizations. The National Council of Women was established in 1983 to meet these objectives and, together with women's interest groups, runs health programmes for women. Information on the minimum legal age at marriage for women is not readily available.

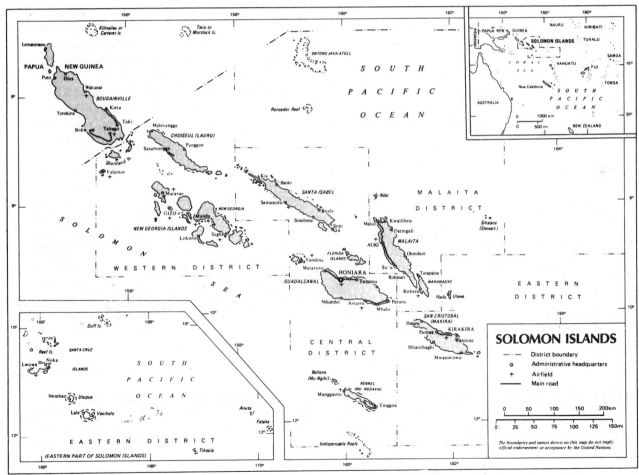

MAP NO. 2960 Rev. 2   UNITED NATIONS
SEPTEMBER 1988

SOMALIA

DEMOGRAPHIC INDICATORS	CURRENT PERCEPTION
SIZE/AGE STRUCTURE/GROWTH	The rate of growth is considered to be satisfactory, while population size is viewed as too small.

Population:
	1985	2025
(thousands)	6 398	18 903
0-14 years (%)	45.9	38.2
60+ years (%)	4.4	5.4

Rate of:
	1980-85	2020-25
growth	3.6	2.0
natural increase	31.7	20.2

MORTALITY/MORBIDITY

Levels of mortality are considered to be unacceptable. There is concern over child and maternal mortality.

	1980-85	2020-25
Life expectancy	43.0	59.0
Crude death rate	22.3	9.5
Infant mortality	143.0	69.0

FERTILITY/NUPTIALITY/FAMILY

Fertility rates are perceived as satisfactory.

	1980-85	2020-25
Fertility rate	6.6	3.6
Crude birth rate	53.9	29.7
Contraceptive prevalence rate	...	...
Female mean age at first marriage	20.1 (1980/81)	

INTERNATIONAL MIGRATION

Immigration is considered to be insignificant and satisfactory, while emigration is significant and satisfactory.

	1980-85	2020-25
Net migration rate	...	...
Foreign-born population (%)	...	...

SPATIAL DISTRIBUTION/URBANIZATION

Spatial distribution is viewed as partially appropriate.

	1985	2025
Urban population (%)	32.5	62.5

Growth rate:
	1980-85	2020-25
urban	5.9	3.1
rural	2.5	0.4

GENERAL POLICY FRAMEWORK

Overall approach to population problems: The Government has not formulated a national population policy.   The official position on population is that, since the country is sparsely populated the major problem facing it is the lack of socio-economic development, rather than population growth.   There is no reported Government intervention to modify levels of population growth or fertility.   Education on population matters has been integrated into school programmes.

Importance of population policy in achieving development objectives: A national population policy has not been adopted as the Government feels that socio-economic development is the most effective means of reducing population problems.   However, the Government is fully aware that demographic phenomena play an active role in the development process.

INSTITUTIONAL FRAMEWORK

Population data systems and development planning: The first nation-wide population census was conducted in 1975 and a second census in 1986-1987 dealt with the settled population in the first phase, and with the nomadic population in the second phase.   Census-taking is the responsibility of the Department of Statistics, in the Ministry of National Planning. Registration of births and deaths is considered to be incomplete and is impeded by the nomadic and semi-nomadic nature of a large segment of the population.   The most recent development plan is the Five-Year Development Plan for the period 1987-1991, which was prepared by the Department of Planning of the Ministry of National Planning.

Integration of population within development planning: Although the Five-Year Development Plan for 1987-1991 does not include a national population policy, the Government has a policy of integrating demographic variables into the development planning process.   The Department of Human Resources and the Department of Statistics within the Ministry of National Planning are responsible for taking into account population variables in planning.   The lack of understanding about the importance of the interrelationship between population and development is considered to be the major obstacle to integrating population factors into development planning.

POLICIES AND MEASURES

Changes in population size and age structure: Although the Government does not report any measures aimed at directly influencing the rate of population growth, it is receiving international assistance to develop a population programme within the framework of its overall objectives.   The activities include establishing a model maternal and child health and child-spacing clinic in eight regions, continuing programmes of population education,

SOMALIA

analysing the results of the 1986-1987 census, eradicating the practice of female circumcision and strengthening the Department of Human Resources to become the policy-making organ in the area of population and human resources. A social security scheme exists only for public employees.

Mortality and morbidity: Articles 55 and 56 of the Constitution confirm the right to health for all and the Govenment is committed to providing free health care. The health system has been reoriented towards primary health care, with emphasis placed, on community involvement. Local committees have been set up at the village and district levels to motivate communities to participate in health activities. Village leaders have been requested to identify health priorities and to select possible remedies. International assistance has been provided to establish a model maternal/child health and child-spacing clinic network in eight regions. Measures have been undertaken to promote oral rehydration salts through primary health care in rural areas. In order to increase immunization coverage, which reached 28 per cent in 1987, strategy has been adopted aimed at mobilizing and training party functionaries to register and report all new-borns. The goal of universal child immunization by 1990 has been endorsed by the Head of State and has been given priority on the social agenda of the Somali Socialist Revolutionary Party. The Government has identified a number of constraints such as the armed conflict, the lack of reliable data, target creation, and monitoring procedure, inadequate co-ordination and the public's poor understanding of primary health care.

Fertility and the family: There is no official policy of intervention to influence the fertility rate. A Family Planning Division created within the Ministry of Health is responsible for co-ordinating all family planning activities. Projects are under way to strengthen child-spacing activities as well as population education. Primary school teachers, community and religious leaders, government officials and others have been trained in population education. The Labour Code of 1972 requires employers to pay maternity leave of 50 per cent of earnings up to 14 weeks to female employees. Access to modern methods of fertility regulation is not restricted and the Government provides indirect support through non-governmental agencies. Abortion is permitted only if the health of the mother or child is endangered. As of 1988 the Government has not formulated a policy governing female sterilization.

International migration: With one of the largest refugee populations in Africa, estimated by the Government to be 840,000 as of early 1989 or about 12 per cent of the population, the Government of Somalia has several times reiterated its position that voluntary repatriation is the most appropriate long-term solution for refugees in Somalia. It has indicated its readiness to facilitate the movement of refugees wishing to repatriate, but also stated that a programme of local settlement would be permitted for refugees not wishing to return. With the aim of expanding the programme of voluntary repatriation within the framework of a wider programme that would include the integration in Somalia of those not wishing to repatriate, the Tripartite Commission, consisting of Ethiopia, Somalia and the United Nations High Commissioner for Refugees, met in mid-1989. The meeting agreed that both self-repatriation where the refugees would make their own way to Ethiopia and report to authorities on arrival and organized repatriation could be contemplated. In both cases, prior clearance by the Government of Ethiopia would be required. There are no reported policies dealing with the significant level of emigration. An estimated 350,000 Somali refugees were in south-eastern Ethiopia at the end of 1988.

Spatial distribution/urbanization: The Government has undertaken measures to modify the spatial distribution of the population. For a number of years the Government has expressed its intention of sedentarizing the nomadic population. Since the mid-1970s, a number of projects have been directed at settlement of nomads through mixed farming systems that combine crop production with livestock rearing. Efforts to settle the population have, however, encountered difficulties. In late 1988 the President of Somalia announced that intensive armed attacks against government installations and administrative centres in the northern regions of West Galbeed and Togdheer had resulted in the massive displacement of population and widespread destruction of public and private property. It was reported that some urban centres in the north had become ghost cities with only limited signs of life.

Status of women and population: The Family Law of 1975 established the legal equality of women and men, granted women the right to hold political office and ensured them equal rights to inheritance and land and access to credit and training. It also abolished the right of a man to divorce his wife at will and would only permit polygamy under certain conditions. The minimum legal age at marriage for women is 18 years.

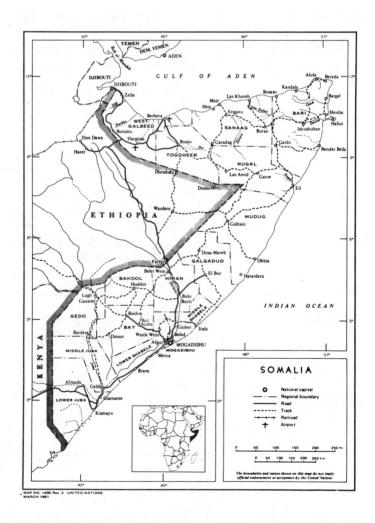

MAP NO. 1406 Rev. 2 UNITED NATIONS
MARCH 1981

SOUTH AFRICA

DEMOGRAPHIC INDICATORS	CURRENT PERCEPTION

SIZE/AGE STRUCTURE/GROWTH
 	
Population: 1985   2025
 (thousands)   31 593   63 232
  0–14 years (%)   37.8   26.1
  60+ years (%)   6.2   11.2
 	
Rate of: 1980–85   2020–25
 growth   2.2   1.1
 natural increase   22.1   11.2
	The Government considers the current population growth rate to be <u>unsatisfactory</u> because it is <u>too high</u>.

MORTALITY/MORBIDITY 1980–85 2020–25 Life expectancy 57.9 72.6 Crude death rate 11.0 6.6 Infant mortality 83.0 22.0	Mortality levels are considered to be <u>unacceptable</u>.
FERTILITY/NUPTIALITY/FAMILY 1980–85 2020–25 Fertility rate 4.8 2.3 Crude birth rate 33.1 17.7 Contraceptive prevalence rate 48.0 (1981) Female mean age at first marriage 25.7 (1980)	Fertility rates are viewed as <u>unsatisfactory</u> because they are <u>too high</u>. Expressed concerns are adolescent fertility and illegal abortions.
INTERNATIONAL MIGRATION 1980–85 2020–25 Net migration rate ... ... Foreign–born population (%) 7.9 (1985)	Immigration is considered to be <u>significant</u> and <u>satisfactory</u>, while emigration is considered to be <u>insignificant</u> and <u>satisfactory</u>. The brain drain is a concern.
SPATIAL DISTRIBUTION/URBANIZATION Urban 1985 2025 population (%) 56.0 77.3 Growth rate: 1980–85 2020–25 urban 3.2 1.7 rural 1.0 −0.6	The spatial distribution pattern is viewed as <u>inappropriate</u>.

GENERAL POLICY FRAMEWORK

<u>Overall approach to population problems</u>: The Government's policy aims to improve the living standards of the population in order to lower rates of population growth and fertility. The policy focuses on improvements in education, manpower training, primary health care, family planning, economic development, housing, controlled urbanization and rural development.

<u>Importance of population policy in achieving development objectives</u>: The Government notes that its Population Development Programme (PDP) aims to improve the living standards of all South Africans; this will contribute to establishing a balance between population size and the country's resources and potential.

INSTITUTIONAL FRAMEWORK

<u>Population data systems and development planning</u>: Population censuses were conducted in 1970, 1980 and 1985 and are the responsibility of the Central Statistical Services. The next census had been provisionally scheduled for 1990. Prepared by the Department of National Health and Population Development and launched in 1984, the PDP is currently in effect.

<u>Integration of population within development planning</u>: The Department of National Health and Population Development established the Population Development Programme, which involves government departments, other public sector bodies, private organizations and individuals. The progress of PDP is monitored annually, mainly with the aid of surveys undertaken by the Human Science Research Council, which is chiefly responsible for providing information on population-development interrelationships. The Government has indicated that high fertility is a major obstacle to integrating population factors into development planning.

POLICIES AND MEASURES

<u>Changes in population size and age structure</u>: The Government views population growth as an area of concern and wants to lower the rate of population growth. It is estimated that in terms of socio-economic potential and natural resources, South Africa can accommodate a population of only 80 million people. It is anticipated, however, that even if the current downward trend in population growth rates continues, the total population will be 116 million by the year 2100. The main objective of the Population Development Programme is to improve the standard of living of all people, so as to lower fertility, by concentrating on education, manpower training, primary health care, orderly urbanization and rural development. The overall goal is to decrease the rate of growth. The target is a population of 80 million by the year 2100. Concerning the social security scheme, coverage is available to residents of limited means, while provisions differ according to race. A special system exists for public employees.

SOUTH AFRICA

Mortality and morbidity: The Government is committed to reducing mortality and morbidity among all population segments. Research into the underlying causes of morbidity and mortality among infants and young children is undertaken by the Medical Research Council, as well as by the various medical schools. Emphasis on health care is being progressively redirected from curative to preventive services and community involvement in health improvement programmes is strongly promoted. There is serious concern over the detrimental effects of adolescent pregnancies and their effect on the health and well-being of both mother and child. Special measures to prevent AIDS have been set up and these include the formation of a nation-wide advisory group and an AIDS action group, health education programmes, screening tests of all blood donations, with free tests available to all high-risk groups, heat treatment of all fractionated blood products, monitoring of the situation by epidemiological surveys and a central confidential register of all cases. Specified targets include a mortality rate equal to that of developed countries by the year 2015.

Fertility and the family: The Government's major objectives in modifying the fertility level are to lower population growth and to improve family health and well-being. One of the goals of the Population Development Programme is to improve the quality of life, thereby lowering fertility, as well as to deal with problems posed by adolescent fertility and illegal abortions. Contraceptives are provided free at government medical facilities. Abortion is permitted for health reasons in the first 12 weeks of pregnancy with the authorization of a physician. Sterilizations require spousal consent and are provided free. A number of targets have been specified such as increasing the number of women using contraceptives from 50 per cent to 70 per cent and a total fertility rate of 2.1 by the year 2010.

International migration: South Africa's immigration policy is based on the country's demand for and supply of skilled labour and it has signed labour agreements with the five African countries that supply it with labour. In its 1986 report, the National Manpower Commission recommended that the Immigrants Selection Board include representatives of employers and workers and that the possibility of State support for immigrants with occupations in short supply and immigrant entrepreneurs be investigated. In June 1986, the Government announced that it would repatriate the 60,000 Mozambican mineworkers employed in South Africa upon the termination of their contracts, but in December 1986 it rescinded the order in the case of more skilled Mozambicans. To stem the tide of Mozambican refugees, the Government had undertaken a policy of forcible repatriation. South Africa reported that it has no legal or institutional mechanism for determining and according refugee status. There is a policy to encourage the return of South Africans who have emigrated by assisting such returnees on the same basis as new immigrants.

Spatial distribution/urbanization: The abolition in 1986 of influx control, which had restricted the movement of blacks into urban areas, has been replaced by a policy of "orderly urbanization", which appears to tie residency to availability of accommodation rather than employment as in the past. However, severe accommodation shortages coupled with high unemployment have limited the movement of blacks. Under the Aliens Act, black residents in homeland areas must obtain work permits to work as migrants or daily commuters in South Africa. To achieve a more balanced distribution of economic activities and incomes as well as promote rural urbanization, incentives have been created to establish industrial projects and relocate projects from overseas and from certain metropolitan areas to identified development areas.

<u>Status of women and population</u>: In South Africa women are considered to be equal to men and are expected to be involved in all aspects of population development. The Women's Affairs Section of the Population Development Programme focuses on educating, informing and communicating with women on demographic issues and emphasizing the role of women in controlling population growth. There are no institutional barriers to women's education, training, employment and access to health care. The 1984 Matrimonial and Properties Affairs Act accords men and women equality in marital affairs. The Women's Bureau conducts research on women's issues and makes recommendations to the Government on legislation for improving the legal rights and status of women. The minimum legal age at marriage for women is 21 years.

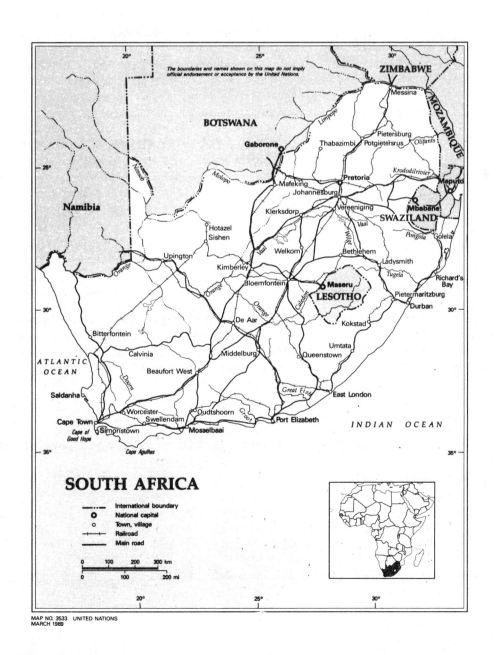

MAP NO. 3533   UNITED NATIONS
MARCH 1989

SPAIN

DEMOGRAPHIC INDICATORS	CURRENT PERCEPTION
SIZE/AGE STRUCTURE/GROWTH	The Government perceives the current growth rate as <u>satisfactory</u>.

Population: 1985 2025
(thousands) 38 602 42 530
 0-14 years (%) 22.9 16.6
 60+ years (%) 17.1 26.1

Rate of: 1980-85 2020-25
 growth 0.6 0.1
 natural increase 5.6 0.8

MORTALITY/MORBIDITY

The Government considers the levels of mortality to be <u>acceptable</u>.

 1980-85 2020-25
Life expectancy 75.8 80.3
Crude death rate 7.7 10.3
Infant mortality 11.0 6.0

FERTILITY/NUPTIALITY/FAMILY

Current fertility rates are viewed as <u>satisfactory</u>.

 1980-85 2020-25
Fertility rate 1.8 1.9
Crude birth rate 13.3 11.0
Contraceptive
 prevalence rate 59.4 (1985)
Female mean age
 at first marriage 23.1 (1981)

INTERNATIONAL MIGRATION

The <u>insignificant</u> immigration levels are considered to be <u>satisfactory</u>. There is concern over the influx of illegal immigrants. Emigration is <u>insignificant</u> and <u>satisfactory</u>.

 1980-85 2020-25
Net migration rate 0.0 0.0
Foreign-born
 population (%) 1.7 (1981)

SPATIAL DISTRIBUTION/URBANIZATION

The spatial distribution of population is felt to be <u>appropriate</u>.

Urban 1985 2025
 population (%) 75.8 88.8

Growth rate: 1980-85 2020-25
 urban 1.4 0.3
 rural -1.8 -1.6

GENERAL POLICY FRAMEWORK

Overall approach to population problems: The demographic situation in Spain is perceived as stable by the Government and there is no official population policy. The Government is aware, however, that its social and economic policies have an effect on demographic trends. Fertility is perceived as an individual matter and the Government has no explicit policies of intervention regarding population growth and fertility.

Importance of population policy in achieving development objectives: Population policy in Spain is viewed as an integral part of socio-economic policies, which are aimed at advancing and protecting the quality of life while protecting and restoring the environment.

INSTITUTIONAL FRAMEWORK

Population data systems and development planning: Census-taking falls under the responsibility of the Instituto Nacional de Estadística. The most recent population census was conducted in 1981 and the next was scheduled for 1991. Vital registration of births and deaths is considered to be complete. Development planning was initiated with the first development plan for the period 1964-1967. The fourth development plan for 1976-1980 was never implemented. A four-year development plan for the period 1983-1986 was prepared, but only the introductory chapters were published.

Integration of population within development planning: An explicit population policy co-ordinated with Government development planning does not exist. Population projections are prepared by the Instituto Nacional de Estadística, which is also responsible for demographic research.

POLICIES AND MEASURES

Changes in population size and age structure: The Government has not reported any explicit policy to influence the rate of population growth, although various socio-economic measures to improve the situation of families with children and working mothers such as family allowances and maternity leave are in place.

Mortality and morbidity: One of the main objectives of the Government is to achieve lower levels of infant and maternal mortality through a better health-care system. The General Law on Health approved by Parliament in 1985 provides the basis for a reorganization and decentralization of the health system in order to give the entire population access to the health-care system. Special emphasis is placed on reaching lower socio-economic groups, certain geographical areas and marginal groups which in the past have not had

SPAIN

access to health centres. Special assistance for maternal health care during pregnancy is also emphasized. Primary health care has been widened to include mental health, oral health and occupational medicine. Health promotion activities include programmes connected with better diet, physical exercise, alcohol consumption, smoking, family planning and sex education. Special programmes have been devoted to the continuous training of primary teachers in health and to informing the rural population about nutrition.

Fertility and the family: Since the legalization of contraception in 1978, fertility has been considered to be a matter of individual conscience. Government priorities are geared towards improving the country's health situation through a national network of family planning centres. The Government believes that instruction, information and assistance should be made accessible to the whole population so that couples may decide the number and spacing of their children. As of 1986 the family allowance was 250 pesetas a month for each child (Ptas 132 = $US 1 as of 1986). To facilitate child-rearing and labour force participation of women, legislation in 1989 extended maternity leave from 14 to 16 weeks and authorized parental leave of up to three years with the guarantee that the job will be kept open for one year. Abortion is permitted only in cases of rape, malformation of the foetus or danger to the mother's physical or mental health. In 1987, the Spanish Parliament defeated a motion to broaden the abortion law to permit the procedure in cases of serious danger to the stability of a woman's physical or mental health or economic, social or family situation. Sterilization was made legal in 1983.

International migration: Spain has gradually been transformed from a country of emigration to one of immigration, often illegal. The main emphasis of the Government's immigration policy is to intensify procedures to prevent the illegal employment of foreign-born workers and restrict the granting of residence permits to the foreign-born. The Government was planning to introduce visa requirements for the North African countries beginning in 1990. Concerning emigration, Spain has traditionally been an exporter of labour, but the character of Spanish emigration is now becoming increasingly temporary. The Government's policy carried out through the Institute of Emigration has been to safeguard the situation of emigrant workers, ensure their acquired rights and promote their integration within the host societies. The Government would like to reduce the level of emigration.

Spatial distribution/urbanization: One of the Government's main objectives is to improve the spatial distribution of the population and reduce internal migration. Government policies concern limiting urban growth and include the promotion of intermediary cities and a revitalization of rural areas. Various programmes have been implemented to decrease the level of rural-to-urban migration and function mainly to increase the level of services, employment and standards of living in rural areas.

<u>Status of women and population</u>: The Government believes that the status and condition of women should be advanced in all judicial, educational, cultural and economic aspects. The National Women's Institute organizes specific courses for women, conducts studies on topics concerning women, and has prepared booklets on labour relations and on women's rights in the home, at work and in society. In 1986 the Ministry of Labour began awarding cash incentives to firms appointing women to jobs in male-dominated fields. A national training and job integration scheme is to include special measures for women over 25 years of age. The minimum legal age at marriage for women is 18 years; however, in individual cases a judge may lower the age to 14 years.

MAP NO. 2771.17   UNITED NATIONS
SEPTEMBER 1990

SRI LANKA

DEMOGRAPHIC INDICATORS	CURRENT PERCEPTION

SIZE/AGE STRUCTURE/GROWTH
 	
Population: 1985   2025
 (thousands)   16 108   24 449
  0–14 years (%)   34.1   21.6
  60+ years (%)   7.1   17.2
 	
Rate of: 1980–85   2020–25
 growth   1.7   0.7
 natural increase   20.5   7.5
	The Government considers the rate of population growth to be <u>unsatisfactory</u> because it is <u>too high</u>.

MORTALITY/MORBIDITY 1980–85 2020–25 Life expectancy 68.9 77.2 Crude death rate 6.3 7.2 Infant mortality 39.0 13.0	Levels are viewed as <u>unacceptable</u>. There is concern over maternal, infant and child mortality and morbidity, particularly among the estate sector, rural groups in poorer districts and urban slum dwellers.
FERTILITY/NUPTIALITY/FAMILY 1980–85 2020–25 Fertility rate 3.3 2.1 Crude birth rate 26.9 14.7 Contraceptive prevalence rate 62.0 (1987) Female mean age at first marriage 24.4 (1981)	Current fertility levels are perceived as <u>unsatisfactory</u> because they are <u>too high</u>.
INTERNATIONAL MIGRATION 1980–85 2020–25 Net migration rate 0.0 0.0 Foreign-born population (%) 0.3 (1981)	Both immigration and emigration levels are considered to be <u>insignificant</u> and <u>satisfactory</u>. There is concern over the brain drain.
SPATIAL DISTRIBUTION/URBANIZATION Urban 1985 2025 population (%) 21.1 42.6 Growth rate: 1980–85 2020–25 urban 1.2 2.7 rural 1.8 -0.6	The overall pattern is viewed as <u>partially appropriate</u>.

GENERAL POLICY FRAMEWORK

Overall approach to population problems: Successive Governments have expressed concern over the implications of population growth for national development and the quality of life. The Government recognizes the importance of a further reduction of fertility to enhance socio-economic development and has sought to strengthen and expand the delivery of family planning services, provide incentives for controlling population growth and increase population education. High priority is also accorded to programmes aimed at reducing infant mortality and to maintaining comprehensive social welfare services.

Importance of population policy in achieving development objectives: The Government recognizes the implications of an unfavourable population growth rate, size and age structure for social and economic development, particularly their effects on social welfare expenditures and problems associated with providing productive employment opportunities. It therefore attaches major importance to population policy as an integral part of socio-economic policy, whose principal objectives are to improve living standards and the quality of life.

INSTITUTIONAL FRAMEWORK

Population data systems and development planning: The last census was held in 1981 under the direction of the Department of Census and Statistics, which also makes population projections. The next census is provisionally scheduled for 1991. Vital registration is considered to be virtually complete. The Population Information Centre acts as the primary resource for the Population Division of the Ministry of Plan Implementation. The current Five-Year Plan for 1987-1991, prepared by the National Planning Division of the Ministry of Finance and Planning, indicates development policy parameters and outlines a national investment strategy.

Integration of population within development planning: The Research Evaluation Unit of the Population Division is chiefly responsible for providing information on population-development interrelationships. The National Planning Division takes into account demographic factors in planning. The Population Division formulates and implements population policy. Other ministries and non-governmental organizations are also responsible for programme implementation, whose management at the regional level has been decentralized through the 24 district population committees. A National Co-ordinating Committee was established in 1983 to supervise these activities. However, the Government has stated that civil disturbances in the northern and eastern regions have adversely affected the implementation of population programmes in those areas.

SRI LANKA

POLICIES AND MEASURES

Changes in population size and age structure: There is an explicit policy of
intervention to reduce growth rates and adjust the age structure by lowering
fertility and infant and child mortality. The family health programme is an
integral element of the extensive health and service delivery network that has
facilitated the provision of family planning services throughout the country.
Other measures include readjusting the spatial distribution pattern, improving
employment prospects and extending social security to rural workers. No
quantitative targets for population growth rates and size have been adopted.
Social security coverage includes employed persons, while excluding family
labour and employees covered under approved private plans. A special pension
system exists for public and local government employees.

Mortality and morbidity: The Government is committed to achieving health for
all, mainly through primary health care with emphasis on preventive
activities. Intervention programmes have been implemented in nutrition
surveillance, the provision of clean water, sanitation and hygiene education,
improvements in primary health care and maternal and child health services,
integrating family planning services and emphasizing community participation.
Communication strategies have been developed as part of an expanded programme
of child immunization for achieving universal coverage by 1990. A diarrhoeal
disease control programme has been undertaken that includes establishing a
plant to manufacture oral rehydration salts. Armed conflict in several
districts has led to a deterioration in health services and increases in
communicable diseases and malnutrition. Consequently, the Government was
formulating programmes of rehabilitation. It was reported that the
resettlement of 250,000 families as part of the Mahaweli River Development
Scheme has contributed to a resurgence of malaria.

Fertility and the family: The policy is to lower fertility, so as to modify
population growth and improve well-being and health. Family planning services
are part of a comprehensive family health service and a range of subsidized
clinical and contraceptive services is provided. The capacity of the existing
maternal and child health and family planning infrastructure is being
enhanced, particularly in rural, estate and poor urban areas. With the wide
acceptance of sterilization, reversible methods and birth-spacing are being
emphasized to encourage younger couples to practise family planning. Since
1988, financial incentives have been offered to women using the intrauterine
device. Emphasis is being given to linking information, education and
communication activities more closely to service delivery and interpersonal
and group approaches. Maternity benefits for certain categories of workers
include six weeks of paid leave, prohibition of dismissal from employment and
provision for nursing breaks at work. Abortion is permitted only to save the
mother's life. Sterilization is permitted without restrictions. Married
acceptors of sterilization with at least two living children qualify for a
monetary incentive.

International migration: Although policy is to halt immigration, in 1987 an
agreement was reached with the Government of India to repatriate Sri Lankan
refugees. As of March 1989, about 36,000 Sri Lankans had returned from
southern India. Concerning emigration, measures aim at facilitating labour
emigration, as it alleviates unemployment and remittances are a major source
of foreign exchange. The Government regulates recruitment, protects the
interests of overseas migrants and acts as an intermediary between migrants

and recruitment agencies. To reduce the brain drain, qualified professionals
in Government employment are entitled to a leave of absence of up to three
years to work abroad, after which they must return to their former posts.

<u>Spatial   distribution/urbanization</u>:   Policies   aim   to   decelerate   internal
migration, curb urbanization, maintain the rural population and relocate
population from crowded urban areas.   Measures include the provision of
adequate urban services and other infrastructure in new towns and communities,
establishing new industries away from urban centres, and State-sponsored land
settlement schemes.   The objective is to resettle people from the densely
populated south-west by providing and developing land, particularly for the
landless and unemployed, in the dry zone in the north, east and south-east
parts of the country.   The Mahaweli River Development Scheme, aims to improve
food self-sufficiency, generate hydro-electric power, create one million new
jobs, and resettle people by relocation and spontaneous migration.

<u>Status of women and population</u>:   Women have equal rights including those
concerning property and inheritance.   The Government has taken steps to
increase female participation in education, productive employment and other
spheres.   Since 1983, the Women's Bureau has directed and co-ordinated
programmes for integrating women into the development process, providing
leadership training in community development, income-generating activities and
health improvement.   The Government has increased the role of women in
population activities, particularly in service delivery and communications.
The minimum legal age at marriage for women is 12 years.

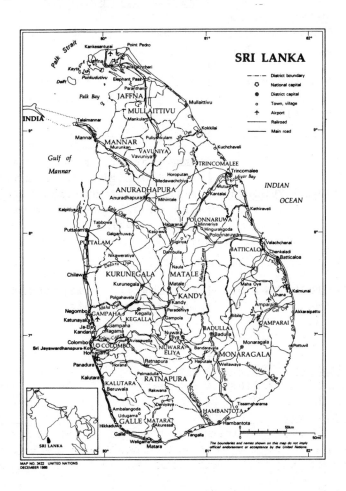

SUDAN

DEMOGRAPHIC INDICATORS	CURRENT PERCEPTION
SIZE/AGE STRUCTURE/GROWTH	The rate of growth is considered to be <u>satisfactory</u>.

Population:

	1985	2025
(thousands)	21 818	59 594
0–14 years (%)	45.2	33.9
60+ years (%)	4.5	6.3

Rate of:	1980–85	2020–25
growth	3.1	1.7
natural increase	28.6	17.4

MORTALITY/MORBIDITY	The levels and trends of mortality are viewed as <u>unacceptable</u>, with special concern for maternal and child mortality.

	1980–85	2020–25
Life expectancy	47.8	63.8
Crude death rate	17.3	7.7
Infant mortality	118.0	51.0

FERTILITY/NUPTIALITY/FAMILY	Levels and trends are perceived as <u>satisfactory</u>.

	1980–85	2020–25
Fertility rate	6.6	3.0
Crude birth rate	45.9	25.1
Contraceptive prevalence rate	4.6 (1978/79)	
Female mean age at first marriage	18.7 (1973)	

INTERNATIONAL MIGRATION	Immigration is perceived as <u>significant</u> and <u>too high</u>, while emigration is also <u>significant</u> and <u>too high</u>. Major concerns are the large influx of refugees and the brain drain.

	1980–85	2020–25
Net migration rate	...	...
Foreign-born population (%)	...	...

SPATIAL DISTRIBUTION/URBANIZATION	The spatial distribution is considered to be <u>inappropriate</u>.

Urban	1985	2025
population (%)	20.6	45.5

Growth rate:	1980–85	2020–25
urban	4.0	3.6
rural	2.9	0.3

GENERAL POLICY FRAMEWORK

Overall approach to population problems: Although the Government has no explicit population policy, the major priority is raising the standard of living with due attention to infant and maternal mortality, mother and child care, and provision of primary health care and basic social services. In addition, the Government aims to improve the status of women, especially in rural areas, and modify the spatial distribution pattern to achieve a better balance between population and resources.

Importance of population policy in achieving development objectives: In 1987 the country's Prime Minister called for the formulation of a population policy. However, as of 1989 no policy had been formulated.

INSTITUTIONAL FRAMEWORK

Population data systems and development planning: Censuses were conducted in 1963, 1973 and 1983 with the next one provisionally scheduled for 1993. Vital registration is considered to be incomplete and projects are under way to strengthen the capabilities of the Department of Statistics for conducting censuses and other demographic surveys. The implementation of the current development plan, the Four-Year Programme for Salvation, Recovery and Development for the period 1988/89 to 1991/92, was adversely affected in its first year by floods and rains which struck the central and northern parts of the country.

Integration of population within development planning: In 1982 the Government endorsed policies proposed by the Second National Population Conference and created the National Population Council to oversee the implementation of the policies. Included were a more active state role in family planning and the extension of such planning to all areas of the country, with emphasis on improvement of maternal and child health, the dissemination of population information and the introduction of population education into all educational institutions. The Department of Statistics prepares population projections. The Population Studies Centre at the University of Gezira conducts research on population-related issues. A project was initiated in 1986 to assist in the formulation and implementation of population policies and planning by strengthening the Department of General Planning and Administration.

POLICIES AND MEASURES

Changes in population size and age structure: While it was noted at the country's Third National Population Conference in 1987 that rapid population growth was hindering development efforts, particularly in the field of education, the Government does not intervene to modify the rate of growth. Policies have been undertaken to strengthen the maternal and child health and family planning clinical network, to promote population education in schools

SUDAN

and out-of-school programmes and to improve the status of women. Social security coverage, which is limited to employees of firms and agricultural establishments with at least 30 workers in eight main provinces, is to be gradually extended.

Mortality and morbidity: Following the revolution in 1985, the entire primary health-care approach was revised with the objective of strengthening the health-care delivery system, by promoting rural and district hospitals and training and reorienting doctors in those hospitals towards primary health care. The Government's objectives are: (a) to achieve an immunization coverage of 90 per cent of all children under the age of one by 1990 against the six most common childhood diseases; (b) to reduce neonatal mortality by 39 per cent; (c) to lower the incidence of fecally transmitted diseases through improved sanitation and personal hygiene; (d) to increase the supply of potable water; and (e) to raise educational levels, particularly of women. Additional community health workers, village midwives and medical assistants, as well as traditional birth attendants, will be trained. To combat acute respiratory infection, a trial programme was launched in 1987 to achieve early diagnosis and sound case management and cut mortality and morbidity by 50 per cent. The programme will also assist in preventing malaria by distributing chloroquine. Other programmes aim to upgrade nutritional status, promote oral rehydration techniques and improve health education among the population.

Fertility and the family: There is no policy of intervention with respect to fertility rates. Measures that have been implemented include family planning, population information, education and communication programmes. The need for more attention to education, particularly women's education, and to health services and a closer integration between family planning and mother and child welfare, has been emphasized. The provision of family planning services to all Sudanese couples and the expansion of programmes to promote child survival and ensure safe motherhood was urged at the Sudan Third National Population Conference in 1987. The provision of contraceptives receives direct Government support. Abortion is legal only to save the mother's life while sterilization is not available.

International migration: The estimated 745,000 refugees in the Sudan as of mid-1989 has severely strained the country's ability to continue to act as a host and provide refugee assistance, and have also threatened its security, stability and development. While the essential needs of the 350,000 Ethiopian refugees assisted at 17 rural settlements and four reception centres in eastern Sudan were being met, measures have been taken to promote self-reliance and enhance their economic independence with various programmes such as linking refugee assistance to development-related activities in refugee-affected areas. Between 1988 and March 1989 almost 85,000 Ugandan refugees had been voluntarily repatriated. Concerned by the substantial loss of skilled and professional workers, the Government has attempted to limit emigration by imposing more stringent passport and visa controls and less favourable exchange rate régimes. A bilateral agreement enable Sudanese civil servants to be seconded to administrative posts in Saudi Arabia. As a consequence of military hostilities, drought and famine, an estimated 330,000 Sudanese refugees had fled to south-western Ethiopia by the end of 1988.

Spatial distribution and urbanization: The Government has tried to deal with major spatial distribution imbalances by means of social infrastructure, investments in rural and desert areas, regional development, sedentarization of nomads, development of new towns, administrative decentralization and legal controls enforced by the police. The current Four-Year Development Plan gives priority to rehabilitating and developing rural areas. Specific objectives include increasing income for small agricultural producers, creating employment in rural areas and halting, if not reversing, urban migration. Following the renewal of hostilities in the south, several years of drought and famine, as well as floods, it is estimated that upwards of 3 million people were displaced during the period 1986-1988. Large numbers of people have moved from Bahr el-Ghazal and the Upper Nile areas into Southern Darfur and Southern Kordofan, as well as forming spontaneous settlements around Greater Khartoum.

Status of women and population: The Government aims to improve the welfare of women, especially in rural areas, in the field of education and employment. Co-ordinated by the Women's Section within the Ministry of Social Welfare, 147 multi-purpose training centres provide women with various skills and grant them small loans. There is no information readily available on the minimum legal age at marriage for women.

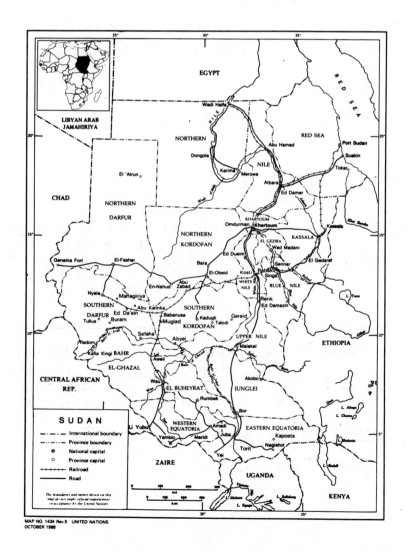

MAP NO. 1434 Rev.5 UNITED NATIONS
OCTOBER 1988

SURINAME

DEMOGRAPHIC INDICATORS	CURRENT PERCEPTION

SIZE/AGE STRUCTURE/GROWTH
 	
 Population: 1985   2025
  (thousands)   375   628
  0-14 years (%)   37.2   22.4
  60+ years (%)   6.6   13.9
 	
 Rate of: 1980-85   2020-25
  growth   1.1   1.0
  natural increase   22.0   9.6
	The Government sees population growth as being <u>satisfactory</u>. It has been noted that substantial unused natural resources might require a larger population in the future.

MORTALITY/MORBIDITY 1980-85 2020-25 Life expectancy 68.0 76.7 Crude death rate 6.8 5.8 Infant mortality 36.0 9.0	Mortality and morbidity levels are viewed as <u>unacceptable</u>. Special concerns are the population in rural areas, mothers and children.

FERTILITY/NUPTIALITY/FAMILY
 	
         1980-85   2020-25
 Fertility rate   3.6   2.1
 Crude birth rate   28.8   15.4
 Contraceptive
  prevalence rate   ...   ...
 Female mean age
  at first marriage   ...   ...
	Fertility is seen as <u>satisfactory</u>.

INTERNATIONAL MIGRATION
 	
         1980-85   2020-25
 Net migration rate   ...   ...
 Foreign-born
  population (%)   ...   ...
	Immigration is seen as <u>insignificant</u> and <u>satisfactory</u>. Emigration is seen as <u>significant</u> and <u>too high</u>. The Government has indicated particular concern with problems associated with the departure of skilled workers.

SPATIAL DISTRIBUTION/URBANIZATION
 	
 Urban   1985   2025
  population (%)   45.7   69.8
 	
 Growth rate: 1980-85   2020-25
  urban   1.5   1.8
  rural   0.8   -0.8
	Spatial distribution of the population is viewed as <u>inappropriate</u> owing to the concentration of population in the coastal area of the capital city.

GENERAL POLICY FRAMEWORK

Overall approach to population problems: The Government has no specifically stated population policy. It has adopted a policy of non-intervention with respect to population growth and fertility. It supports the availability of accessible, affordable and acceptable health services to the population with a focus on the development of primary health care and it supports the provision of contraceptives. Measures have been taken to reduce international emigration and to shift spatial distribution towards the country's interior.

Importance of population policy in achieving development objectives: There is no explicit population policy. Following major political changes in 1980, development policies were reoriented towards modifying the political-administrative and socio-eonomic order and education system. Health policies have been aligned within this context. The redistribution of the population towards the interior of the country has been identified as a national development goal.

INSTITUTIONAL FRAMEWORK

Population data systems and development planning: Censuses were conducted in 1971 and 1980. As of 1989 no new census had been scheduled. The registration of births and deaths is considered to be virtually complete. Coverage of mortality data has improved partly as a result of direct reporting on causes of death from the interior; this improvement, however, makes comparisons with previous periods difficult. Separate mortality, epidemiological and health service coverage data exist for groups in coastal and interior areas. The health information system is being reorganized, standardized and centralized.

Integration of population within development planning: The Ministry of Health has a regulatory, legislative, co-ordinating and initiating role with respect to health policy. In 1985 a health policy for 1985-1990 was being formulated in line with strategies for health for all. In 1986 a National Advisory Committee on Family Planning of the Ministry of Health was established.

POLICIES AND MEASURES

Changes in population size and age structure: The Government has adopted a policy of non-intervention with respect to population growth. Policies that are in place that may influence population growth include health programmes to lower mortality and those aiming to integrate family planning services into government clinics. Information on the status of pension schemes is not readily available.

SURINAME

Mortality and morbidity: The Government has actively intervened to address mortality and morbidity differentials. More attention is being given to the development of primary health care as the capacity for secondary and tertiary care is thought to be adequate. A major ongoing initiative to increase child immunization coverage began in 1982 and a diarrhoeal disease control programme was launched in 1984. Family health is seen as a focus around which primary health care has been organized with special attention given to women and children. Eradication programmes aimed at malaria, schistosomiasis and leprosy have also been undertaken and disease control activities have been successfully transferred from vertical programmes to primary health-care services. In 1980 the availability of acetic acid was curtailed to address the incidence of suicide, a leading cause of mortality in the country. Accident prevention programmes have addressed the problem of death from traffic accidents, another important cause of death. The development of human resources in the health sector is a priority. A state health insurance foundation has existed since 1981 covering curative medical services for government employees and their families; this coverage is to be extended to other groups including the underprivileged.

Fertility and the family: The Government is supportive of family planning activities, although it has not yet adopted an official policy towards rates of fertility. It gives direct support to the distribution of contraceptives and there are no major limits to access. The Government supports the country's private family planning association, Stichting Lobi, which works to integrate family planning into the Government's primary health-care system and to include sex education in the school curriculum. A project was initiated in 1985 to increase awareness of population issues and expand family planning services by integrating such services into all existing government polyclinics, assessing the demand for contraceptives through prevalence surveys, creating awareness of contraceptive demand through information campaigns and supplementing the Government's primary health-care activities for women of fertile age. It is technically illegal to provide family planning information and services to adolescents, although the laws are not strictly enforced. Abortion is legal if there is a risk to the health of the woman. Information on the status of sterilization is not readily available.

International migration: The Government's policy is one of maintaining immigration and lowering emigration. At independence in 1976 close to one third of the country's population emigrated to the Netherlands. Subsequently, the Government hoped that development programmes would depress emigration as well as encourage the return of emigrants. Emigration has, however, continued, although visa requirements after 1980 reduced this trend. Civil strife in 1986 led to the flight of nearly 5,000 Surinamese from the interior of Suriname to neighbouring French Guyana. Within the framework of a Tripartite Commission, composed of representatives of Suriname, France and the United Nations High Commissioner for Refugees, the possibilities for voluntary repatriation of the refugees were being explored in 1989. In 1988 the Netherlands had formulated a plan to repatriate about 5,000 Surinamese who had entered the Netherlands without proper documentation.

Spatial distribution/urbanization: The redistribution of the population towards the interior has been identified as a national development goal which is to be accomplished by the creation of agricultural settlements and housing projects in the interior. This goal has occurred in light of the concentration of two thirds of the entire population in and around the coastal capital city of Paramaribo. The remaining population, which is distributed in the interior of the country, is ethnically and culturally distinct from that of the urban coastal area. These interior population groups have been singled out for special attention with respect to health and development programmes.

Status of women and population: Suriname participated in a regional Caribbean workshop for the training of young women in health development. Information on the minimum legal age at marriage for women is not readily available.

Other issues: The Action Programme announced by the Government in May 1982 called for the encouragement of small-scale industry, establishment of industrial parks, development of rural electrification and water supply projects, liberalization of land distribution, and worker participation in management of government enterprises.

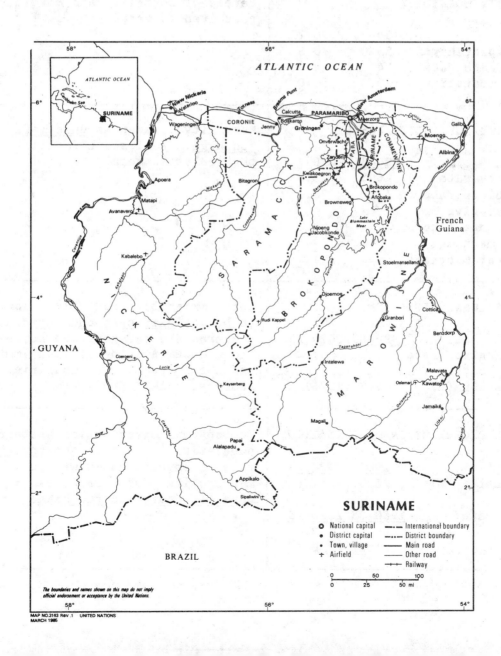

SURINAME

⊙ National capital	▬·▬· International boundary
● District capital	▬··▬·· District boundary
• Town, village	▬▬ Main road
+ Airfield	▬▬ Other road
	▬+▬+ Railway

0   50   100
0   25   50 mi

The boundaries and names shown on this map do not imply official endorsement or acceptance by the United Nations.

MAP NO.3163 Rev.1   UNITED NATIONS
MARCH 1985

SWAZILAND

DEMOGRAPHIC INDICATORS	CURRENT PERCEPTION
SIZE/AGE STRUCTURE/GROWTH	Population growth is seen as <u>unsatisfactory</u> and <u>too high</u>.

Population:	1985	2025
(thousands)	665	2 206
0-14 years (%)	46.8	35.3
60+ years (%)	4.7	5.7

Rate of:	1980-85	2020-25
growth	3.3	2.0
natural increase	32.9	20.4

MORTALITY/MORBIDITY

Levels of mortality and morbidity are perceived as <u>unacceptable</u>.

	1980-85	2020-25
Life expectancy	53.0	70.3
Crude death rate	14.1	4.9
Infant mortality	129.0	51.0

FERTILITY/NUPTIALITY/FAMILY

Fertility is seen as <u>unsatisfactory</u> and <u>too high</u>. Adolescent fertility is a particular concern.

	1980-85	2020-25
Fertility rate	6.5	3.0
Crude birth rate	47.0	25.3
Contraceptive prevalence rate	...	...
Female mean age at first marriage	...	...

INTERNATIONAL MIGRATION

Both immigration and emigration are felt to be <u>insignificant</u> and <u>satisfactory</u>. Concerns are refugees and asylum-seekers and undocumented or illegal immigrants and the emigration of qualified professionals.

	1980-85	2020-25
Net migration rate	...	...
Foreign-born population (%)	5.3 (1976)	

SPATIAL DISTRIBUTION/URBANIZATION

The spatial distribution pattern of the population is seen as <u>appropriate</u>. The rate of population growth in the metropolitan and urban areas is seen as <u>unsatisfactory</u> and <u>too high</u>.

Urban	1985	2025
population (%)	26.3	62.6

Growth rate:	1980-85	2020-25
urban	9.0	3.1
rural	1.6	0.4

GENERAL POLICY FRAMEWORK

<u>Overall approach to population problems</u>: Although Swaziland has no explicit and comprehensive population policy, a number of programmes are being promoted that aim at lowering population growth and fertility through provision of family planning services, maternal and child health care and socio-economic development.

<u>Importance of population policy in achieving development objectives</u>: The impact of the country's rate of population growth is perceived as having a negative impact on the achievement of social and economic development objectives. The inclusion of specific population issues in the country's development plans indicates an awareness and concern about the relationships between demographic trends and national social and economic development. The 1986 census clearly reflected the importance the country has attached to demographic data in relation to socio-economic and housing planning. A parliamentary group on population and development has been formed.

INSTITUTIONAL FRAMEWORK

<u>Population data systems and development planning</u>: Censuses have been held at approximately 10-year intervals since 1898 with the last occurring in 1986, and are the responsibility of the Central Statistical Office (CSO). Efforts are being made to train national personnel so that analysis of the 1986 census may be carried out as much as possible by Swazis. Immigration statistics are routinely collected at 14 border points that convey data to CSO. A civil registration project has been ongoing since 1984 within the Ministry of Justice and population surveys of homesteads, family expenditure and labour migration have also been undertaken. The Fifth National Development Plan for the period 1989/90-1991/92, prepared by the Department of Economic Planning and Statistics, is to be updated annually. It represents a departure from the previous practice of five-year plans in that it covers only three years.

<u>Integration of population within development planning</u>: There is no government agency responsible for formulating or co-ordinating population policy nor is any agency charged with integrating population variables in planning. Since its establishment in 1967, however, the Central Statistical Office has been responsible for the collection, processing and publication of statistical data required for development planning. CSO constitutes a wing of the Department of Planning and Statistics within the Prime Minister's Office. The Fourth National Development Plan for 1984-1988 addressed population issues of health and education. In 1988 a programme was initiated to promote knowledge among policy makers and also community and traditional leaders of the capabilities of integrating demographic variables into development planning and to encourage self-sufficiency in the design, implementation and co-ordination of national population policies and programmes.

SWAZILAND

POLICIES AND MEASURES

Changes in population size and age structure: The Government has a policy to lower the rate of population growth. In 1987 the country's Prime Minister cited the high population growth rate and the depressed economy as constituting the main causes of unemployment in the country. The growth rate is to be reduced by programmes of maternal and child health and family planning and socio-economic development. The social security scheme covers employed persons, excluding casual employees, domestic servants and aliens. A special scheme exists for public employees.

Mortality and morbidity: The country's development plans have provided for the increase of preventive health services and integration with curative services, emphasizing vulnerable groups and the expansion of health education. Maternal and child health services have been strengthened, and programmes enacted in young child care, women and development, and malaria control. Specific programmes have involved the training of rural health motivators, expansion of immunization programmes, an oral rehydration salts campaign, nutrition and growth monitoring, and training of pre-school teachers. A law was enacted in 1986 making parents punishable in court if their children were not immunized. There are 6,000 traditional medical practitioners in Swaziland and the use of traditional medicine is encouraged by the Government. Educational and information campaigns to create public awareness of AIDS prevention have been instituted. In 1989 a conference was held to establish a medium-term plan for the prevention and control of AIDS. A number of specific disease reduction targets have been specified, as well as increasing full immunization coverage of infants to 80 per cent by 1990 and lowering infant mortality to 50 per thousand births by the year 2000.

Fertility and the family: The Government's policy is to lower fertility levels to improve family well-being and the health of mothers and children, although no quantitative targets have been set for future fertility levels. The Government has implemented a maternal and child-care programme, a family planning programme, child-care centres and measures for improving the status of women. The National Family Planning Programme launched in 1973 provides family planning services at all health service delivery centres, as well as mobile units in isolated areas. The Government continues to provide contraceptives through government facilities and indirectly supports provision through non-governmental organizations; oral pills and injectables are provided free. Fertility among adolescents is a major concern and access to contraception is permitted to them regardless of marital status. A male-oriented family planning programme is receiving international assistance. Access to female sterilization is prohibited and abortion is legal on eugenic grounds to preserve the physical and mental health of the mother.

International migration: The Government is very concerned by the presence of Mozambican and South African refugees, who have placed additional pressure on the country's social infrastructure. While there were approximately 28,000 registered refugees in Swaziland as of June 1989, the Government estimates that a much larger, but undetermined, number of Mozambicans have spontaneously settled within the country. The Malindza Reception Centre, which provides care and maintenance, continued to expand in 1988 to accommodate the increase in Mozambican asylum-seekers. The Government announced a policy to relocate the spontaneously settled Mozambicans to the Ndzevane settlement and the Malindza Reception Centre in late 1989 and 1990 and has appealed to the United

Nations High Commissioner for Refugees to find another country to which Swaziland could refer additional refugees. The Government does not discourage emigration, given that emigration for employment is an important means of alleviating some of the pressure on the domestic labour market.

Spatial distribution/urbanization: Although rates of growth in the country's metropolitan and urban areas are seen as too high, an official policy to address these concerns has not been formulated. Rural development has, however, been promoted. The Rural Area Development Programme seeks to bring about higher levels of production and consumption among rural families. By promoting a more commercially oriented approach to agriculture and by narrowing the gap in living standards between rural and urban areas, the programme tries to raise the overall level of living in rural areas.

Status of women and population: The Government has not adopted any specific measures relating to the status of women aimed at influencing demographic trends. The capacity of rural women to earn suppplementary income and thereby enhance their ability to care for their children has been promoted; training centres have been established in income-generating activities such as blockmaking, simple construction techniques, water and grain storage, welding, sewing and handicrafts. Information on the minimum legal age at marriage for women is not readily available.

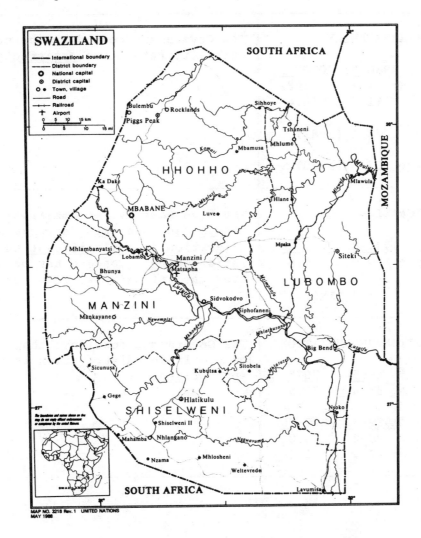

SWEDEN

DEMOGRAPHIC INDICATORS	CURRENT PERCEPTION
SIZE/AGE STRUCTURE/GROWTH	The Government considers the current rate of population growth to be <u>satisfactory</u>.

Population:	1985	2025
(thousands)	8 350	8 136
0-14 years (%)	17.5	15.6
60+ years (%)	23.6	30.0

Rate of:	1980-85	2020-25
growth	0.1	-0.2
natural increase	0.3	-2.3

MORTALITY/MORBIDITY	The Government considers current levels and trends to be <u>acceptable</u>, although environmental questions and unhealthy life-styles continue to be issues of concern.

	1980-85	2020-25
Life expectancy	76.3	80.6
Crude death rate	11.0	12.7
Infant mortality	7.0	5.0

FERTILITY/NUPTIALITY/FAMILY	The Government considers the current fertility rate to be <u>satisfactory</u>.

	1980-85	2020-25
Fertility rate	1.7	1.8
Crude birth rate	11.3	10.4
Contraceptive prevalence rate	78.1 (1981)	
Female mean age at first marriage	27.6 (1980)	

INTERNATIONAL MIGRATION	The Government views immigration as <u>significant</u> and <u>satisfactory</u>, while emigration is <u>insignificant</u> and <u>satisfactory</u>. Concern has been expressed over the influx of asylum-seekers.

	1980-85	2020-25
Net migration rate	0.0	0.6
Foreign-born population (%)	7.9 (1985)	

SPATIAL DISTRIBUTION/URBANIZATION	The Government considers that the pattern of population distribution is <u>partially appropriate</u>.

Urban	1985	2025
population (%)	83.4	90.5

Growth rate:	1980-85	2020-25
urban	0.2	0.0
rural	-0.3	-1.9

GENERAL POLICY FRAMEWORK

Overall approach to population problems: The debate on population trends extends to a wide range of issues including equality between the sexes, the changing role of women at home, regional variations in employment opportunities and social welfare, and the higher unemployment rate among new immigrants. Despite concern over low population growth and falling fertility, the Government does not intervene to influence those rates. There is a clear recognition that population issues cannot be addressed fully and adequately within the context of the confined aspects of demography. Hence, population policies have been framed as part of socio-economic policies. There is a desire to limit future levels of immigration and to adjust the urban-rural balance.

Importance of population policy in achieving development objectives: The Government does not have an explicit population policy designed to achieve specific demographic objectives. Nevertheless, population aging is seen as a problem hindering future economic development. Regional policies are in place to reduce the imbalance of employment opportunities among regions. Measures have been implemented to remove remaining obstacles to female labour force participation.

INSTITUTIONAL FRAMEWORK

Population data systems and development planning: The Central Bureau of Statistics is responsible for the continuous collection of data on population and for conducting censuses, which have been held at five-year intervals. The most recent was held in 1985 and the next is scheduled for 1990. Vital statistics registration is considered to be complete. No institutions focusing solely on demographic issues exist. However, there are national universities, institutions and committees involved in demographic research.

Integration of population within development planning: Various government bodies are responsible for taking into account population variables in planning, among which are: the Ministry of Health and Social Affairs, the Ministry of Labour and the Ministry of Industry. Other bodies involved in population planning are the National Boards of Social Health and Welfare, Labour, and Education. Under Sweden's decentralized social welfare system, municipal governments and county councils are also involved in population planning matters. The Central Bureau of Statistics is responsible for the preparation of population projections.

POLICIES AND MEASURES

Changes in population size and age structure: Although there is mounting concern over the low and continuously declining growth rate, no specifically designed countermeasures have been taken. Rather, the Government and

SWEDEN

localities have sought to remove impediments that may discourage families from having children. The major objective is to permit females to have children and participate in labour market activities. To deal with the growing elderly population, the national and local governments have been advancing social programmes and health care geared to their needs. The basic aim of old-age care is to provide economic security, adequate housing and greater opportunities to be active in the community and society.

<u>Mortality and morbidity</u>: Based on the 1983 Act on Health and Medical Care, responsibility for the provision of health and medical care rests with the county councils. Lacking an explicit and consistent national health policy, the Government in 1985 presented a Public Health Bill emphasizing primary health care, preventive measures, equity with special attention to high-risk groups, intersectoral co-operation and care for the elderly and mentally handicapped focusing on home care rather than institutionalization. Problems that remain to be resolved are a relocation of resources for primary health care during a period of economic stagnation, the training of personnel and the provision of housing and services for the elderly and handicapped. A system to forecast future demand for and supply of health personnel was under development. The Government has appointed a special national AIDS Commission.

<u>Fertility and the family</u>: The Government does not intervene to modify fertility, but within the scope of family policy, a number of measures have been implemented to allow families to adopt a life-style of their choice. Under the Government's "cradle-to-grave" social welfare system, there is an attempt to lessen the financial burdens of child-bearing and child-rearing. Maternity or paternity leave is available for up to 290 days, during which time 90 per cent of wages are paid. A family is also entitled to 60 days of paid leave a year to care for a sick child. A family allowance scheme pays 485 Swedish kronor a month until the child reaches the age of 16 for one child (SKr 6.8 = $US 1 as of 1986), SKr 970 for two, SKr 1,698 a month for three children, SKr 2,668 for four children, and a family with five or more chidren receives SKr 3,638. A network of family planning services integrated with maternal and child health has been established throughout the country. Emphasis is on preventive measures and reducing the number of abortions, which are free on request up to 12 weeks of pregnancy and in certain circumstances between 13 and 18 weeks of pregnancy. After 18 weeks an abortion must be approved by the National Board of Health and Welfare. In 1976 the Sterilization Act went into effect, making sterilization available upon request to those over 25 years of age and to those under age 25 with medical approval.

<u>International migration</u>: While immigration to Sweden from Nordic countries is unrestricted, immigration from non-Nordic countries for employment has virtually ceased. Labour market considerations underlie the current restrictive immigration policy. In June 1989 the Riksdag passed legislation creating new guidelines on immigration and refugee policy, which permit labour immigration only in exceptional cases and after the Employment Service has determined that a particular job cannot be filled with the labour already available in Sweden. Immigration for family reunification is still permitted. The Government supports measures that encourage immigrants to return to their countries of origin, as well as international co-operation to stimulate employment growth in emigration countries. Concerning the influx of asylum-seekers, the Government accepts refugees for humanitarian reasons,

within a fixed annual refugee quota. In July 1989 new measures were announced
to expedite the processing of asylum-seekers. The Government has repeatedly
emphasized the need for international co-operation in handling refugee
movements, and border controls have been strengthened.

Spatial distribution/urbanization: Evolving from a policy of
decentralization, regional policy has taken the form of a welfare policy to
eliminate differences in living standards between the various regions, by
focusing on job creation, particularly in the north, which has had relatively
high unemployment. The 1982 Regional Policy Act aimed to create conditions so
that stable populations can be maintained in different regions and to provide
employment, services and a healthy environment. Local governments in
development areas receive higher tax grants and other types of benefits. Aid
is offered to industries in development areas usually in the form of location
grants and loans if new investments will contribute to employment growth.

Status of women and population: The 1980 Act on Equality between Women and
Men at Work covers both public and private sector employment, prohibits
employment discrimination because of sex and obliges employers to take
affirmative action to achieve further equality. The Government also tries to
eliminate the self-fulfilling images associated with the stereotyped roles of
women and men. In schools, both boys and girls are obliged to learn domestic
science and child care. In addition, the parental insurance scheme, which
grants parental leave with pay to either parent, attempts to promote shared
responsibility for child care. The minimum legal age at marriage for females
is 18 years.

MAP NO. 2771.18 UNITED NATIONS
SEPTEMBER 1980

SWITZERLAND

DEMOGRAPHIC INDICATORS	CURRENT PERCEPTION

SIZE/AGE STRUCTURE/GROWTH
 	
Population: 1985   2025
 (thousands) 6 470 6 118
  0–14 years (%) 16.9 14.3
  60+ years (%) 19.6 33.7
 	
Rate of: 1980–85 2020–25
 growth   0.4   –0.4
 natural increase 2.3   –4.2
	The Government views the rate of population growth as <u>satisfactory</u>, although it acknowledges problems associated with population aging.

MORTALITY/MORBIDITY 1980–85 2020–25 Life expectancy 76.3 80.6 Crude death rate 9.3 13.5 Infant mortality 8.0 5.0	Current levels are perceived as <u>acceptable</u>.
FERTILITY/NUPTIALITY/FAMILY 1980–85 2020–25 Fertility rate 1.5 1.7 Crude birth rate 11.6 9.3 Contraceptive prevalence rate 71.2 (1980) Female mean age at first marriage 25.0 (1980)	Current levels of fertility are considered to be <u>unsatisfactory</u> because they are <u>too low</u>.
INTERNATIONAL MIGRATION 1980–85 2020–25 Net migration rate 0.0 0.0 Foreign-born population (%) 16.7 (1980)	The Government views the <u>significant</u> level of immigration as <u>satisfactory</u>. Emigration is <u>insignificant</u> and <u>satisfactory</u>. Concern is voiced at the influx of refugees and undocumented immigrants.
SPATIAL DISTRIBUTION/URBANIZATION Urban 1985 2025 population (%) 58.2 69.5 Growth rate: 1980–85 2020–25 urban 0.9 0.0 rural –0.1 –1.4	The overall spatial distribution is perceived as <u>partially appropriate</u>.

GENERAL POLICY FRAMEWORK

Overall approach to population problems: The Government's policy objectives include raising fertility through indirect measures to improve the situation of families and children and imposing stiffer regulations on immigration in order to curb the number of undocumented immigrants, asylum-seekers and refugees.

Importance of population policy in achieving development objectives: The Government does not have an explicit population policy intended to influence the demographic structure of the population. The Government, however, is aware that measures to improve the situation of families may have a demographic impact.

INSTITUTIONAL FRAMEWORK

Population data systems and development planning: Censuses are conducted under the direction of the Federal Statistical Office and were held in 1951, 1961, 1971 and 1981, with the next scheduled for 1991. Vital registration is considered to be complete. A formalized system of development plans does not exist.

Integration of population within development planning: There is no governmental body charged with the formulation or co-ordination of population policy. The Interdepartmental Commission for Economic and Demographic Studies is responsible for taking demographic variables into account in the planning process. The Government regularly informs the public on the demographic situation in the country.

POLICIES AND MEASURES

Changes in population size and age structure: Switzerland has no policy to influence directly the size and composition of the population, believing that population growth no longer contributes to economic growth. A major concern is the large number of immigrants and foreign workers and their impact on population growth. The Government seeks to establish policies that ensure the health and well-being of children and families, thus indirectly influencing demographic trends. The large proportion of the aged in the population is posing problems related to the viability of pension schemes.

Mortality and morbidity: In the area of health care the Government's main objectives are to control the spread of the AIDS virus, to stop the abuse and sale of illegal drugs and to work towards the advancement of genetic technology. There is no centralized planning of health services due to the fact that the country is divided into 26 autonomous cantons. About 95 per cent of the population is covered by public or private medical schemes. The entire population has access to primary health care, which is supplemented by other services such as domiciliary treatment of the sick and the aged, advisory centres for mothers, emergency and ambulance service and medical and dental services in the schools. As a result of the country's decentralized structure, there is a very high degree of community involvement in the health-care system at both the cantonal and the community level.

Fertility and the family: The Government's main objective is to increase the rate of fertility indirectly by establishing an atmosphere of economic security and well-being, especially for children and families in all sectors. In the 1980s there was a substantial expansion of family assistance services, family counselling, marriage guidance centres and pregnancy advisory services. Responsibility for family policy is shared by the cantons and the municipalities. Following the rejection, in a 1984 referendum, of the establishment of maternity insurance and parental leave, and the Parliament's refusal to introduce compulsory insurance against loss of earnings in the event of sickness - including maternity - maternity allowances were introduced through a partial revision of the sickness insurance scheme in 1987. Entitlement is for 16 weeks beginning at the time of confinement. A system of family allowances exists at both the Federal and cantonal level with the amounts varying according to region, occupation, canton and number of children. Abortion is legal only in cases of preserving the life and health of the mother. Sterilization is legal.

International migration: The Government's policy is to reduce the flow of immigrants given that about one third of the labour force is foreign-born. Stiffer regulations on immigration have been in force since January 1988, as estimates of unauthorized workers in Switzerland range from 50,000 and upwards. Despite a second revision of the country's refugee law that went into effect in early 1988 and that was designed to accelerate the determination procedure and deter the arrival of asylum-seekers without a valid claim, the number of requests increased by almost 50 per cent from the previous year to 16,700. As an immediate response, new measures were announced in 1989 stipulating that anyone not submitting a claim for asylum status at one of the 289 frontier posts designated for this purpose will not have the right to work, and that anyone entering the country illegally without submitting an asylum request would be immediately expelled. Emigration is not a major concern and there is no official policy encouraging the return of Swiss nationals. The Government has established a placement service for Swiss returning to Switzerland and keeps a register of Swiss skilled professionals abroad who might at some time seek employment in their own country.

Spatial distribution/urbanization: The Government has adopted a policy to modify the population distribution pattern. The main objectives are to adjust the population distribution between rural and urban areas and to achieve a better balance between population and local resources. Migration into metropolitan areas is not a problem in Switzerland, as such areas do not exist in the country; however, certain measures are being currently implemented to influence internal migration and spatial distribution. These measures include rural development to attract more population to rural areas, promoting the growth of existing small towns and cities and the development of lagging and border regions. Mountain regions, which are the focus of rural policy, are eligible for grants for investment under the 1974 Federal law on aid for investments in mountain regions.

<u>Status of women and population</u>: In the 1980s substantial improvements were made concerning the rights and treatment of women. In 1985 an amendment to the Civil Code affecting the laws governing marriage and succession was adopted by referendum. The law that came into effect on 1 January 1988 gives women equal rights in marriage, whereas previously a husband could lawfully manage his wife's inheritance and savings and prevent his wife from working. The minimum legal age at marriage for women is 17 years.

The boundaries shown on this map do not imply official endorsement or acceptance by the United Nations.

MAP NO. 2771.19   UNITED NATIONS
SEPTEMBER 1990

SYRIAN ARAB REPUBLIC

DEMOGRAPHIC INDICATORS	CURRENT PERCEPTION
SIZE/AGE STRUCTURE/GROWTH Population: 1985 2025 (thousands) 10 458 32 271 0-14 years (%) 48.1 30.8 60+ years (%) 4.3 6.5 Rate of: 1980-85 2020-25 growth 3.5 1.8 natural increase 36.9 17.8	The Government views the rate of population growth as <u>satisfactory</u>.
MORTALITY/MORBIDITY 1980-85 2020-25 Life expectancy 62.6 74.3 Crude death rate 8.6 3.7 Infant mortality 59.0 15.0	Current levels are considered <u>acceptable</u>, although the Government is concerned with improving health services for the rural population, children, mothers and the aged.
FERTILITY/NUPTIALITY/FAMILY 1980-85 2020-25 Fertility rate 7.2 2.6 Crude birth rate 45.5 21.5 Contraceptive prevalence rate 19.8 (1978) Female mean age at first marriage 21.5 (1981)	The Government regards fertility as <u>satisfactory</u>.
INTERNATIONAL MIGRATION 1980-85 2020-25 Net migration rate 0.0 0.0 Foreign-born population (%)	Levels and trends of immigration are considered to be <u>insignificant</u> and <u>satisfactory</u>. Emigration is considered to be <u>significant</u> and <u>too high</u>.
SPATIAL DISTRIBUTION/URBANIZATION Urban 1985 2025 population (%) 49.5 72.0 Growth rate: 1980-85 2020-25 urban 4.3 2.5 rural 2.7 0.0	The Government views the pattern of spatial distribution as being <u>partially appropriate</u>. The major concern is migration from rural areas to Damascus, the capital.

GENERAL POLICY FRAMEWORK

<u>Overall approach to population problems</u>: The Government has not formulated any explicit population policies. It is, however, aware of the impact that high rates of population growth have on development efforts. Policies are in place to improve health and educational, cultural and housing conditions, particularly in rural areas, and to channel resources better to different sectors of the economy.

<u>Importance of population policy in achieving development objectives</u>: No comprehensive population policy has been expressed, although population factors have been taken into account in various development plans. Government measures in the areas of health care, education, productivity, migration and the status of women have been influenced by population factors.

INSTITUTIONAL FRAMEWORK

<u>Population data systems and development planning</u>: The major sources of population data for the Syrian Arab Republic are national censuses, vital registration of births and deaths, which is considered to be incomplete, and various surveys. The first census was carried out in 1960, with subsequent censuses taken in 1970 and 1981 and the next provisionally scheduled for 1990. The Ministry of the Interior is charged with vital registration. Since 1968, the Central Bureau of Statistics has prepared population projections, and since 1972 the Centre for Population Studies and Research within the Central Bureau of Statistics has provided information on population matters and conducted special demographic surveys to meet planning needs. The Government has received international co-operation for basic data collection and training in demographic research. Formal economic planning has existed since the late 1950s. The Sixth Five-Year Plan covers the period 1986-1990.

<u>Integration of population within development planning</u>: The State Planning Commission, headed by the Minister of State for Planning Affairs, plays an important role as a policy- and decision-making body in population matters. Under the Commission, the Directorate of Comprehensive Planning and the Directorate of Manpower Planning are involved in population and manpower planning. A project was initiated in 1986 in order to strengthen the national capability to formulate population policies and to integrate population factors into development planning.

POLICIES AND MEASURES

<u>Changes in population size and age structure</u>: While the Government recognizes the problems associated with a high rate of population growth, there is no intervention to modify the rate. However, other policies such as raising the educational attainment of women are expected to have an indirect impact on

SYRIAN ARAB REPUBLIC

growth by decreasing rates of fertility. The Government's Five-Year Development Plan for 1981-1985 took the implications of population growth into account, particularly in relation to labour force and sectoral strategies. The country's very young population (48 per cent under age 15 in 1985) has diverted a substantial amount of the country's resources to the health and education sectors. The social security scheme covers employees in industry, commerce and agriculture, while excluding domestic servants, temporary and casual workers and family labour.

Mortality and morbidity: The Government's policies are to continue to improve the health conditions of the entire nation, with special attention paid to the rural population, in order to narrow the gap in health services between urban and rural areas. The Government is committed to increasing maternal and child health-care services, including child-spacing throughout the country, in order to provide free services for mothers and children. Efforts are under-way to train traditional birth attendants to refer high-risk cases to health centres and hospitals, to provide antenatal care and care to the mother during childbirth at home, post-natal care and advice on child care. In 1986 a campaign was launched to vaccinate 1.4 million children under five years of age against poliomyelitis, measles, whooping cough, tuberculosis, diphtheria and tetanus. Given the success of the 1986 media campaign in promoting vaccination, Syrian television in 1987 mounted an anti-smoking campaign.

Fertility and the family: The Syrian Arab Republic has traditionally had a pro-natalist policy. In view of the rapid growth of population, the young population, and the attendant problems these pose for development, this policy has been modified. In 1986, the Syrian National Assembly repealed a decree passed in 1952 that awarded "the Syrian Family Badge of Honour" to families with large numbers of children. As population has increased threefold since 1952, the Government considers that the objective of the award has been achieved. The Government now maintains a policy of non-intervention concerning fertility. Population information, education and communication campaigns are under way. Other government programmes, as well as social and economic changes, have indirectly had a significant impact on fertility. The Government supports family planning activities through a network of maternal and child health centres. Abortion is available only to save a woman's life. Information on the status of sterilization is not readily available.

International migration: Immigration is not an active policy concern, given its insignificant level. Emigration, however, is an area of active policy concern. Until the early 1970s, emigration was unrestricted, but the Government, in view of its concern over the departure of skilled workers, has placed restrictions on emigration. Government employees who leave their jobs without official approval, for example, are subject to serious penalties. Out-migration of unskilled and semi-skilled labour had been substantial, particularly of young people, to the oil-exporting countries of the Gulf.

Spatial distribution/urbanization: The Government reports that policies are in place to reduce rural-to-urban migration by improving public services such as education and overall living conditions in rural areas. By reducing migration it is hoped to reduce shortages of services, particularly housing in Damascus and Aleppo, the two largest cities, as well as to improve agricultural productivity, which has fallen as a result of the migration of young men. Less investment is being concentrated in large cities and the channelling of resources to different sectors of the economy is being improved. It is expected that the recommendations from a study on internal migration will be taken into account in preparing the Seventh Five-Year Development Plan for 1991-1995.

Status of women and population: The Government recognizes the importance of integrating women into the development process. A project was being prepared in 1987 with international assistance to develop educational and training programmes for women in order to create and strengthen a cadre of female social workers and specialists. The project, which would be undertaken by the Ministry of Social Affairs, the Ministry of Education and the Ministry of Culture, would facilitate the integration of women in the activities of existing rural development centres and local units of the Syrian Women's General Unit. Information on the minimum legal age at marriage for women is not readily available.

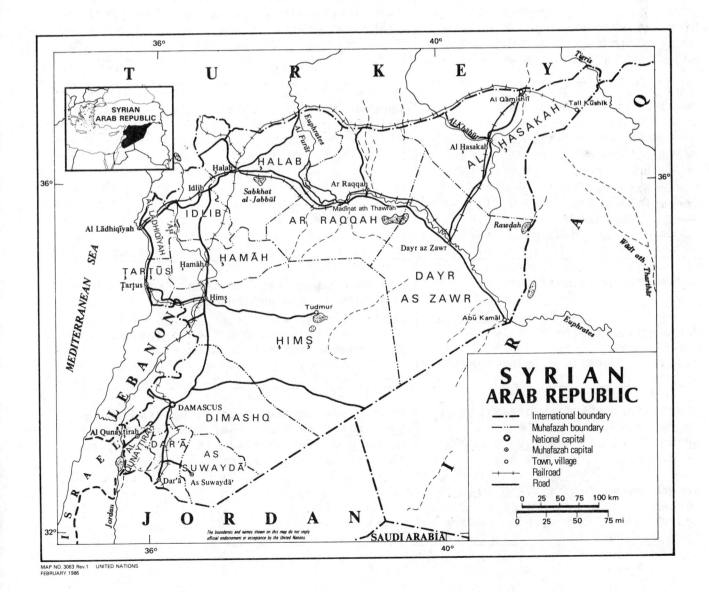

THAILAND

DEMOGRAPHIC INDICATORS	CURRENT PERCEPTION

SIZE/AGE STRUCTURE/GROWTH
 	
Population: 1985   2025
 (thousands)   51 604   80 911
  0-14 years (%)   36.5   21.0
  60+ years (%)   5.6   15.5
 	
Rate of: 1980-85   2020-25
 growth   2.0   0.7
 natural increase   19.9   7.0
	The Government considers the current growth rate to be <u>unsatisfactory</u> and <u>too high</u>.

MORTALITY/MORBIDITY 1980-85 2020-25 Life expectancy 62.7 74.6 Crude death rate 8.0 7.4 Infant mortality 48.0 13.0	Levels and trends are viewed as <u>unacceptable</u>. There is concern over cardio-vascular diseases, neoplasms and gastro-enteritis.
FERTILITY/NUPTIALITY/FAMILY 1980-85 2020-25 Fertility rate 3.5 2.1 Crude birth rate 27.8 14.4 Contraceptive prevalence rate 65.5 (1987) Female mean age at first marriage 22.7 (1980)	Current fertility rates are perceived as <u>unsatisfactory</u> because they are <u>too high</u>.
INTERNATIONAL MIGRATION 1980-85 2020-25 Net migration rate ... ... Foreign-born population (%) 0.6 (1980)	The Government regards levels of both immigration and emigration as <u>insignificant</u> and <u>satisfactory</u>. Concern has been expressed over the large numbers of refugees and asylum-seekers.
SPATIAL DISTRIBUTION/URBANIZATION Urban 1985 2025 population (%) 19.8 49.2 Growth rate: 1980-85 2020-25 urban 4.7 2.4 rural 1.4 -0.8	Spatial distribution is considered to be <u>inappropriate</u> because of the extreme primacy of the capital city, Bangkok, and the existence of regional imbalances.

GENERAL POLICY FRAMEWORK

Overall approach to population problems: The Government has adopted a policy to reduce population growth through voluntary acceptance of family planning. An active national programme sponsored by the Government provides family planning services and increases awareness of population matters and the desire for small families. The scope of population policy has been broadened to encompass wider health, social and economic objectives, and now also intends to effect a more balanced population distribution within the limits of available resources, to improve the quality of life and to develop human resources.

Importance of population policy in achieving development objectives: The Government accords high priority to population issues and recognizes that population policy is an important element in the overall socio-economic development of the country. Major development objectives outlined in the Sixth National Economic and Social Development Plan (1987-1991) are to accelerate economic growth, increase income levels and equalize income distribution, improve the quality of life and increase social development through such measures as raising the level of education, health and other services, and ensuring their widespread distribution.

INSTITUTIONAL FRAMEWORK

Population data systems and development planning: The National Statistical Office conducts censuses and surveys, including the decennial population and housing census, an intercensal survey of population change, as well as surveys of contraceptive prevalence, the labour force and the socio-economic situation. The last census was held in 1980 and the next was scheduled for 1990. Vital registration is incomplete. The Institute of Population Studies at Chulalongkorn University, Bangkok, is a major research and training centre for population studies and also conducts surveys concerning family planning, demographic and socio-economic issues. The National Economic and Social Development Board (NESDB), attached to the Office of the Prime Minister, is the central planning agency and is responsible for formulating both population policy and the five-year plans. The Sixth National Economic and Social Development Plan for 1987-1991 is the most recent plan. A major development plan was announced in 1989 to transform southern Thailand into an industrial centre.

Integration of population within development planning: Government policy is to integrate population variables into development planning. The Sixth Five-Year Plan (1987-1991) focuses on issues such as labour absorption, the rapid increase in the working-age population, unemployment, urbanization and population distribution. The awareness and capacity of government agencies to integrate population and development planning has been strengthened. The Thailand Development Research Institute has since 1986 been responsible for providing information on population-development interrelationships. The Population Planning Section of the National Economic and Social Development Board takes into account population variables in planning.

THAILAND

POLICIES AND MEASURES

Changes in population size and age structure: The Government has a policy to modify population growth and improve well-being and health. The goal of reducing population growth has been operationalized by setting progressively lower growth rate targets. The Sixth National Development Plan aims to reduce the growth rate from under 1.7 per cent per year in 1986 to 1.39 per cent in 1991. A variety of policy instruments has been implemented to that effect, including an extensive family planning programme, information, education and communication activities, and other measures to reduce the desired number of children and infant and child mortality rates. With regard to social security, there is a scheme only for public employees.

Mortality and morbidity: Health policy objectives are to achieve Health for All by the Year 2000 and to secure basic minimum needs. Health facilities at all levels have been reoriented towards primary health care, which is part of a wider basic minimum needs programme extending beyond the health sector and involving three other ministries in addition to the Ministry of Public Health. Strategies include the improvement of access to primary health care, particularly in rural areas; decentralization of the health-care management system; community participation; intersectoral collaboration; development of alternative approaches for health financing and enforcement of health-related regulations. The target is an infant mortality rate of 39 per thousand live births by 1991. Despite the small number of confirmed cases, in 1989 the Government formulated Asia's first national medium-term plan to combat AIDS.

Fertility and the family: The policy is to reduce fertility primarily by expanding family planning services. The national family planning programme is the major source of contraceptive services and has played an important role in facilitating the national fertility decline. It is characterized by the constant expansion of service provision, co-operation with non-governmental agencies and integration of activities with maternal and child health services. Measures include the expansion of family planning services with a focus on addressing the needs of underserved groups, particularly Muslims in the four southern border provinces, the hill tribes in the north-west, adolescents, factory and construction workers and slum residents; a greater stress on service quality; improved programme management and information, education and communication efforts; increased community involvement; and stronger linkages between governmental and private sectors. Sterilization is allowed only for women with at least three living children, although in practice, women with two living children can apply for sterilization, which is the most common method of contraception. Abortion is permitted to save the life of the woman, for rape, incest or eugenic reasons.

International migration: As of July 1989, there were about 106,000 Indo-Chinese asylum-seekers in nine refugee camps and centres in Thailand. This figure does not include Laotians ineligible for entry to the camp and who are awaiting repatriation, nor does it include an estimated 300,000 displaced Cambodians housed along the Thai-Cambodian border. The Thai authorities are considering for citizenship several thousand persons from Cambodia and the Lao People's Democratic Republic who claim recent ancestry in Thailand. Thai workers, whose supply exceeds demand, are being encouraged to find employment abroad. To prevent shortages of skilled manpower in Thailand, a new Recruitment and Protection Law for workers was enacted in 1985. It provided for the licensing of private recruitment agencies and forbade the departure of Thai workers without the approval of the Department of Labour.

<u>Spatial distribution/urbanization</u>: The Government considers controlling the growth of the Bangkok Metropolitan Area to be an important national priority. Spatial policies are being implemented through physical planning measures, e.g., land use controls and zoning regulations. In addition, the Government has divided the Bangkok metropolitan region into four strategic areas, for which complementary investment strategies will be implemented. Beyond Bangkok, after more than a decade of discussion, the Government's Eastern Seaboard strategy is finally under way. To promote regional equity, the Government intends to develop other industrial estates in peripheral areas, as outlined in previous five-year plans. In 1989, a new long-term development strategy was announced for southern Thailand.

<u>Status of women and population</u>: The status of women is viewed as an important factor contributing to development. The Government has established the National Commission on Women's Affairs, chaired by a deputy Prime Minister, to monitor and co-ordinate development activities related to women and has formulated the Long-Term Development Plan for Women, 1982-2001. National development plans identify labour, education and health as problems pertaining to female status. Programmes include improving the living conditions of rural women through education and training in business skills and extending credit for income-generating activities. The joint sharing of responsibilities between men and women in family life, child-rearing and family planning is being promoted. The minimum legal age at marriage for women is 17 years.

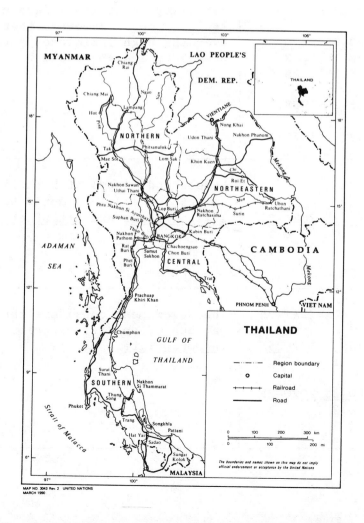

TOGO

DEMOGRAPHIC INDICATORS	CURRENT PERCEPTION

SIZE/AGE STRUCTURE/GROWTH
 	
Population: 1985 2025
 (thousands) 2 960 9 500
  0-14 years (%) 44.8 38.4
  60+ years (%) 5.1 5.6
 	
Rate of: 1980-85 2020-25
 growth 3.0 2.3
 natural increase 29.5 22.6
	The Government considers the current rate of growth to be <u>satisfactory</u>.

MORTALITY/MORBIDITY 　　　　　　　　　1980-85 2020-25 Life expectancy 50.5 67.0 Crude death rate 15.7 6.3 Infant mortality 102.0 40.0	Levels are considered to be <u>unacceptable</u>. The Government is concerned by high mortality levels, particularly of children aged 0-4, respiratory and gastro-intestinal infections, malaria and malnutrition.
FERTILITY/NUPTIALITY/FAMILY 　　　　　　　　　1980-85 2020-25 Fertility rate 6.1 3.6 Crude birth rate 45.2 28.9 Contraceptive prevalence rate 33.1 (1988) Female mean age at first marriage 18.5 (1971)	Fertility rates are viewed as <u>satisfactory</u>. However, there is concern over the high incidence of teen-age pregnancy and abortion.
INTERNATIONAL MIGRATION 　　　　　　　　　1980-85 2020-25 Net migration rate 0.0 0.0 Foreign-born population (%)	Levels and trends of both immigration and emigration are considered to be <u>insignificant</u> and <u>satisfactory</u>.
SPATIAL DISTRIBUTION/URBANIZATION Urban 1985 2025 population (%) 22.1 53.0 Growth rate: 1980-85 2020-25 urban 6.2 3.7 rural 2.1 0.7	The Government considers the present pattern of spatial distribution to be <u>inappropriate</u>.

GENERAL POLICY FRAMEWORK

Overall approach to population problems: The Government does not have an official policy to modify fertility, although it is broadly supportive of family planning and interested in employment aspects and in population redistribution. It seeks to reduce mortality, particularly infant mortality, and to modify patterns of spatial distribution by reducing in-migration to Lomé and to other urban centres, particularly Kara in the north.

Importance of population policy in achieving development objectives: The Government had not adopted an official population policy as of early 1989, although it has modified its traditional pro-natalist position. A draft national population policy statement was prepared following a conference on population and development in Lomé in 1987. Rapid population growth is increasingly perceived as an obstacle to development efforts. Policies have been formulated that are essential aspects of a population policy, such as those aimed at providing integrated health and family planning services, improving female status and adjusting the spatial distribution pattern.

INSTITUTIONAL FRAMEWORK

Population data systems and development planning: Togo has held three censuses, the last of which was conducted in 1981. The next census was provisionally scheduled for 1991. Census-taking is the responsibility of the Bureau Central du Recensement. Vital registration remains incomplete. Development planning had been affected by the serious economic crisis of the early 1980s. The Fifth Five-Year Plan for the period 1986-1990 was superseded by a structural adjustment programme. A number of action programmes had been drawn up for different sectors over the period 1986-1990, at the end of which it is hoped that economic and social conditions will have improved. A Population Research Unit has been established at Lomé University.

Integration of population within development planning: Although there is neither an explicit population policy nor a single organization for formulating such policy, the Government is now attempting to integrate demographic variables in the planning process. Preparations were under way in 1989 for a Population Planning Unit within the Ministry of Planning. Both the Division of Manpower and the Division of Demography and Statistics take population variables into account in planning. A project was begun in 1986 with international assistance to strengthen the demographic data analysis and research capabilities of the Division of Demography and Statistics to assist the Government in formulating and monitoring population policies and to improve knowledge of the country's demographic situation.

TOGO

POLICIES AND MEASURES

Changes in population size and age structure: There is no policy of intervention. The Government seeks to improve maternal and child health and to attain a more equitable population distribution. Sectoral programmes in primary health care education, rural and regional development, population education and family planning are expected to have indirect effects on population dynamics. A draft national population policy statement was prepared in 1988. Under the social security scheme, coverage is extended to employed persons, members of co-operatives, apprentices and students. There is also a special system for public employees, and voluntary insurance is available to persons with six months of previous social security coverage.

Mortality and morbidity: The Government's stated policy is to achieve Health for All by the Year 2000. There is increased emphasis on preventive and primary health care, with communities mobilized to deal more effectively with a range of diseases. Specific programmes include malaria control, an expanded programme of immunization, diarrhoeal disease control, public drinking water supply and environmental health, and improving the supply of essential drugs. The Expanded Programme on Immunization was initiated in 1980 and now serves all of Togo. An Inter-ministerial Planning Committee was to have been created in 1985 under the direction of the Ministry of Health with the intention of designing, implementing and evaluating health programmes. The Government intends to increase the number of maternal and child health-care centres to 84 by 1992.

Fertility and the family: There is no explicit policy with respect to the levels of fertility. The advantages of a planned family are being publicized as part of the increased efforts to combat maternal and child mortality and morbidity, and to promote family well-being. The Government is concerned by adolescent pregnancies, and population and sex education has been integrated into secondary school curricula. The Togolese Family Welfare Association, established in 1976, provides family planning information and education and has medical and clinical programmes. Contraceptives are available in both government and private facilities. Government plans are to strengthen the family planning clinic network and make family planning services available in all facilities supervised by physicians or midwives. Maternity benefits are available, as well as an employment-related scheme of pre-natal and family allowances. Abortion is permissible to preserve the mother's life or health. There are no specific legal provisions concerning sterilization.

International migration: No explicit policy has been formulated concerning the insignificant levels of either immigration or emigration. Visa and border check-points have been relied on to control both immigration and emigration. Most of the migrant workers repatriated from Nigeria in early 1983 came from south-east Togo and are now considered to be self-sufficient and reintegrated. As of early 1989 there were an estimated 3,500 refugees in Togo.

Spatial distribution/urbanization: The Government is very conscious of the need to promote a more balanced urban structure and regional and rural development. To assist in regional planning, regional planning offices have been created in the country's five regions, and a regional development plan

was prepared as well as a master plan for 1985-1990. An Integrated
Development Programme for Northern Togo was undertaken to improve the living
and working conditions of the rural population. Infrastructure such as roads
and buildings was developed, work methods were adopted to the region's
socio-economic conditions, and rural medical and social centres were
constructed. With international assistance, a Special Programme of
Labour-Intensive Public Work was established to stem the rural exodus and to
reduce urban unemployment by developing new agricultural, forest and pastoral
areas.

Status of women and population: The Government has adopted a number of
measures to improve the status of women. A new Personal and Family Code was
enacted in January 1980, harmonizing laws on marriage, divorce and the custody
of children. Both parties must consent to a marriage and polygyny is allowed
only if the husband declares this option before the marriage ceremony. The
role of head of household is to be shared by both spouses, and the wife is
given full legal rights. The Code also abolished the unilateral divorce of a
wife by repudiation. The minimum legal age at marriage for women is 17 years.

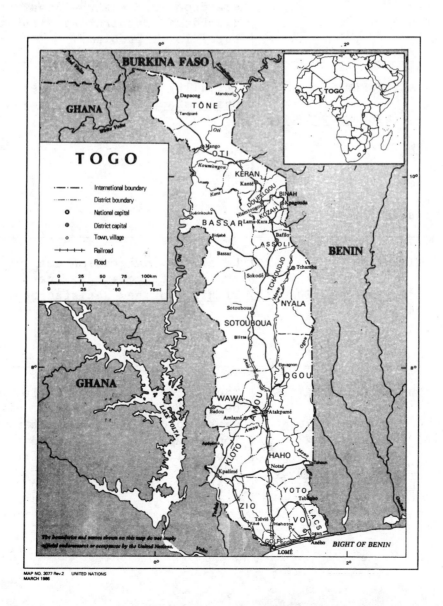

MAP NO. 3077 Rev.2   UNITED NATIONS
MARCH 1986

TONGA

DEMOGRAPHIC INDICATORS	CURRENT PERCEPTION
SIZE/AGE STRUCTURE/GROWTH	The rate of population growth is viewed as <u>unsatisfactory</u> because it is <u>too high</u>.

Population:	1985	2025
(thousands)	109	177
0-14 years (%)	...	...
60+ years (%)	...	...

Rate of:	1980-85	2020-25
growth	2.4	0.6
natural increase	...	...

MORTALITY/MORBIDITY		Present levels and trends are considered to be <u>unacceptable</u>. Major concerns are maternal and child care, including diarrhoea and gastro-intestinal disorders, respiratory diseases and nutritional problems.

	1980-85	2020-25
Life expectancy	...	...
Crude death rate	...	...
Infant mortality	...	...

FERTILITY/NUPTIALITY/FAMILY		Fertility levels are viewed as being <u>unsatisfactory</u> because they are <u>too high</u>.

	1980-85	2020-25
Fertility rate	...	...
Crude birth rate	...	...
Contraceptive prevalence rate	...	...
Female mean age at first marriage	...	...

INTERNATIONAL MIGRATION		Levels of immigration are <u>insignificant</u> and <u>satisfactory</u>. Emigration levels are <u>significant</u> and <u>satisfactory</u>.

	1980-85	2020-25
Net migration rate	...	...
Foreign-born population (%)	1.2 (1976)	

SPATIAL DISTRIBUTION/URBANIZATION		The spatial distribution is considered to be <u>partially appropriate</u>. The Government seeks to decelerate migration to Tongatapu, the main island group, and especially to Nuku'alofa, the capital.

Urban	1985	2025
population (%)	19.7	43.9

Growth rate:	1980-85	2020-25
urban	2.4	2.5
rural	2.4	-0.8

GENERAL POLICY FRAMEWORK

<u>Overall approach to population problems</u>: Concerned by population pressures, the Government has implemented policies to lower population growth and fertility through programmes of maternal and child health and family planning and population education. The Government also hopes to reduce the movement of population from the outer islands to Tongatapu.

<u>Importance of population policy in achieving development objectives</u>: The Government has designated population policy as an important and integral component of economic and social planning. Demographic factors are perceived as having an important bearing on development objectives because of the increasing disparities between the islands and the greater salience of employment and manpower issues in development planning. These considerations have added to the urgency of development programmes directed towards increasing employment, especially in fisheries, tourism and small-scale industry, as well as strengthening agricultural extension services.

INSTITUTIONAL FRAMEWORK

<u>Population data systems and development planning</u>: Censuses have been conducted on a decennial basis since the first modern census was held in 1956. A national mini-census was carried out in December 1984 in addition to the full census that was held in 1986. Vital registration remains incomplete with mortality data being most deficient. The Central Planning Department is responsible for formulating implementing and reviewing the five-year development plans, as well as population policy. The Fourth Five-Year Development Plan for the period 1980-1985 paid greater attention to the need for rural and regional development, but was interrupted by a major cyclone and drought. The Fifth Five-Year Development Plan for 1986-1990 was the first to deal with employment and manpower issues explicitly in the form of a separate chapter.

<u>Integration of population within development planning</u>: The Government recognizes the need to integrate population policy within development planning. National development plans have consistently included as goals the reduction of population growth through a lowering of the birth rate, together with more balanced development between and within the island groups. Inter-ministerial committees are responsible for co-ordinating many population-related programmes, such as those related to regional development that span several ministerial domains. The Fifth Five-Year Development Plan called for the establishment of a Human Resources and Employment Planning Co-ordination Committee.

TONGA

POLICIES AND MEASURES

Changes in population size and age structure: As part of overall development
strategy, the Government's policy is to lower rates of population growth. The
country has a long history of being concerned by population growth because of
the implications of increasing population pressure for the land distribution
system mandated by the Constitution. Under the Constitution, every male
Tongan taxpayer above the age of 16 is entitled to a small plot of land, but
this entitlement has not been fulfilled because of the growing shortage of
land. Programmes in family planning, population education and development of
the outer islands have been undertaken. In the mid-1980s legislation for the
provision of social security was under consideration.

Mortality and morbidity: Current health policies reflect the goal of health
for all and are consistent with rational development objectives. An important
development has been the gradual shift to a community-based approach to health
care. Priority areas now include the improved provision of planning and the
equitable distribution of health services and resources between and within the
island groups. By 1986 coverage of the six immunizable diseases was more than
80 per cent, improvements had been made in environmental sanitation, and
essential health services within one hour's walking distance were available to
at least 80 per cent of the population. Voluntary village health workers have
been trained in very small, peripheral areas. Health education in schools is
being improved and contributes to increasing public awareness of health
matters. To contribute to the development of a comprehensive health-care
delivery service for the total health needs of the population and to promote
social and economic productivity through primary health-care activities,
programmes were undertaken in 1988 to strengthen community participation,
information, education, motivation, and maternal and child care and family
planning services.

Fertility and the family: The Government has had a policy of intervention to
lower the fertility level. The Tongan Family Planning Association was formed
in 1969 and the Prime Minister agreed to serve as its patron. This
non-governmental organization provides contraceptive services mostly through
private clinics. Government family planning services are available at
hospitals, health centres and clinics, and have been fully integrated with
maternal and child health services. There has been a move towards
community-based distribution; in-service training of health personnel,
traditional birth attendants and health educators in family planning matters;
and an emphasis on motivation through women's development groups.
Information, education and communication activities are carried out, including
broadcasts on the national radio. Abortion is permitted to save the mother's
life and sterilization is allowed.

International migration: Because of a shortage of land, immigration is not
encouraged. Those wishing to reside in Tonga must obtain a permit and
permission is granted only to those taking up approved employment. Emigration
of Tongan workers, both skilled and unskilled, has long been of concern to the
Government. Despite these concerns, emigration is not discouraged as it
lowers population growth, while remittances provide an important source of
foreign exchange receipts. The Government hopes that development will create

additional employment possibilities that will reduce the loss of the country's most dynamic manpower. The Fifth Five-Year Development Plan included a project to develop a system for the continuous monitoring of emigration and return migration, as well as a scheme for channelling remittances and overseas savings into productive investments.

Spatial distribution/urbanization: With substantial migration to the major island group of Tongatapu and particularly to Nuku'alofa, the capital, national development plans have contained projects directed at preventing additional migration by fostering economic opportunities, communications and social services in the outer island groups. The Government is attempting to narrow differences in living standards between urban and rural areas and to promote a more balanced regional development. In 1979 the Rural Development Unit was established within the Central Planning Unit.

Status of women and population: Both the Fourth and the Fifth Development Plans sought to increase women's participation in the development process. Within the Central Planning Department, a Woman's Informal Working Committee acts as the co-ordinating body between the Women's Development Programme and overall development planning and policy. At the village level, women's development committees are quite active and play an important role in health care. Information is not readily available on the legal age at marriage for women.

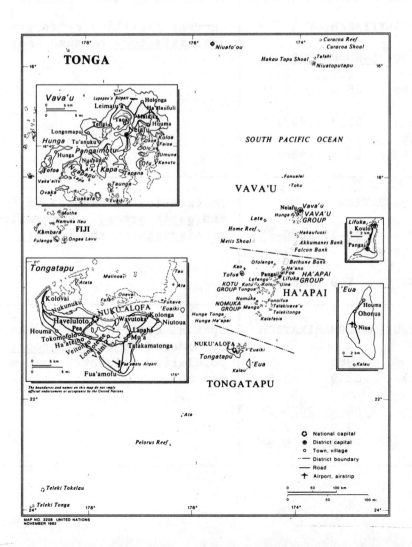

TRINIDAD AND TOBAGO

DEMOGRAPHIC INDICATORS	CURRENT PERCEPTION
SIZE/AGE STRUCTURE/GROWTH	The Government perceives current growth rates as <u>unsatisfactory</u> and <u>too high</u>.

Population:	1985	2025
(thousands)	1 185	1 918
0-14 years (%)	32.9	22.0
60+ years (%)	7.9	16.9

Rate of:	1980-85	2020-25
growth	1.6	0.8
natural increase	18.4	8.3

MORTALITY/MORBIDITY	Current levels are considered to be <u>acceptable</u>.

	1980-85	2020-25
Life expectancy	68.7	77.2
Crude death rate	7.0	6.7
Infant mortality	24.0	9.0

FERTILITY/NUPTIALITY/FAMILY	Current fertility rates are viewed as <u>unsatisfactory</u> because they are <u>too high</u>.

	1980-85	2020-25
Fertility rate	2.9	2.1
Crude birth rate	25.4	15.1
Contraceptive prevalence rate	52.7 (1987)	
Female mean age at first marriage	22.3 (1980)	

INTERNATIONAL MIGRATION	Immigration is seen as <u>insignificant</u> and <u>satisfactory</u>. Emigration is viewed as <u>significant</u> and <u>too high</u>.

	1980-85	2020-25
Net migration rate	...	...
Foreign-born population (%)	5.8 (1980)	

SPATIAL DISTRIBUTION/URBANIZATION	Spatial distribution of the population is considered to be <u>inappropriate</u> due to population concentration in metropolitan centres.

Urban	1985	2025
population (%)	63.9	83.8

Growth rate:	1980-85	2020-25
urban	3.9	1.2
rural	-1.9	-0.9

GENERAL POLICY FRAMEWORK

<u>Overall approach to population problems</u>: The Government's population policy since the late 1960s has consisted mainly of a national family planning programme aimed at reducing rapid population growth so as to make it commensurate with the country's resources. Through various sectoral measures it has sought to address other areas affecting the population such as housing, health, education, employment, the status of women, immigration and the spatial distribution of the population.

<u>Importance of population policy in achieving development objectives</u>: The Government has indicated that although the country's rate of population growth in some ways had contributed to the achievement of economic and social development, it has been basically too high, placing excessive pressure on the country's natural resources and contributing to problems of unemployment and an unfavourable income distribution. Development plans since 1960 have included a commitment to reducing population growth.

INSTITUTIONAL FRAMEWORK

<u>Population data systems and development planning</u>: The most recent population census was taken in 1980 and the next was provisionally scheduled for 1990. Vital registration is considered to be virtually complete and is the responsibility of the Central Statistical Office. Family planning and fertility surveys were conducted in 1977 and 1987 and an adolescent fertility survey was initiated in 1984. It appears that the Government has not published development plans in recent years.

<u>Integration of population within development planning</u>: The National Population Council, established in 1967, served as the initial advisory body on matters of population policy, which centred mainly on family planning services. This Council was disbanded in 1978 and reconstituted in 1989. In 1986 the national family planning programme was encompassed by the newly formed Ministry of Health, Welfare and the Status of Women in an attempt to link population with the wider area of community development. Population matters are co-ordinated with other sectoral organizations in various fields. Demographic estimates and projections are prepared by the Central Statistical Office.

POLICIES AND MEASURES

<u>Changes in population size and age structure</u>: The Government's policy directly supports family planning measures and a more diversified economy in order to reduce growth rates that are felt to place a burden on the Government's resources. Government benefits for the aged have been increased and include free public transportation, an increased pension, food stamps and

financial assistance to non-governmental agencies that provide care for the aged. The Government has a social insurance scheme covering employed persons, including agricultural and domestic workers, apprentices and public employees.

Mortality and morbidity: The Government has actively sought to improve the health of the population of the country and provides the majority of health care to its citizens. The main goals are to provide Health for All by the Year 2000 and restructure health services to orient them more towards a primary health-care approach. A second National Health Plan was being developed in 1987 to provide policy guidelines, strategies and priorities. In 1989 the Government noted that the continuous drop in the gross national product had necessitated the adjustment of the Government's policies in sectors such as health. Improvement of health conditions for mothers and children is the target of numerous health projects and activities. Recent measures have included evaluating pre-natal and perinatal care at the primary health-care level, publication of a maternal and child health-care manual and control of acute respiratory and diarrhoeal diseases among children. Additional measures are improvements in the management of health centres and the maintenance of plant and equipment, upgrading water supplies and the sewage system, rationalizing the financing of services and greater community participation. The Government has established a model child-care centre in an area of high infant and child mortality. A special facility to be used as a counselling centre for AIDS patients and their families has been created.

Fertility and the family: The National Family Planning Programme, which began in 1967, has formed the major part of the country's policy to lower fertility and has consisted of three co-ordinating branches: the Ministry of Health and two non-governmental organizations, namely, the country's private family planning organization, the Family Planning Association of Trinidad and Tobago, (FPATT), and the Catholic Marriage Advisory Council. In the 1980s the programme was reappraised and restructured in order to make it more effective. In 1988 family planning services were available in 103 government centres throughout the country and two FPATT clinics in urban centres. Family planning objectives in the 1980s have aimed at expanding integrated maternal and child health and information and education programmes at the community level. A study was initiated in 1984 on the cultural patterns underlying adolescent pregnancy in order to determine the most effective strategy for introducing population education and information on responsible parenthood to teenagers. Abortion is legal to protect the mother's physical or mental health. Voluntary sterilization is not provided for by law, but female sterilization occurs in practice, although spousal consent is required.

International migration: No explicit policy exists concerning immigration. However, as a consequence of deteriorating employment conditions, spouses of foreigners who have not yet received residence status are required to obtain a permit to work. Although the Government has participated in sponsored emigration schemes for unskilled labour, it has enacted measures to reduce the emigration of skilled labour such as programmes to expand training facilities and employment opportunities.

Spatial distribution/urbanization: Government measures aim to improve the spatial concentration of population in metropolitan areas and they include provision for employment and development of industries outside major urban areas, low-income housing in rural areas, the development of a network of highways and the decentralization of public service activities'. The Government has also enacted a Town and Country Plan to facilitate the development and implementation of comprehensive housing and settlement policy. The Government's concern over the homeless has led to the funding of housing associations, expanding the private rental sector and targeting resources more effectively in the public sector.

Status of women and population: From 1980 to 1986 an Intersectoral Commission on the Status of Women functioned and was responsible for laws affecting women. In 1986 this responsibility was transferred to the newly created Ministry of Health, Welfare and the Status of Women, which aimed to place the status of women in the context of community development. The legal age at marriage for women varies between 12 and 14 years depending on the religious group.

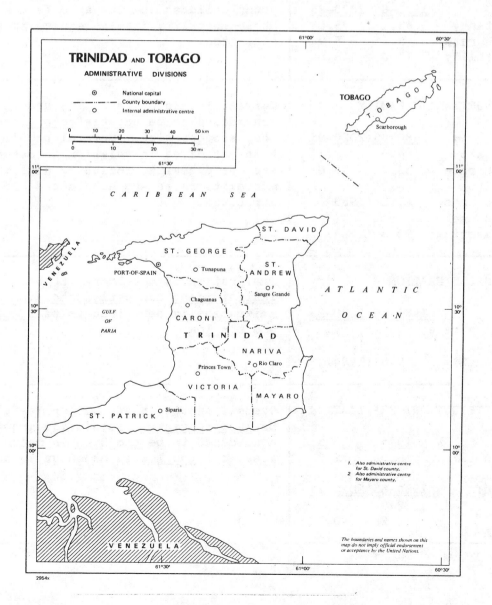

2954x

TUNISIA

DEMOGRAPHIC INDICATORS	CURRENT PERCEPTION

SIZE/AGE STRUCTURE/GROWTH
 	
Population: 1985   2025
  (thousands) 7 261 13 284
  0-14 years (%) 39.6   22.5
  60+ years (%)   6.0   13.1
 	
Rate of: 1980-85 2020-25
 growth   2.6   1.0
 natural increase 25.3   10.2
	The Government considers the present rate of population growth to be <u>unsatisfactory</u> because it is <u>too high</u>.

MORTALITY/MORBIDITY 1980-85 2020-25 Life expectancy 63.1 75.0 Crude death rate 8.4 5.9 Infant mortality 71.0 16.0	Levels of mortality are <u>unacceptable</u>. The Government has identified infants, young children and the aged as the groups whose mortality levels require special attention.
FERTILITY/NUPTIALITY/FAMILY 1980-85 2020-25 Fertility rate 4.9 2.1 Crude birth rate 33.7 16.0 Contraceptive prevalence rate 41.1 (1983) Female mean age at first marriage 24.3 (1984)	Current levels of fertility are considered to be <u>unsatisfactory</u> because they are <u>too high</u>. Several problems have been perceived in relation to maternal and child health, including high infant mortality rates and unbalanced age structure.
INTERNATIONAL MIGRATION 1980-85 2020-25 Net migration rate ... ... Foreign-born population (%) 0.6 (1984)	Immigration is considered to be <u>insignificant</u> and <u>satisfactory</u>. Emigration is perceived to be <u>significant</u> and <u>too low</u>.
SPATIAL DISTRIBUTION/URBANIZATION Urban 1985 2025 population (%) 53.0 72.6 Growth rate: 1980-85 2020-25 urban 2.9 1.7 rural 2.2 -0.7	Overall spatial distribution is felt to be <u>inappropriate</u>. Population growth is considered to be <u>too high</u> in metropolitan areas but <u>too low</u> in other urban areas.

GENERAL POLICY FRAMEWORK

<u>Overall approach to population problems</u>: The Government's population
policy objectives include lowering the birth rate and extending family
health services in rural areas, improving living conditions and
health-care facilities for infants and small children, decreasing
migration to the metropolitan areas, and adjusting the spatial
distribution pattern.

<u>Importance of population policy in achieving development objectives</u>:
Population policy is viewed as essential in meeting the goals of economic
growth and in harmonizing labour supply with the employment possibilities
in Tunisia. The Government is aware that a reduction of population growth
is necessary to speed up socio-economic development which, in turn, can
contribute to alleviating the unemployment problem. In 1987 Tunisia
received the United Nations Population Award for the work of the National
Office of Population and the Family.

INSTITUTIONAL FRAMEWORK

<u>Population data systems and development planning</u>: Nine censuses have been
conducted since 1921, with the most recent held in 1984. Vital
registration, which is the responsibility of the National Institute of
Statistics, is believed to be complete. The seventh Plan National de
Développement Economique et Social (1987-1991), prepared by the Ministry
of Planning, is currently in effect.

<u>Integration of population within development planning</u>: The National
Office of Population amd the Family and the Ministry of Planning are
responsible for integrating demographic variables in development planning,
as well as for the formulation and co-ordination of population policies.
In 1985 the Consultative Commission on the Family and Population was
created to evaluate the impact of population and family policies.
International assistance was initiated in 1980 to assist the National
Institute for Demographic Research and Studies to strengthen the
institutionalization of demographic studies, formulate population policies
and integrate population in national development planning.

POLICIES AND MEASURES

<u>Changes in population size and age structure</u>: Concerned by the impact of high
population growth on economic development, unemployment and the health of
mothers and children, the Government has undertaken policies to reduce natural
increase, population size and population growth with programmes to lower
fertility levels, increase emigration, adjust the spatial distribution pattern
and modify social and economic factors. Targets in terms of both total
population size and population growth rates have been specified. Under the
social security scheme, coverage includes employees in industry, commerce,
construction, transportation, liberal professions, agricultural workers,
public employees and fishermen.

TUNISIA

<u>Mortality and morbidity</u>: Government priorities in the area of health include preventive care; health protection of vulnerable population groups, particularly mothers and children; reduction of health hazards related to the environment and industrialization; strengthening the training of medical personnel; and expanding peripheral and rural infrastructure. Programmes have been undertaken to promote oral rehydration therapies, child growth monitoring and public awareness of maternal and child health care. Beginning in 1987 annual national immunization days have been declared with the goal of vaccinating all children under the age of five against the six immunizable diseases. The Seventh Five-Year Development Plan specified a target of reducing the infant mortality rate by 50 per cent by 1991.

<u>Fertility and the family</u>: To lower population growth and improve family well-being, the Government has aggresively pursued a co-ordinated policy of decreasing fertility levels. Direct measures include Government provision of family planning integrated with maternal and child care, information, education and communication programmes. Indirect measures consist of raising educational levels, improving the status of women and increasing employment opportunities. A number of projects have been undertaken such as those to expand family planning services in rural areas and to study the use of traditional birth attendants. Family allowances were limited to four children in 1987 and to three children in 1988. A maternity leave of two months at full pay, followed by four months at half pay, was also limited in 1988 to the first three confinements. Abortion is permitted on demand and sterilization is legal. Targets to be achieved by 1991 are a general fertility rate of 116 per thousand and a contraceptive rate of 51 per cent (42 per cent using modern methods).

<u>International migration</u>: The Government reports that it does not have any policy concerning the insignificant level of immigration. Given the persistence of high unemployment, the Government seeks to increase the significant level of emigration, while being concerned by the return of Tunisian emigrants from abroad. Remittances from Tunisian expatriates fell sharply following the expulsion of 30,000 Tunisian workers from the Libyan Arab Jamahiriya in 1985. However, the signing of a bilateral agreement providing for Tunisian workers to live, work and own property in the Libyan Arab Jamahiriya has helped to reverse this trend. In addition, in late 1988 the Libyan Arab Jamahiriya agreed to recruit 10,000 Tunisian workers.

<u>Spatial distribution</u>: One of the Government's priorities is to stem the influx of people into urban areas. To achieve this goal, measures have been implemented to promote the agricultural sector, improve the living conditions in rural areas and decentralize services and investments. The Seventh Development Plan proposed to provide 20,000 additional jobs in the rural sector through programmes of integrated rural development. Desert farming is also being encouraged by developing new land in the southern part of the country, where a huge underground lake has been discovered. In 1986 work was launched on a new town near Tunis, which should increase the capital's area by one third. The town is expected to have a population of 350,000 people in the twenty-first century.

<u>Status of women and population</u>: The Government has adopted several measures to improve the status of women. An employment code for women has been established, the minimum legal age at marriage for women has been raised to 17 years, access to contraception is being facilitated and emphasis is being given to women's education. The Government is also promoting the sharing of responsibilities between men and women. Radio and television, as well as other mass media and the various ministries, are also playing an important role in improving the status of women.

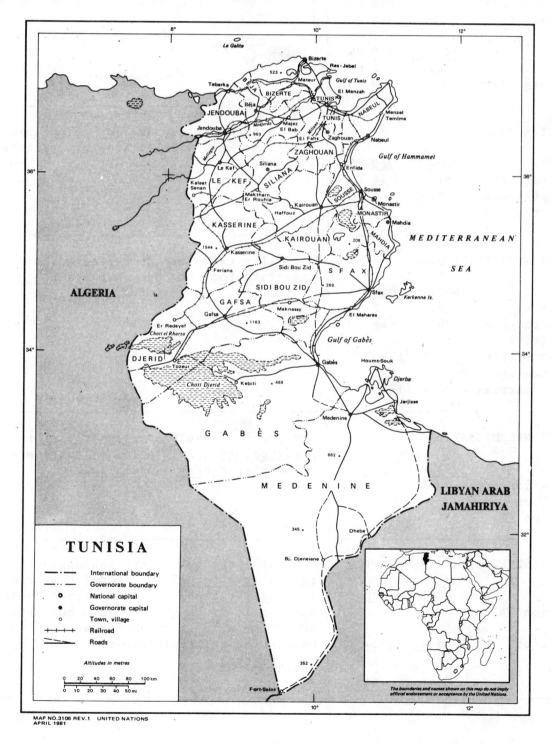

TURKEY

DEMOGRAPHIC INDICATORS	CURRENT PERCEPTION

SIZE/AGE STRUCTURE/GROWTH
 	
Population: 1985   2025
 (thousands) 50 345 89 646
  0-14 years (%) 36.4 22.9
  60+ years (%)   6.4 13.6
 	
Rate of: 1980-85 2020-25
 growth   2.5   1.0
 natural increase 20.8   9.0
	The Government considers the present rate of population growth to be <u>unsatisfactory</u> and <u>too high</u>.

MORTALITY/MORBIDITY 1980-85 2020-25 Life expectancy 61.6 74.6 Crude death rate 9.4 6.7 Infant mortality 92.0 19.0	Levels of mortality are <u>not acceptable</u>. Infant mortality is an area of specific concern.
FERTILITY/NUPTIALITY/FAMILY 1980-85 2020-25 Fertility rate 3.9 2.1 Crude birth rate 30.2 16.3 Contraceptive prevalence rate 51.0 (1983) Female mean age at first marriage 20.7 (1980)	Fertility rates are perceived to be <u>unsatisfactory</u> because they are <u>too high</u>.
INTERNATIONAL MIGRATION 1980-85 2020-25 Net migration rate 0.0 0.0 Foreign-born population (%) 1.9 (1980)	Immigration levels are <u>significant</u> and <u>satisfactory</u>. Emigration is considered to be <u>significant</u> and <u>too low</u>.
SPATIAL DISTRIBUTION/URBANIZATION Urban 1985 2025 population (%) 45.9 69.8 Growth rate: 1980-85 2020-25 urban 3.4 1.8 rural 1.7 -0.8	Spatial distribution is considered to be <u>partially appropriate</u>. Population growth is <u>unsatisfactory</u> in metropolitan areas because it is <u>too high</u>. In other urban areas and also in rural areas, the population growth is viewed as <u>satisfactory</u>.

GENERAL POLICY FRAMEWORK

Overall approach to population problems: The Government considers the rates of population growth and fertility to be unsatisfactory and has adopted a policy of decreasing the growth rate by family planning measures and a range of family welfare provisions. To reduce mortality, Government public health services have been expanded throughout the country with emphasis on the provincial and village levels. Other policies are to reduce migration to large urban areas and to increase emigration.

Importance of population policy in achieving development objectives: The Government views rapid population growth as an obstacle to achieving its development objectives. Population policies are an integral part of Turkey's development objectives, the aim being to ensure that population change is compatible with social and economic development. Government pronouncements and documents have indicated the objectives, targets and measures designed to influence fertility, mortality and migration.

INSTITUTIONAL FRAMEWORK

Population data systems and development planning: Turkey has a tradition of census-taking. The first of its quinquennial censuses was taken in 1927 and the most recent in 1985. The next was scheduled for 1990. Several socio-economic and demographic surveys have been conducted in the past two decades, notably the 1983 fertility survey. The vital registration system is considered to be incomplete and efforts are under way to improve the population register. The last published development plan is the Fifth Five-Year Plan for the period 1985-1989 prepared by the State Planning Organization.

Integration of population within development planning: The Social Planning Department of the State Planning Organization (SPO) is the key unit for formulating population policy and for integrating population into development planning. The essentials of population policy are elaborated by the Population Section of the Department, in consultation with various ministries and non-governmental organizations. Integration of population variables into sectoral planning is accomplished through the collaborative effort of various sections in the Department. Population variables are integrated into comprehensive planning by the Economic Planning Division of SPO. The Fifth Five-Year Development Plan (1985-1989) incorporated population projections into both the national and sectoral plans.

POLICIES AND MEASURES

Changes in population size and age structure: The Government's basic objective in lowering population growth is to facilitate the development process. Measures enacted include national family planning campaigns, liberalizing the availability of contraception, upgrading and extending

TURKEY

maternal and child health services to remote areas and reducing migration to urban areas. Specified targets include a total population of 66 million by the year 2000 and a population growth rate of 1.76 by the period 1995-2000. In 1984 social security was extended to agricultural workers and farmers, thus covering most types of workers.

<u>Mortality and morbidity</u>: The Five-Year Development Plan for 1985-1989 calls for extending health services throughout the country, emphasizing preventive services, reducing infant mortality, improving health management, preventing public bodies and insurance institutions from creating their own health services and strengthening the health insurance scheme. In 1986 the health system was modified to make it less socialized and centralized, by establishing two types of health centres, one to serve populations over 10,000 and one for populations under 10,000, thus minimizing problems created by specialization that concentrated physicians at larger hospitals. In 1985 a major immunization campaign was launched, with the goal of maintaining an immunization coverage of 90 per cent of all infants by 1992. In 1986 the country's President initiated the accelerated national oral rehydration therapy programme. Programmes of child growth monitoring, child nutrition, breast-feeding motivation and water and sanitation were also undertaken. The two-year compulsory service for medical and paramedical personnel has helped to eliminate a shortage of staff. Targets include a mortality rate of 6.4 per thousand and an infant mortality rate of 34 per thousand by the period 1995-2000.

<u>Fertility and the family</u>: Perceiving that high fertility poses both economic and health problems, the Government vigorously pursues a policy of lowering fertility through programmes of family planning combined with maternal and child health, information, education and communication, and extending social welfare and social security. In 1984 a project was begun to widen the scope of family planning and maternal and child health in regions of high fertility in the eastern and south-eastern provinces. One objective of the project was the training of midwives and nurses to insert intrauterine devices. In 1986 the President of Turkey announced a national family planning campaign, the largest in the country's history, in order to increase the number of couples using modern methods of contraception from 18 per cent to 25 per cent. The campaign included plans to establish a family planning clinic in each of the 200 Government-run general hospitals and 25 maternity hospitals and to institutionalize 25 maternal and child health and family planning training centres. A 1983 law liberalized abortion, permitting it on request up to the tenth week of pregnancy and beyond the tenth week on medical grounds. The Government's target is a total fertility rate of 2.9 by the period 1995-2000.

<u>International migration</u>: The sudden influx of Bulgarians that began in May 1989 has placed enormous strains on Turkey's infrastructure. With the unemployed rate hovering at 15 per cent, the Government has found it extremely difficult to find employment for the estimated 300,000 people that entered from Bulgaria as of September 1989. In August 1989 Turkey reversed its policy and said that it could no longer absorb additional people in such a short time. In addition, the country wants to confront problems posed by large numbers of undocumented Iranian refugees, who have been permitted to enter Turkey until asylum in third countries could be found. Emigration policy seeks to increase the level of emigration, while protecting Turkish workers abroad through multilateral and bilateral agreements with host Governments.

These agreements cover social security benefits, educational and cultural services to second generation migrants, and provision of just compensation and assistance to those migrants who decide to return to Turkey.

Spatial distribution/urbanization: A number of programmes have been undertaken to reduce rural-to-urban migration. A major effort has been the Priority Development Areas Programme, focusing on the southern and south-eastern regions. Its goal is to initiate self-sustained development in these regions and thus reduce interregional differentials in development by integrated rural development, supported by developing an agro-industrial sector and by the promotion of labour-intensive industries utilizing locally available materials and skills. To make villages and small towns more attractive, 4,319 villages were designated as central villages in 1983 and were slated to receive additional social services. The Cukurova Metropolitan Region Urban Development Project seeks to develop five major urban centres, with an integrated approach to improving the provision of infrastructure, urban services and housing.

Status of women and population: The Government reported in 1990 that women's status in Turkey was not satisfactory. Although the role of women in development is recognized, it has not been given full attention in development plans. Attention to women in national development plans has been in the form of measures related to maternal and child health and family planning.

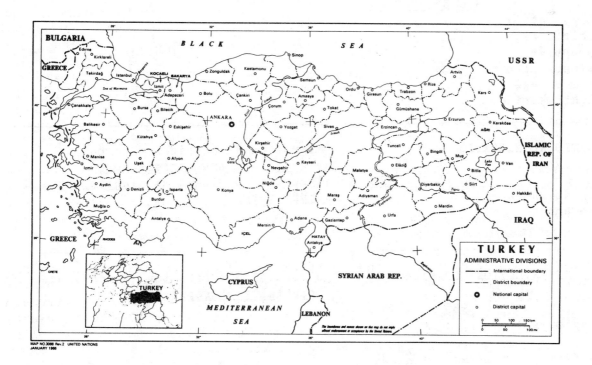

TUVALU

DEMOGRAPHIC INDICATORS	CURRENT PERCEPTION
SIZE/AGE STRUCTURE/GROWTH Population: 1985 2025 (thousands) 8 11 0-14 years (%) ... ... 60+ years (%) ... ... Rate of: 1980-85 2020-25 growth 1.6 0.3 natural increase	The Government perceives current growth rates as <u>unsatisfactory</u> and <u>too high</u>.
MORTALITY/MORBIDITY 1980-85 2020-25 Life expectancy ... ... Crude death rate ... ... Infant mortality	The levels of mortality are considered to be <u>unacceptable</u>.
FERTILITY/NUPTIALITY/FAMILY 1980-85 2020-25 Fertility rate ... ... Crude birth rate ... ... Contraceptive prevalence rate ... ... Female mean age at first marriage	Current fertility rates are <u>unsatisfactory</u> and <u>too high</u>.
INTERNATIONAL MIGRATION 1980-85 2020-25 Net migration rate ... ... Foreign-born population (%) ...	Immigration is considered to be <u>insignificant</u> and <u>satisfactory</u>. Emigration is viewed as <u>significant</u> and <u>satisfactory</u>.
SPATIAL DISTRIBUTION/URBANIZATION Urban 1985 2025 population (%) ... ... Growth rate: 1980-85 2020-25 urban ... ... rural	The spatial distribution is considered to be <u>partially appropriate</u>.

GENERAL POLICY FRAMEWORK

<u>Overall approach to population problems</u>: The Government has undertaken policies to reduce population growth, lower fertility, improve the provision of medical services and reduce migration to urban areas through development of the outer islands.

<u>Importance of population policy in achieving development objectives</u>: An effective policy to control population growth is considered essential for achieving the primary national objectives. The objectives consist of strengthening and diversifying the economy as a means of obtaining national self-reliance and raising standards of living to levels that will ensure a secure, healthy and productive family life within the traditional social system and customs.

INSTITUTIONAL FRAMEWORK

<u>Population data systems and development planning</u>: The first census was conducted in 1973 when Tuvalu was still part of the Gilbert and Ellice Islands. A subsequent census was held in 1979 following independence in 1978. A census had been scheduled for 1989. Vital registration is the responsibility of the Statistics Division of the Ministry of Finance. The latest available development plan is the Third Development Plan for the period 1984-1987.

<u>Integration of population within development planning</u>: Population variables have been integrated in national development plans by the Ministry of Finance.

POLICIES AND MEASURES

<u>Changes in population size and age structure</u>: Concerned by the fact that the demand for resources is outstripping the supply, the Government intervenes to lower growth. Policies are in place to provide health services consistent with resource availability and the needs of the population, in addition to family planning services. Information on the status of pension schemes is not readily available.

<u>Mortality and morbidity</u>: Government objectives as stated in the Third Development Plan are to develop and maintain preventive health services for all islands; to improve the quality of basic health services; to promote and strengthen activities relating to family planning and maternal and child health; and to develop and maintain dental health services. Specific programmes are the improvement of water and sanitation facilities, disease prevention and control, immunization schedules, prevention of dental cavities, health manpower development and nutrition. Health education programmes are broadcast three times a week over the radio. Health committees were established on each island and were given responsibility for village

TUVALU

environmental health. The Division of Health carries out health surveys whenever sufficient funds are available. Traditional health skills have been introduced into general health services.

Fertility and the family: The Government intervenes to lower fertility. The Third Development Plan aimed for the improvement of family health services by continuing personnel training in midwifery and family health technology. Emphasis was placed on motivating the target population. The programme's target was to have 40 per cent of women in the child-bearing ages practising family planning. To improve the family planning programme, health education programmes were intensified in order to motivate the population, the target population was broadened to include unmarried women, staff were encouraged to have more frequent contacts with family planning acceptors and specific problem areas were identified. Maternal and child health services have also been upgraded.

International migration: There are no reported policies to deal with the insignificant level of immigration. Concerning emigration, remittances from Tuvaluans working abroad represent an important source of foreign exchange. At the time of the 1979 census, about 1,500 Tuvaluans, or approximately 20 per cent of the population, were living in Kiribati and Nauru. The country has been subject to waves of emigration and return migration, which are a consequence of overseas employment opportunities. Return migration has contributed to increased population pressures and higher unemployment. The Tuvalu Maritime School is expected to provide additional opportunities for young men to obtain overseas employment.

Spatial distribution/urbanization: To redress urban-rural imbalances in per capita income and to stem the drift of young people from the outer islands to the urban centre of Funafuti, a programme of rural development and rural employment creation has been undertaken. Each island has its own Island Council, which identifies development priorities and projects. Projects include those to construct new health, education and welfare facilities as well as housing and transport facilities, and to improve sanitation. As enunciated in the Third Development Plan, a programme of urban development is under way to ensure the continued orderly and planned development of Funafuti and to provide those basic amenities and services which are essential for urban settlements. The Government proposes to resolve problems associated with rents in Funafuti, to reclaim unproductive land, to relieve the land shortage and to assist residents of Funafuti to establish settlements on the other islets of Funafuti atoll, thereby relieving pressure on the main islet of Fongafale.

Status of women and population: The Women's Council plays an active role with regard to family welfare and women's issues. It has organized seminars and workshops to provide education and training to Council members who then disseminate information to local communities. Information on the minimum legal age at marriage for women is not readily available.

Other issues: Tuvalu is the smallest least developed country in terms of area and population. Given its poor endowment of natural resources, small population size and the almost total lack of domestic sources of savings and investment, the country depends on foreign assistance for financing both its

recurrent budget and its development budget. In order to diminish the
uncertainty related to its extremely high external dependence and to free
other funds for development projects, the Government invited donors to
contribute to a trust fund, the interest of which would then be used for
covering Government recurrent expenditures. The Tuvalu Trust Fund was set up
with $19 million in 1987. It is expected to yield up to $1.5 million
annually, which would finance about 45 per cent of the country's recurrent
budget.

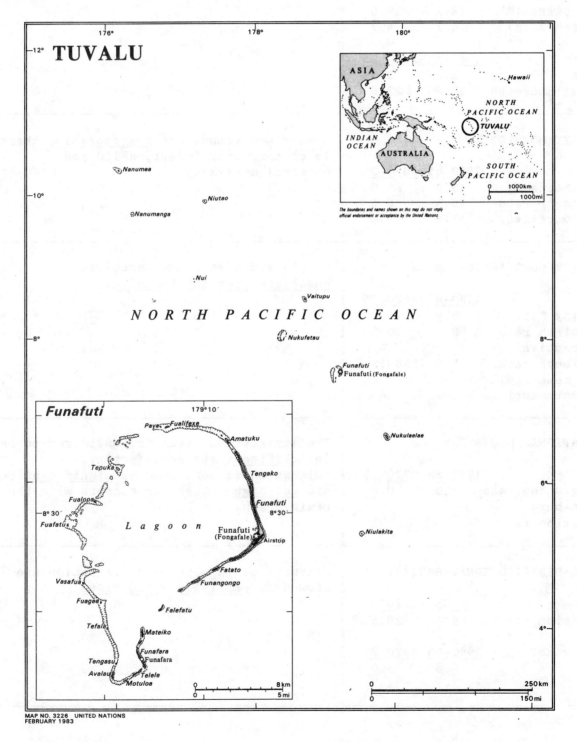

MAP NO. 3226   UNITED NATIONS
FEBRUARY 1983

UGANDA

DEMOGRAPHIC INDICATORS	CURRENT PERCEPTION
SIZE/AGE STRUCTURE/GROWTH	The rate of growth is considered to be <u>unsatisfactory</u> because it is <u>too high</u>.

Population: 1985   2025
 (thousands)   15 491   55 198
   0–14 years (%)   48.1   39.0
   60+ years (%)   4.1   4.7
 	
Rate of: 1980–85   2020–25
   growth   3.3   2.3
   natural increase 33.4 23.0	

MORTALITY/MORBIDITY	Levels and trends are <u>unacceptable</u>; there is concern over infant, child and maternal mortality.
1980–85 2020–25 Life expectancy 49.0 65.0 Crude death rate 16.8 6.6 Infant mortality 112.0 47.0	
FERTILITY/NUPTIALITY/FAMILY	Levels and trends are perceived as <u>unsatisfactory</u> and <u>too high</u>.

1980–85   2020–25
Fertility rate   6.9   3.6
Crude birth rate   50.3   29.5
Contraceptive
   prevalence rate   5.5 (1989)
Female mean age
   at first marriage	

INTERNATIONAL MIGRATION	The immigration level is considered to be <u>insignificant</u> and <u>satisfactory</u>. Emigration is perceived as <u>significant</u> and <u>too high</u>. There is concern with the brain drain.
1980–85 2020–25 Net migration rate 0.0 0.0 Foreign–born population (%)	
SPATIAL DISTRIBUTION/URBANIZATION	Patterns of population distribution are viewed as <u>partially appropriate</u>.

Urban   1985   2025
   population (%)   9.4   29.6
 	
Growth rate: 1980–85   2020–25
   urban   4.8   5.0
   rural 3.2 1.3	

GENERAL POLICY FRAMEWORK

<u>Overall approach to population problems</u>: The Government gives priority to a multi-sectoral approach to population problems through integrated socio-economic development. Emphasis is placed on lowering mortality and morbidity by focusing on maternal and child health through primary health care and health education. The official view is that lowering infant mortality, combined with a long-term modification of reproductive behaviour, will reduce fertility levels. The Government also believes that maintaining peace is a vital pre-condition for the formulation and implementation of a population policy.

<u>Importance of population policy in achieving development objectives</u>: There is no explicit national population policy. However, the Government considers that rapid population growth increases the dependency ratio to such an extent that it can become a constraint to development by directing investment resources away from productive activities and towards the provision of social infrastructure to meet the needs of a rapidly growing population. In September 1989 a new national Technical Committee on Population and Development was launched with the responsibility of formulating a national population policy.

INSTITUTIONAL FRAMEWORK

<u>Population data systems and development planning</u>: The last reliable population census was conducted in 1969. A census was held in 1980, but most of the collected data were lost. In order to remedy the lack of up-to-date demographic data, the Government has prepared a comprehensive four-year census operation plan (1988-1992), with a census tentatively scheduled for 1990. Vital registration is still incomplete. The Institute of Statistics and Applied Economics (ISAE), Makerere University, is responsible for analysing population data. A Population Unit has recently been created within ISAE, which is responsible for training in population education. The National Rehabilitation Development Plan for 1987/88-1990/91 is currently in effect.

<u>Integration of population within development planning</u>: The Social Services Section in the Ministry of Planning and Economic Development is charged with taking into account population variables in planning. Major obstacles remain to the formulation of a population policy integrated into planning: the lack of adequate data and an institutional framework and the shortage of trained personnel. The Government is receiving international assistance for the creation of a population secretariat and a national population committee to serve as the national machinery for integrating population into development planning and for co-ordinating national population programmes. In September 1989 the National Technical Committee on Population and Development was established.

UGANDA

POLICIES AND MEASURES

<u>Changes in population size and age structure</u>: There is a policy aimed at lowering the growth of the population. Although the Government does not view the size of the population as too large in relation to natural resources, it is fully aware of the long-term serious consequences of a high rate of population growth on per capita income and the provision of social services. Since the major changes in population size have resulted from civil disturbances and their consequences, the Government believes that the maintainance of peace is a priority for controlling population growth. In addition, maternal and child health is viewed as an important means of reducing growth. Under the social security scheme, employees of firms with at least five workers and public employees are covered, while voluntary affiliation is available for those not compulsorily covered.

<u>Mortality and morbidity</u>: The Government's health policy emphasizes the primary health-care approach as a strategy to improve the health status of the population by the year 2000. As a result of the civil war, most health facilities are not functional or lack basic equipment, handicapping the Government in its attempt to undertake health programmes. Malaria, measles, complications of child-bearing, respiratory and diarrhoeal diseases, and AIDS are considered to be the major concerns from the viewpoint of mortality policy. A five-year vaccination programme was set up in 1987. A national campaign against AIDS was begun in 1988 and is conducted by the Ministry of Health. The programme, established by the AIDS Control Committee, concentrates on health education, the creation of uncontaminated blood banks and support for research. A national health policy was under consideration in 1988. The target is to lower infant mortality to 50 per thousand and raise life expectancy to at least 60 years by the year 2000.

<u>Fertility and the family</u>: The Government considers that fertility and mortality policies cannot be separated, since the improvement of family well-being and maternal and child health, as well as the voluntary choice of family size, are dependent upon reducing mortality, particularly infant mortality. Consequently, the policy calls for the strengthening of maternal and child health and family planning services and the expansion of population and family life education campaigns in order to reduce fertility. Family life educational programmes have been established in primary and high schools to lower the incidence of induced abortions and high levels of maternal and infant mortality. Contraceptives are directly provided by governmental services. Female sterilization is permitted only for women who are at least 30 years of age and have a certain number of children. Abortion is illegal, except to protect the life or physical or mental health of the mother.

<u>International migration</u>: Although immigration is not a major concern of the Government, the latter views the repatriation of refugees in Uganda as the most desirable solution to the refugee problem. There were estimated to be about 120,000 refugees in Uganda as of March 1989. Concerning the substantial number of Ugandans who have emigrated as a consequence of the country's political, economic and social disruptions, presidential appeals have been made to encourage their return. Employment and improved conditions of service

have been promised to the returnees. It is estimated that from 1986 to the end of 1988, approximately 320,000 Ugandans were repatriated from the Sudan and Zaire. In addition, the Government constantly seeks to review civil service salaries and conditions of service in order to retain potential emigrants.

Spatial distribution/urbanization: The Government reported in 1988 that it has no comprehensive policy on population distribution, mainly owing to the fact that the total population size is still small and the available land is capable of supporting increased population. Land pressure is acute in a few selected districts only. Support is given by the Government to settlers in new regions. Civil disturbances in the recent past have led to displacement of Uganda's populations in parts of the country. The Government's task has been to resettle these populations to their district of origin, to halt internal migration by creating employment opportunities in districts of out-migration and to give support to those settling in new regions.

Status of women and population: The Government attaches importance to the promotion of functional literacy and the education of women. Income-generating activities for women are envisaged through credit and agricultural extension services directed to rural women. The Government is striving to remove traditional and cultural practices and attitudes which impede the improvement of women's status. The minimum legal age at marriage for women is 18 years.

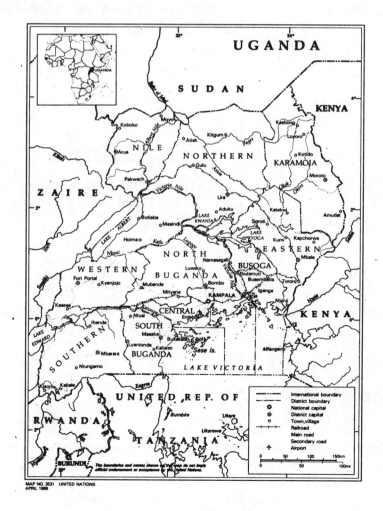

MAP NO. 3531   UNITED NATIONS
APRIL 1989

UKRAINIAN SOVIET SOCIALIST REPUBLIC

DEMOGRAPHIC INDICATORS	CURRENT PERCEPTION
SIZE/AGE STRUCTURE/GROWTH	The Government considers the rate of growth of the population to be <u>satisfactory</u>, although there is concern over the large proportion of aged persons.

Population:	1985	2025
(thousands)	51 300	...
0–14 years (%)	...	...
60+ years (%)	...	...

Rate of:	1980–85	2020–25
growth	0.4	...
natural increase	4.5	...

DEMOGRAPHIC INDICATORS	CURRENT PERCEPTION
MORTALITY/MORBIDITY	The current level of mortality is viewed as <u>unacceptable</u>. Concerns are infant mortality and men in the working-age population.

	1980–85	2020–25
Life expectancy	...	...
Crude death rate	11.1	...
Infant mortality	...	...

DEMOGRAPHIC INDICATORS	CURRENT PERCEPTION
FERTILITY/NUPTIALITY/FAMILY	Fertility levels are perceived as <u>satisfactory</u>.

	1980–85	2020–25
Fertility rate	...	...
Crude birth rate	15.5	...
Contraceptive prevalence rate	...	...
Female mean age at first marriage	...	...

DEMOGRAPHIC INDICATORS	CURRENT PERCEPTION
INTERNATIONAL MIGRATION	Levels of both immigration and emigration are considered to be <u>insignificant</u> and <u>satisfactory</u>.

	1980–85	2020–25
Net migration rate	...	...
Foreign-born population (%)	...	...

DEMOGRAPHIC INDICATORS	CURRENT PERCEPTION
SPATIAL DISTRIBUTION/URBANIZATION	Spatial distribution is viewed as <u>partially appropriate</u>.

Urban	1985	2025
population (%)	66.4	...

Growth rate:	1980–85	2020–25
urban	...	...
rural	...	...

GENERAL POLICY FRAMEWORK

Overall approach to population problems: In order to improve the
demographic situation, the Government feels that it is necessary to pursue
a demographic policy aimed at increasing life expectancy and labour force
activity, strengthening the family and creating more favourable conditions
for educating the young population and for combining motherhood with the
active participation of women in the labour market and public life.

Importance of population policy in achieving development objectives:
Given that demographic processes are felt to be closely linked to
socio-economic development, population policy has been incorporated into
socio-economic development plans.

INSTITUTIONAL FRAMEWORK

Population data systems and development planning: Censuses were carried
out in 1979 and 1989. Vital registration is considered to be complete.
Demographic policies are included in the formulation of the economic and
social development plan. The latest plan is the State Plan for the
Economic and Social Development of the Ukrainian SSR for the period
1986-1990, prepared by the State Planning Committee of the Ukrainian SSR.

Integration of population within development planning: Formulation and
co-ordination of population policies and their integration within
development planning are the responsibility of the State Planning
Committee (Gosplan), established in 1921, and the State Committee on
Labour (Goskontrud) established in 1987. Demographic variables are
analysed and taken into account by the Labour Department and Gosplan.
Research on the relationship between population and development is carried
out by many scientific organizations such as the Economic Research
Institute of Gosplan, the Ukrainian branch of the Statistical Institute of
Goskontrud of the USSR, the Economic Institute of the Academy of Sciences,
the Council for the Study of Production Forces, the Academy of Sciences
and the Institute of Gerontology of the Academy of Medical Sciences of the
USSR. Demographic indicators are incorporated as an essential part of
social and economic development plans, which are drawn up for modifying
the structure of the population, increasing the effectiveness of labour
resources and expanding the participation of citizens in social and labour
activities.

POLICIES AND MEASURES

Changes in population size and age structure: The Government attaches great
importance to population size, structure and growth. It aims to maintain the
existing rate of population growth and possibly to increase it, but no
quantitative targets have been specified. Modifications are desired in the
age structure, especially concerning the large proportion of the population

UKRAINIAN SOVIET SOCIALIST REPUBLIC

aged 60 years and above. Measures for the protection of the elderly are constantly being improved. In 1985 pension entitlements were increased, the system of social services for the elderly was extended, funding for the construction of additional housing for the elderly was approved, and medical, social and cultural activities were upgraded.

Mortality and morbidity: The State Plan of the Ukrainian SSR for 1986-1990 describes the further development of the health-care system, which is an integral part of socio-economic development. The right of citizens to health care is laid down in the Constitution of the Ukrainian SSR. All basic types of medical services, including hospital treatment, are provided free of charge. The Republic has created and operates an extensive system of health care. It includes institutions providing treatment and preventive care (polyclinics, hospitals, dispensaries, ambulance service, blood transfusion stations, etc.), institutions providing sanitary preventive care (sanitary-epidemiological stations, disinfecting stations, etc.), and institutions providing sanitarium and health spa facilities. Measures have been taken to improve industrial hygiene and industrial safety procedures. The State system of public health care interacts with the continually developing and expanding physical culture and sports system, which forms one of the principal means of improving the health of citizens. To protect the health of mother and child, the system provides a wide network of antenatal clinics, children's clinics and hospitals, day nurseries, kindergartens and other facilities. To render qualified medical assistance more accessible to the rural population, further efforts are being made to improve travelling paediatric and antenatal clinics.

Fertility and the family: The Government's policy is to maintain the level of fertility by encouraging child-bearing through a host of moral and material incentives. Working mothers are entitled to a partially paid maternity leave of 18 months and an additional unpaid leave of six months. Women are also granted paid leave of up to 14 days a year to care for a sick child. Large families are granted allowances and benefits and priority in housing. Families with at least four children pay reduced fees for crèches. Low-income families receive additional allowances and are exempt from certain school fees. Opportunities for part-time work, flexible work schedules and employment at home are being expanded. To improve family well-being, there are family and marriage clinics, maternity and young fathers' schools and family and marriage advisory services attached to registry offices. Abortion is permitted up to the twelfth week of pregnancy, with medical authorization required beyond that period. Concerned by the adverse consequences of abortion on women's health, the Government is attempting to reduce the incidence of abortion by making available modern methods of contraception. Sterilization is not considered to be a contraceptive method and is performed only on medical grounds.

International migration: The insignificant levels of immigration and emigration are not active policy concerns of the Government.

Spatial distribution/urbanization: The policy for development of urban areas is to restructure the agro-industrial development of the regions, based on the mobility of the population and the distribution of labour resources. Internal migration is linked to career transfers and the desire to change the place of residence.   The Government influences migration by encouraging the movement of the population to areas necessary for the development of the national economy.   Government bodies recruit workers and specialists on a contractual and voluntary basis.   Graduates of higher educational establishments, technical colleges and vocational and technical establishments are given employment on a planned basis.   Migrants are settled in new locations and provided with work in their area of specialization by government agencies.   In rural areas migrants receive preferential credit and other financial assistance for settling in.

<u>Status of women and population</u>:   In accordance with article 33 of the Constitution of the Ukrainian SSR, women and men have equal rights.   Those rights are ensured by granting women the same opportunities as men in respect of education and vocational training, employment remuneration and socio-political activities.   Measures have been taken to create conditions enabling women to combine labour force participation with motherhood.   There is legal protection, as well as material and moral support, for working mothers.   The legal minimum age at marriage is 17 years for females.   In accordance with the marriage and family code, the minimum age for marriage may be reduced by one year in exceptional cases.

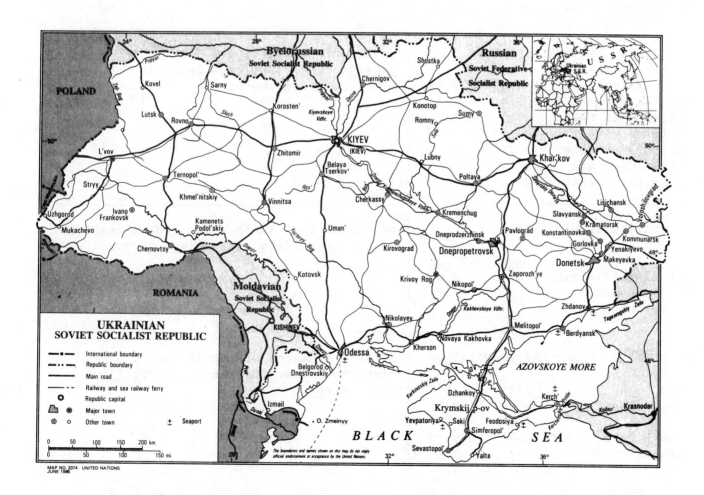

UNION OF SOVIET SOCIALIST REPUBLICS

DEMOGRAPHIC INDICATORS	CURRENT PERCEPTION
SIZE/AGE STRUCTURE/GROWTH	The rate of population growth is considered to be <u>satisfactory</u>.

Population:	1985	2025
(thousands)	276 946	351 450
0–14 years (%)	25.2	20.8
60+ years (%)	13.5	20.6

Rate of:	1980–85	2020–25
growth	0.8	0.5
natural increase	8.4	4.7

DEMOGRAPHIC INDICATORS	CURRENT PERCEPTION
MORTALITY/MORBIDITY	Levels and trends are viewed as <u>unacceptable</u>. Special concerns are infant mortality and mortality of working age males.

	1980–85	2020–25
Life expectancy	67.9	76.7
Crude death rate	10.7	9.4
Infant mortality	26.0	8.0

DEMOGRAPHIC INDICATORS	CURRENT PERCEPTION
FERTILITY/NUPTIALITY/FAMILY	Levels of fertility are felt to be <u>satisfactory</u>. The high level of induced abortions is a concern.

	1980–85	2020–25
Fertility rate	2.4	2.1
Crude birth rate	19.1	14.1
Contraceptive prevalence rate	...	...
Female mean age at first marriage	21.9 (1985)	

DEMOGRAPHIC INDICATORS	CURRENT PERCEPTION
INTERNATIONAL MIGRATION	Levels of both immigration and emigration are <u>insignificant</u> and <u>satisfactory</u>.

	1980–85	2020–25
Net migration rate	0.0	0.0
Foreign-born population (%)	...	...

DEMOGRAPHIC INDICATORS	CURRENT PERCEPTION
SPATIAL DISTRIBUTION/URBANIZATION	Current patterns of population distribution are felt to be <u>partially appropriate</u>.

Urban	1985	2025
population (%)	65.6	74.1

Growth rate:	1980–85	2020–25
urban	1.6	0.6
rural	–0.6	0.2

GENERAL POLICY FRAMEWORK

Overall approach to population problems: The Government wants to maintain the rate of population growth and possibly to increase it in some regions. The policy aims to maintain population growth and fertility, to reduce infant mortality and the level of morbidity, to adjust the pattern of spatial distribution, to improve the status of women, to ensure a further increase in the well-being of all strata and social groups of the population, and to curb the growth of large cities.

Importance of population policy in achieving development objectives: Population policy is felt to be an integral part of the State's social policy aimed at further improving the well-being of the population, protecting health and strengthening maternity and child care. In the course of implementing those objectives, the basic aim is to secure the steady reproduction of the population. Population policies are incorporated in development planning and all development plans include demographic indicators.

INSTITUTIONAL FRAMEWORK

Population data systems and development planning: Censuses were conducted in 1959, 1970 and 1989 by the Central Statistical Board of the USSR. The 1989 census, which obtained data not previously collected, will be used in drafting the development plan for 1990-1994. The State Plan for the Economic and Social Development of the USSR for the period 1986-1990, prepared by the State Planning Committee of the USSR (Gosplan, USSR), is currently in effect.

Integration of population within development planning: Gosplan, USSR, which is charged with development planning, together with the State Committee of the USSR on Labour and Social Questions (Goskontrud, USSR), is responsible for the formulation and co-ordination of population policies. The Division for the Comprehensive Planning of Social Development of Gosplan takes population variables into account in planning. The Central Statistical Board prepares population projections used for development planning, as well as demographic surveys. Three institutions produce information on population-development interrelationships: the Economic Research Institute of Gosplan, the Scientific Research Institute of the Central Statistical Board and the Institute of Sociological Research of the Academy of Sciences.

POLICIES AND MEASURES

Changes in population size and age structure: Great importance is attached to questions of the size, distribution and structure of the population. The policy is to maintain the rate of growth and possibly increase it in some regions. A series of measures has been put into effect that takes into

UNION OF SOVIET SOCIALIST REPUBLICS

consideration the characteristics of the different regions and aims to reduce infant mortality and increase life expectancy, to improve the working conditions and well-being of the population, to strengthen the family and to facilitate motherhood. Concern for the living conditions of the elderly has led to pension increases, further discounts on the cost of medicines, improved services to the elderly living alone and the construction of homes for the elderly.

Mortality and morbidity: The Government's primary objective of reducing mortality and morbidity is to be achieved by improving the public health-care system, strengthening disease prevention activities, and also improving the environment and working conditions. All basic types of medical care, including hospital treatment, are provided free of charge. Hospitals have established special departments for pre-natal care and children under one year of age are subject to monthly observations by local medical staff. An extensive public education campaign, bolstered by tough new legislation, was launched to improve nutrition and reduce alcohol consumption. The objective was to improve health conditions and raise labour productivity. In 1987 Soviet officials indicated that as a result of increased Government efforts, alcohol consumption dropped significantly, contributing to a sharp decline in job-related injuries and in deaths due to cardio-vascular diseases. Concerning AIDS, a series of stringent measures was adopted, which includes mandatory testing of anyone suspected of having AIDS, and prison sentences for carriers of the AIDS virus who knowingly infect others. Also, all foreigners residing in the country for at least three months are required to undergo testing.

Fertility and the family: The policy to maintain the level of fertility is supported by a series of measures facilitating motherhood. Working mothers are entitled to a maternity leave of 112 days with full pay, a partially paid maternity leave of 18 months and an additional six months of unpaid leave, and up to 14 days of annual paid leave to care for a sick child. Families with children receive birth grants, family allowances beginning with the fourth child and priority in housing, while the children may attend pioneer camps at State expense. Low-income families receive additional benefits and subsidies. To allow women to combine motherhood with labour market activities, part-time, flexible time and work-at-home opportunities are available. Families with children under three years of age can choose between either municipal day-care centres or home-care allowances. To lower the significant incidence of induced abortion, which is permitted up to the twelfth week of pregnancy and afterwards for medical reasons, the use of modern methods of contraception is being promoted by the Government. Sterilization, which is not viewed as a contraceptive method, is performed only on medical grounds.

International migration: Immigration is composed of relatively small numbers of workers from other Council for Mutual Economic Assistance (CMEA) countries who have come to the USSR to work on specific co-operative projects. Recent political changes in the USSR have led to a modification of policies regulating emigration, and as a result a large increase in those travelling abroad occurred in 1988 and 1989. There are indications that the requirement that those seeking to emigrate must receive invitations from close family members living abroad may eventually be repealed.

<u>Spatial distribution/urbanization</u>: The Government reports that it has a policy to modify the pattern of spatial distribution. Policies aim to limit rural-to-urban migration, curb the growth of large cities and favour the development of small and medium-sized towns. The tempo of internal migration is expected to increase as the country moves to a more intensive course of development and accelerated rates of economic growth. Internal migration is mainly linked to career transfers and the desire to change the place of residence. The Government influences migration by encouraging the movement of population to areas that are necessary for achieving national objectives. Organized relocations are on a contractual basis and the expenditures involved are assumed by the State. The State assists migrants to settle in new locations and provides them with employment according to their skills and qualifications. Workers in remote or newly developed areas receive incentives, including higher pay, extended vacations and early retirement. Migrants to agricultural areas receive preferential credit terms.

<u>Status of women and population</u>: The country's President indicated in 1987 that women's progress in society was still an acute socio-political problem and that further progress was linked to the pace of socio-economic reforms under the economic programme of <u>perestroika</u>. Equality between men and women is anchored in the Constitution and a system of legal measures guarantees observance. Attention has focused on raising the status of women, particularly in regard to combining motherhood with active participation in public life and labour market activities. It is illegal to refuse to hire or to dismiss a woman, or to lower her wages, because of pregnancy. The minimum legal age at marriage is 18 years, although it is one or two years lower in some Republics.

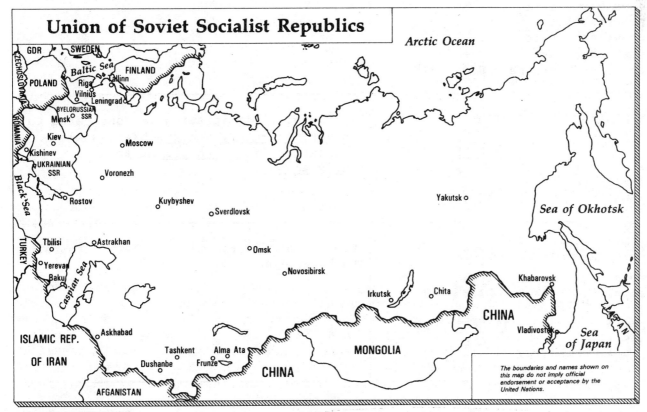

MAP NO. 3581.1   UNITED NATIONS
SEPTEMBER 1990

UNITED ARAB EMIRATES

DEMOGRAPHIC INDICATORS	CURRENT PERCEPTION

SIZE/AGE STRUCTURE/GROWTH
 	
Population: 1985   2025
 (thousands)   1 350   2 692
  0-14 years (%)   31.0   24.8
  60+ years (%)   2.4   18.6
 	
Rate of: 1980-85   2020-25
 growth   5.7   0.9
 natural increase   23.0   8.6
	The Government considers the growth rate to be <u>unsatisfactory</u> and <u>too high</u>.

MORTALITY/MORBIDITY 1980-85 2020-25 Life expectancy 69.2 77.6 Crude death rate 3.6 8.1 Infant mortality 32.0 7.0	The levels of mortality and morbidity are viewed as <u>acceptable</u>.
FERTILITY/NUPTIALITY/FAMILY 1980-85 2020-25 Fertility rate 7.2 3.6 Crude birth rate 26.6 16.8 Contraceptive prevalence rate ... ... Female mean age at first marriage 18.0 (1975)	The Government regards the levels of fertility as <u>satisfactory</u>.
INTERNATIONAL MIGRATION 1980-85 2020-25 Net migration rate ... ... Foreign-born population (%) 63.9 (1975)	The level of immigration is considered to be <u>unsatisfactory</u> and <u>too high</u>, while emigration is <u>insignificant</u> and <u>satisfactory</u>.
SPATIAL DISTRIBUTION/URBANIZATION Urban 1985 2025 population (%) 77.8 84.9 Growth rate: 1980-85 2020-25 urban 4.8 1.2 rural 9.0 -0.9	Population distribution patterns are felt to be <u>appropriate</u>.

GENERAL POLICY FRAMEWORK

Overall approach to population problems: No formal population policy has as yet been formulated. However, the Government places special emphasis on raising the standard of living through economic development and social changes. Special attention is focused on statistics, maintaining a high fertility rate among the native-born population, lessening the country's dependence on immigrants by progressively decreasing the size of the foreign population and reducing migration to urban areas.

Importance of population policy in achieving development objectives: Although the Government has not adopted an explicit population policy, population issues were accorded high priority in the First Five-Year Development Plan for 1981-1985. The need to increase the size of the national population, to plan for manpower development and continuously to monitor and evaluate the population situation is considered to be crucial for the country's development.

INSTITUTIONAL FRAMEWORK

Population data systems and development planning: Censuses are conducted every five years and were held in 1975, 1980 and 1985, with the next provisionally scheduled for 1990. Registration of births is considered to be virtually complete, while deaths are felt to be under-registered. Data collection is the responsibility of the Central Statistics Department of the Ministry of Planning. The First-Five Year Development Plan for the period 1981-1985, prepared by the Ministry of Planning, is the latest available development plan.

Integration of population within development planning: The Central Statistics Department is responsible for taking into account population variables in planning and for providing information on population-development interrelationships.

POLICIES AND MEASURES

Changes in population size and age structure: Although the Government reports that it does not have a policy to modify the rate of population growth, it had specified a target population size in excess of 2 million to be reached by 1991. The target is to be achieved by restricting immigration and confining growth to the national population. Human resource development is to take place through the expansion of education and training facilities. Information on the status of pension schemes is not readily available.

Mortality and morbidity: The primary health-care approach has been adopted as the country's long-term health strategy. A detailed health strategy and plan of action was to have been completed by 1987. Health policies are characterized by primary health care, a new health registration system, the

UNITED ARAB EMIRATES

issuance of family and individual health records to reduce unnecessary visits to health institutions and to limit drug consumption, nominal payment of fees to enhance the sense of responsibility and participation of beneficiaries and pre-employment health examinations of expatriate labour. Special clinics have been established for providing occupational health services. A 1985 report to the Ministry of Health recommended that no additional hospitals be built until at least 1990 and that a Central Hospital Administration be established. The Government's target of immunizing 95 per cent of all infants by 1990 is being undertaken through maternal and child health centres and district Departments of Preventive Health with the use of mobile teams.

Fertility and the family: While the Government reports that it does not have a policy to adjust fertility rates, various measures are in place to encourage fertility among the national population. Those measures take the form of family allowances, day-care facilities and maternity or paternity benefits and tax exemptions to families. The Government does not support the provision of contraception. Abortion is forbidden except to save the life of the mother. Information on the status of sterilization is not readily available.

International migration: With one of the world's highest proportions of non-nationals, 64 per cent of the total population in 1975, immigration has had a profound impact on shaping the country's population. Believing that a large national population is essential for the country's rapid socio-economic development and future political stability, the Government has established a policy to reduce immigration and to restrict it to those migrants with essential skills. The entry of the dependants of migrants with work permits is still permitted. Federal ministries have been asked to increase their employment of nationals. Nationals who have emigrated are offered incentives to return such as receiving assistance in finding high paying employment.

Spatial distribution/urbanization: Explicit spatial planning at the national level does not exist, although at the urban level there has been comprehensive physical planning. Under a project begun in 1985, physical development plans will be produced for the urban and rural centres of the Dubai Emirate Area. The plan has served as a blueprint for similar projects in Abu Dhabi, Al Fujayrah and Sharjah and is likely to be eventually carried out in the other Emirates. Environmental concerns have led the larger cities to locate industrial sites outside urban areas. Within the context of housing policy, one aim is the sedentarization of nomads, preferably on the urban periphery, by providing them with a plot of land and an expandable house free of charge.

Status of women and population: As part of the country's objective of increasing the share of nationals in the work force, programmes and activities for the integration of women in society and eradication of illiteracy are under way. Labour laws guaranteeing equality between men and women in pay and promotion have been established. The minimum legal age at marriage for women is 15 years.

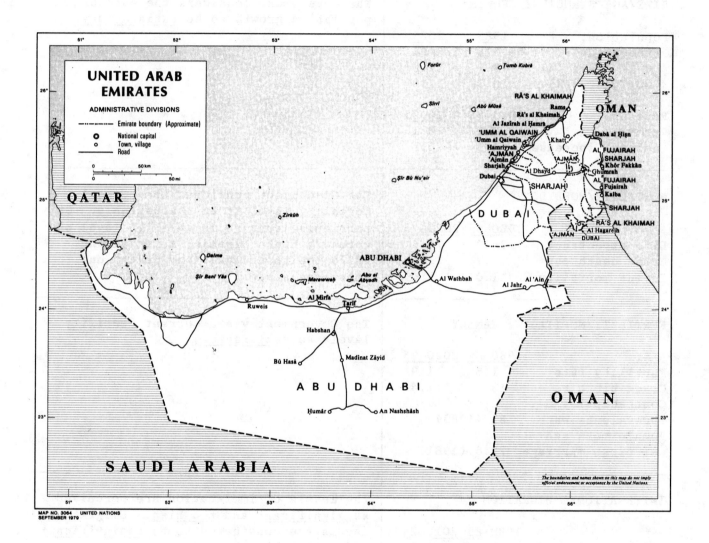

UNITED KINGDOM OF GREAT BRITAIN
AND NORTHERN IRELAND

DEMOGRAPHIC INDICATORS	CURRENT PERCEPTION
SIZE/AGE STRUCTURE/GROWTH	The Government considers the rate of population growth to be <u>satisfactory</u>.

Population:	1985	2025
(thousands)	56 618	57 464
0-14 years (%)	19.2	17.2
60+ years (%)	20.7	27.5

Rate of:	1980-85	2020-25
growth	0.1	-0.1
natural increase	1.3	-0.1

MORTALITY/MORBIDITY

The Government considers the current mortality level to be <u>unacceptable</u>. Of particular concern is the high level of coronary heart disease, maternal and child health diseases and deaths due to substance abuse.

	1980-85	2020-25
Life expectancy	74.0	79.6
Crude death rate	11.7	11.5
Infant mortality	11.0	5.0

FERTILITY/NUPTIALITY/FAMILY

The Government views current fertility levels as <u>satisfactory</u>.

	1980-85	2020-25
Fertility rate	1.8	1.9
Crude birth rate	13.0	11.4
Contraceptive prevalence rate	83 (1983)	
Female mean age at first marriage	22.8 (1981)	

INTERNATIONAL MIGRATION

The levels of immigration are perceived as <u>significant</u> and <u>too high</u>. Emigration levels are considered to be <u>insignificant</u> and <u>satisfactory</u>.

	1980-85	2020-25
Net migration rate	0.0	-0.5
Foreign-born population (%)	8.7 (1981)	

SPATIAL DISTRIBUTION/URBANIZATION

The spatial distribution patterns are viewed as <u>appropriate</u>.

Urban	1985	2025
population (%)	91.7	95.8

Growth rate:	1980-85	2020-25
urban	0.3	0.0
rural	-2.0	-1.7

GENERAL POLICY FRAMEWORK

Overall approach to population problems: The Government has no official policy with regard to overall population size and components of change, except in the area of immigration where recent legislation has sought to decrease the number of foreigners entering the country. The main concerns of the Government are to: provide individuals with information and the means necessary for family planning so that they may make effective decisions and avoid unwanted pregnancy, provide funding for health programmes to decrease morbidity and mortality, and promote health services to improve the prevention, diagnosis and treatment of illness.

Importance of population policy in achieving development objectives: Although the Government has not expressed any specific policy in terms of population size or growth, population issues are taken into account in formulating economic and social policy. Population trends influence programmes concerning education, housing, health and social security.

INSTITUTIONAL FRAMEWORK

Population data systems and development planning: Censuses were conducted in 1951, 1961 and 1971. The most recent census held in 1981 was administered by the Office of Population, Censuses and Surveys (OPCS) (England and Wales), the General Register Office (Scotland) and the General Register Office (Northern Ireland). A census has been scheduled for 1991. A formal system of development planning does not exist.

Integration of population within development planning: Although the Government does not have a centralized planning organization, considerable use is made of demographic factors in a wide range of policy areas such as the allocation of government expenditures, planning social services, social security and manpower planning, and in regional policy. Government departments most directly involved in formulating and co-ordinating population policies include the Departments of Health and Social Security concerning fertility and mortality issues, the Department of the Environment for population distribution and the Home Office for matters relating to international migration. Population variables are also integrated in town and country planning at the district level.

POLICIES AND MEASURES

Changes in population size and age structure: There is no explicit policy of intervention with respect to population growth or size, as the Government believes that decisions concerning fertility and child-bearing should be left to the individual. Policies are pursued in order to improve the well-being of the population and are not intended to influence the population structure. Included are maternity benefits and a comprehensive social security system to combat the impact of poverty and low income on the health of vulnerable groups, such as children, the elderly and the disabled. The Government has indicated that while at present there are no strong sentiments to boost fertility, a substantial and prolonged population decline may lead to a change in attitudes.

Mortality and morbidity: The overall health policy is to improve both the quality of health services and equality of access to them. To achieve this goal emphasis continues to be placed on prevention and on health care for the growing elderly population, the young, the mentally ill and the handicapped. In 1989, the Government proposed far-reaching changes in the organization of the National Health Service (NHS), which currently provides comprehensive health-care services. The proposed reforms are aimed at improving efficiency and applying free-market methods to the currently publicly financed system. Health education is a key part of the Government's strategy to combat AIDS, and other activities include the "Look after your heart" campaign to encourage healthier life-styles. A campaign was launched in 1988 to immunize children against measles, mumps and rubella with a single vaccine.

Fertility and the family: The Government does not intervene to influence levels of fertility. The Government's reluctance to implement measures designed to raise fertility is reinforced by doubts concerning the effectiveness of such measures. It is felt that the proper role of the Government is to provide the information and methods necessary for individuals to make decisions regarding optimal family size. Among the measures that have been taken are a campaign to reduce unwanted fertility among young women and to encourage greater male responsibility regarding contraception. Family planning services are widely available free of charge through the National Health Service. Under the Social Security Act of 1986, a new maternity pay scheme was introduced, consisting of the payment of an earnings-related allowance for six weeks, followed by a flat rate payment for an additional 12 weeks. Payment is made by the employer who is reimbursed by the national insurance system. Since 1967, abortion has been legal up to the 28 weeks of pregnancy on broad medical grounds, for eugenic reasons and generally in cases of rape and incest. Socio-economic factors are taken into account in the medical assessment of the request for abortion. An attempt to reduce the time limit for legal abortion to the eighteenth week of pregnancy was defeated in Parliament in 1988. Sterilization is available free of charge through the National Health Service.

International migration: Immigration policy is based on the broad objectives of family reunification, entry to those with a connection to the United Kingdom, as well as entry to refugees with a justified fear of returning to their own country. New primary immigration is strictly limited, given the current situation of high unemployment. The Immigration Act of 1971 and the Nationality Act of 1981 form the basis for the Government's policy on immigration. Recent legislation has included an amendment to the immigration rules in 1985 to equalize the situation of prospective entrant spouses/fiancés and new visa rules in 1986 requiring that citizens from Bangladesh, Ghana, India, Nigeria and Pakistan obtain visas from their own country to visit the United Kingdom. As of June 1986, a policy of "exceptional leave to remain" was implemented for certain refugees already in the country who have sought asylum. More recent concern has focused on the immigration rights of residents of Hong Kong who wish to migrate to the United Kingdom. The Government is concerned about the problems associated with the emigration of skilled workers and professionals and has taken a number of initiatives that, while not specifically aimed at reducing the flow, may assist in retaining highly skilled professionals. For example, a new salary structure has been introduced for academic staff at universities.

Spatial distribution/urbanization: The Government has no explicit policy to modify population distribution, although programmes aimed at regional development, inner city regeneration and a revival of rural areas may indirectly influence population patterns. Successive Governments have relied on two major instruments of regional policy: financial inducements to companies to move to assisted areas and direct public investment in assisted areas. Regional policy has been down-played since 1983 as a result of a major review of policy, coupled with attempts to reduce public expenditure and to rely on free-market solutions to regional inequalities.

Status of women and population: Various efforts have been made to improve the status of women. The Sex Discrimination Act of 1975 prohibits employers from discriminating on the grounds of sex in recruitment, training and promotion. The Act also provides for affirmative action to train women so that they can compete for jobs in occupations traditionally occupied by men and to rejoin the labour force after a period of absence. Given the lack of child-care facilities, the Government believes that more employers should provide workplace nurseries to retain women workers. The minimum legal age at marriage for women is 16 years.

UNITED REPUBLIC OF TANZANIA

DEMOGRAPHIC INDICATORS	CURRENT PERCEPTION
SIZE/AGE STRUCTURE/GROWTH	The Government perceives the current growth rate as <u>unsatisfactory</u> and <u>too high</u>.

Population:
	1985	2025
(thousands)	22 751	84 784
0–14 years (%)	48.6	39.0
60+ years (%)	3.8	4.6

Rate of:
	1980–85	2020–25
growth	3.7	2.4
natural increase	35.4	23.5

MORTALITY/MORBIDITY

Present conditions of health and levels of mortality are considered to be <u>unacceptable</u>. Infants and women in reproductive ages are of special concern.

	1980–85	2020–25
Life expectancy	51.0	66.5
Crude death rate	15.3	5.8
Infant mortality	115.0	49.0

FERTILITY/NUPTIALITY/FAMILY

Current fertility levels are viewed as <u>unsatisfactory</u> and <u>too high</u>.

	1980–85	2020–25
Fertility rate	7.1	3.6
Crude birth rate	50.6	29.4
Contraceptive prevalence rate	...	...
Female mean age at first marriage	19.2 (1978)	

INTERNATIONAL MIGRATION

Levels of both immigration and emigration are <u>insignificant</u> and <u>satisfactory</u>.

	1980–85	2020–25
Net migration rate	...	...
Foreign–born population (%)	2.4 (1978)	

SPATIAL DISTRIBUTION/URBANIZATION

The spatial distribution is considered to be <u>appropriate</u>.

Urban	1985	2025
population (%)	24.4	64.2

Growth rate:	1980–85	2020–25
urban	11.6	3.4
rural	1.7	0.7

GENERAL POLICY FRAMEWORK

Overall approach to population problems: The Government believes that poverty is the root problem to be tackled and although no official population policy had been formulated as of 1988, the necessity for a policy to reinforce national development, especially human resource development, and improve the quality of life of the people has been recognized. A draft national population policy was prepared in 1988.

Importance of population policy in achieving development objectives: One of the objectives of the Government's policy is to enhance the process of integrating population variables in planning through the provision, dissemination and utilization of population-development data. There is an increasing appreciation in political and policy circles of the impact of demographic trends on development and the need for a comprehensive population policy as part of development planning and policies.

INSTITUTIONAL FRAMEWORK

Population data systems and development planning: The United Republic of Tanzania is one of the few African countries with a relatively long history of demographic data collection. The third national census was conducted in 1988. The Government hopes that periodic large-scale demographic and fertility sample surveys will be taken in the intercensal period. The National Demographic Survey of Tanzania was conducted in 1973. Vital registration is still incomplete and efforts are under way to introduce a comprehensive system. Ministries and various agencies and institutions collect population-related data pertaining to their areas of operation. The latest development plan is the Second Union Fifth Five-Year Development Plan covering the period 1987/88-1991/92, prepared by the Ministry of Finance, Economic Affairs and Planning.

Integration of population within development planning: The Population and Development Planning and Policy Unit of the Ministry of Finance, Economic Affairs and Planning, which was established in 1986, is carrying out the groundwork for the formulation of a national population policy that the Government intends to promulgate. There is no research institution which focuses on the population-development interrelationship, although the National Population Committee advises the Government on population matters.

POLICIES AND MEASURES

Changes in population size and age structure: The Government feels that the rate of population growth is too high and the resulting age structure unfavourable in relation to the prevailing social and economic conditions. The Government has responded to these concerns by the creation of the Population and Development Planning and Policy Unit in order to strengthen the institutional framework for the integration of population and development.

UNITED REPUBLIC OF TANZANIA

Social security coverage is limited to employees of firms with at least four workers, with coverage to be gradually extended to smaller firms. A special system exists for public employees.

Mortality and morbidity: The major objective of health policy is to provide comprehensive basic health services to all people as close as possible to where they live. Preventive health care rather than curative care is stressed, with a shift of emphasis from constructing large hospitals to smaller and simpler service units. The national primary health-care strategy underscores the importance of community involvement in planning, implementing and evaluating health activities. Since 1985 a national child-spacing programme has been an integral component of maternal and child health services. Targets are to immunize all children and 90 per cent of pregnant women by the year 1992. To combat the spread of the AIDS virus, a National Committee on AIDS has been established, health education campaigns have been held and provision has been made for diagnostic facilities at all referral hospitals.

Fertility and the family: Although the Government does not intervene with respect to fertility rates, it is concerned with the impact of high fertility on the attainment of development objectives. To improve the health of mother and child and permit families to have the number of children that they can adequately support, family planning in the form of child-spacing is being promoted. A project was undertaken in 1987 to introduce population and family life education into the curricula of schools and teacher training colleges. To encourage smaller families, tax exemption and other benefits are available only to families with fewer than five children. Family planning services are being integrated into all hospitals, rural health centres and dispensaries. Abortion is permitted only to save the life of the mother, while there are no restrictions placed on sterilization.

International migration: As of mid-1989, it was estimated that the country was host to over 267,000 refugees, mostly of rural origin from Burundi, Mozambique, Rwanda and Zaire. In co-ordination with the Ministry of Home Affairs, which is the Government's focal point for refugee matters, assistance provided by the Office of the United Nations High Commissioner for Refugees is directed towards consolidating the self-sufficiency of rural refugees in settlements, promoting employment opportunities for urban refugees, and providing subsistence and counselling to those few who are still dependent due to poverty or illness. While there are no policies directed to emigration, the Government is concerned by the emigration of skilled workers and professionals.

Spatial distribution/urbanization: The Government continues to establish nucleated villages (ujamma) in order to facilitate the provision of social services and to promote co-operative development. To contain problems of squatter development and improve living conditions, programmes of sites, services and squatter upgrading have been undertaken. Since 1973 the Government has been planning to transfer the country's capital from Dar es Salam on the eastern coast to Dodoma, in the country's interior. The city's actual growth has fallen below expectations and the master plan originally prepared in 1974 is being reviewed and may be revamped along less ambitious lines. As of 1988 the Parliament and most key ministries were still located in Dar es Salam.

<u>Status of women and population</u>: In order to avoid all forms of discrimination against women, the Government has passed legislation, such as a law in 1971, which enabled women to own and dispose of property. The Employment Amendment Act of 1975 gave equal opportunities to work in all areas with equal pay, as well as the right to receive maternity leave regardless of marital status. The Union of Tanzanian Women has, as its mandate, the objective of facilitating the participation of women in development activities. The minimum legal age at marriage for women is 16 years.

MAP NO.1960 REV.2   UNITED NATIONS
MARCH 1978

UNITED STATES OF AMERICA

DEMOGRAPHIC INDICATORS	CURRENT PERCEPTION

SIZE/AGE STRUCTURE/GROWTH
 	
 Population: 1985   2025
   (thousands)   239 283   300 796
   0-14 years (%)   21.7   18.1
   60+ years (%)   16.5   26.3
 	
 Rate of: 1980-85   2020-25
   growth   1.0   0.4
   natural increase   7.1   2.1
	The Government considers the rate of population growth to be <u>satisfactory</u>.

MORTALITY/MORBIDITY 1980-85 2020-25 Life expectancy 74.5 79.7 Crude death rate 8.6 9.8 Infant mortality 11.0 5.0	Levels and trends of mortality are considered to be <u>acceptable</u>. The Government views AIDS as a major public health concern.

FERTILITY/NUPTIALITY/FAMILY
 	
     1980-85   2020-25
 Fertility rate   1.8   2.0
 Crude birth rate   15.7   11.9
 Contraceptive
   prevalence rate   68.0 (1982)
 Female mean age
   at first marriage   23.3 (1980)
	Levels and trends of fertility are <u>satisfactory</u>. However, adolescent child-bearing is of particular concern.

INTERNATIONAL MIGRATION
 	
     1980-85   2020-25
 Net migration rate   0.0   1.5
 Foreign-born
   population (%)   6.2 (1980)
	Immigration is perceived as <u>significant</u> and <u>satisfactory</u>. Concern is expressed over illegal immigration. Emigration is considered to be <u>insignificant</u> and <u>satisfactory</u>.

SPATIAL DISTRIBUTION/URBANIZATION
 	
 Urban   1985   2025
   population (%)   73.9   77.0
 	
 Growth rate: 1980-85   2020-25
   urban   1.0   0.5
   rural   0.8   -0.1
	The spatial distribution of the population is viewed as <u>appropriate</u>.

GENERAL POLICY FRAMEWORK

Overall approach to population problems: The Government intervenes only to lower mortality and morbidity and to regulate the flow of immigration.

Importance of population policy in achieving development objectives: There is no national policy to influence demographic trends directly. The Government feels that data collection on population growth and internal population distribution is very important for effective planning.

INSTITUTIONAL FRAMEWORK

Population data systems and development planning: The Bureau of the Census conducts a decennial census of population, with the latest taken in 1990. Births, deaths and other vital events are registered by each State and compiled by the National Center for Health Statistics. The Center for Population Research of the National Institute of Child Health and Human Development is responsible for the primary Federal efforts in population research. In addition, the Office of Population Affairs in the Department of Health and Human Services develops policy and co-ordinates activities pertaining to population research, voluntary family planning and related concerns. The Federal Government does not have an institutionalized system of development planning.

Integration of population within development planning: There is no agency charged with the integration of population within development planning.

POLICIES AND MEASURES

Changes in population size and age structure: Although there is no official policy concerning population size and growth, accurate data on population growth are felt to be essential for planning. Confronted with population aging and its social and economic consequences, the Federal Government has recently taken measures to implement health-care services and to limit unnecessary expenses. The Medicare Insurance Programme, the national health insurance scheme for the aged and disabled, provides payments for a variety of hospital, physician, nursing and home-care services. The Medicare Catastrophic Coverage Act of 1988, which had been expanded to cover the high medical costs of acute illnesses, was repealed in 1989 following controversy surrounding the additional costs of the programme. Legislation that eliminated mandatory retirement at age 70 in companies with 20 or more employees and in state and local governments was enacted both to permit older people a greater choice of life-styles and to lessen the financial burden on the social security system.

Mortality and morbidity: The Public Health Service, the Federal agency charged by law with promoting the highest level of health attainable for every American, has since 1980 pursued a specific set of health objectives, with

UNITED STATES OF AMERICA

five major goals to be achieved by 1990 in 15 priority areas. Among the
targets are an infant mortality rate of less than 9 per thousand live births,
fewer than 34 deaths per thousand among children aged 1 to 14, and reducing
the average annual number of days of restricted activity due to acute and
chronic conditions to fewer than 30 days per year for those aged 65 and over.
In mid-1988 health officials indicated that significant problems persist in
terms of infant and maternal mortality and that the targets unlikely to be met
by 1990 are those for pre-natal care and infant, perinatal and maternal
mortality among some racial and ethnic groups. The 1989 Healthy Birth Act
under consideration by the United States Congress in mid-1989 would implement
additional programmes to lower infant mortality. In 1982 and 1984 Federal
block grants were introduced for programmes in maternal and child health,
preventive health, alcohol and drug abuse, mental health and community health
centres for the medically needy population. The objective is to moderate the
level of Federal funding and regulatory involvement, while granting
flexibility to States. The Government has expressed serious concern over the
spread of the AIDS virus and has responded in various ways such as by
supporting epidemiological and biomedical research and testing and counselling
centres, as well as undertaking information and educational campaigns.

Fertility and the family: There is no explicit policy designed to influence
fertility. The Government is seriously concerned by adolescent
child-bearing. The Adolescent Family Life Program (AFL) funds services aimed
at preventing adolescent pre-marital sexual relations and supporting services
that address the needs of pregnant and parenting youth. AFL also promotes
adoption as an alternative among pregnant adolescents. Subsidized family
planning services, including information on contraception and birth control,
are provided for individuals with financial or other difficulties. During the
first trimester, there are virtually no restrictions on abortion. During the
second trimester, abortions must be performed in a hospital and in the third
trimester, abortions are permitted only if there is a grave risk to the mental
or physical health of the mother. From the second trimester, grounds for an
abortion may be subject to state regulation; in 1989 a Supreme Court decision
upheld the state's right to regulate access to abortion. Federal funding for
abortion is not permitted, except if the physical health of the mother is
seriously endangered. Moreover, clinics that conduct abortion counselling are
prohibited from receiving Federal funds even if such counselling is financed
with private money. Female sterilization is permitted as a method of family
planning, although certain restrictions apply if Federal funds are involved.

International migration: In view of the Government's concern over the
substantial numbers of undocumented migrants, the Immigration Reform and
Control Act of 1986 sought to curb undocumented immigration. The legislation
penalizes employers of undocumented migrants. It established a process for
aliens living in the United States unlawfully since before 1 January 1982 to
qualify for legal status. Under the legalization programme, aliens had to
submit proof before 4 May 1988 that they had resided in the United States
since before 1 January 1982 and that they were financially responsible. More
than 1.7 million aliens applied for the programme. The 1986 Act also
contained provisions for legalizing the status of farm workers who could prove
that they had engaged in harvesting activities for at least 90 days in a
one-year period ending 1 May 1986. With a deadline for application of 30
November 1988, more than 1 million workers had applied by early November 1988,
far exceeding the 600,000 expected applications. Legislation that went into

effect in November 1988 contained provisions for a lottery system in 1989 and 1990 to award permanent residency to certain "disadvantaged" nationalities. To accommodate a larger than expected influx of refugees, the President of the United States in 1989 proposed increasing the number of refugees admitted into the United States for fiscal year 1990 to 125,000, including 50,000 from the Union of Soviet Socialist Republics.

Spatial distribution/urbanization: Although there is no official policy concerning spatial distribution, the Government feels that accurate data on population distribution are important for social and economic institutions that respond to the needs of various population subgroups. The Government has sought to reverse urban decline and to revitalize local economies by decentralizing national programmes and by strengthening the authority of state and local governments as well as by stimulating public-private partnership.

Status of women and population: There are no policies to promote the sharing of responsibilities between men and women with respect to family life, child-rearing and family planning. However, Federal programmes dealing with these matters support and encourage the sharing of responsibilities. To guarantee women equal employment opportunities, a series of statutes have been enacted to prevent discrimination. It has, however, been acknowledged that the lack of adequate child-care facilities continues to hamper mothers seeking education and training as well as those employed or seeking employment. The minimum legal age at marriage for women is 18 years in most states.

MAP NO. 2768.1   UNITED NATIONS
SEPTEMBER 1990

URUGUAY

DEMOGRAPHIC INDICATORS	CURRENT PERCEPTION
SIZE/AGE STRUCTURE/GROWTH	The Government perceives population growth as <u>unsatisfactory</u> and <u>too low</u> and is very concerned by the aging of the population.

Population:	1985	2025
(thousands)	3 012	3 875
0–14 years (%)	26.9	22.1
60+ years (%)	15.3	17.4

Rate of:	1980–85	2020–25
growth	0.7	0.5
natural increase	9.3	5.2

MORTALITY/MORBIDITY

Levels and trends of mortality and morbidity are considered to be <u>acceptable</u>.

	1980–85	2020–25
Life expectancy	70.3	73.4
Crude death rate	10.2	10.2
Infant mortality	30.0	16.0

FERTILITY/NUPTIALITY/FAMILY

Current fertility rates are felt to be <u>unsatisfactory</u> because they are <u>too low</u>.

	1980–85	2020–25
Fertility rate	2.8	2.2
Crude birth rate	19.5	15.4
Contraceptive prevalence rate	...	...
Female mean age at first marriage	22.4 (1975)	

INTERNATIONAL MIGRATION

Immigration is <u>insignificant</u> and <u>too low</u>, while emigration is <u>significant</u> and <u>too high</u>.

	1980–85	2020–25
Net migration rate	...	...
Foreign-born population (%)	3.5 (1985)	

SPATIAL DISTRIBUTION/URBANIZATION

The spatial distribution of the population is seen as <u>inappropriate</u>.

Urban	1985	2025
population (%)	84.6	91.6

Growth rate:	1980–85	2020–25
urban	0.9	0.6
rural	-0.3	-1.2

GENERAL POLICY FRAMEWORK

<u>Overall approach to population problems</u>: The Government has adopted a policy to increase population growth and fertility, improve morbidity and mortality conditions, decelerate migration and increase immigration.

<u>Importance of population policy in achieving development objectives</u>: Population policy is perceived as forming an essential component of the socio-economic development process and is aimed at promoting the well-being and prosperity of all Uruguayans.

INSTITUTIONAL FRAMEWORK

<u>Population data systems and development planning</u>: Censuses were conducted in 1963, 1975 and 1985. Vital registration of births and deaths is considered to be virtually complete. The Department of General Statistics and Census is responsible for the preparation of population projections and conducting demographic surveys. To support the National Agreement signed on 1 April 1986 between the Government and other political parties, which places emphasis on economic growth and social development, the Government has designed a series of political, economic and social guidelines. Its objectives were to be achieved on the basis of medium- and long-term planning implemented in the period 1986-1988.

<u>Integration of population within development planning</u>: In 1974 the Government designated the Ministry of Housing and Social Welfare as the national body to deal with population policy. In 1974 an inter-ministerial commission was established to study the country's population problems and to formulate an integrated population policy. The Commission, however, was reported as inactive in 1982. The Government had prepared, on the basis of medium- and long-term planning, a series of political, economic and social guidelines which were designed to cover a period of three years starting in 1986. There does not appear to be an agency responsible for the formulation and co-ordination of population policy.

POLICIES AND MEASURES

<u>Changes in population size and age structure</u>: Concerned by the most aged population structure in Latin America and a very high dependency ratio, the Government has a policy of boosting population size, natural increase and the rate of population growth by increasing levels of fertility and immigration, reducing emigration, encouraging return migration and adjusting economic and social factors. The Ministry of Health had developed a programme aimed at giving priority to the care of the elderly, by stressing improved geriatric care and developing centres for the care of the elderly. The social security scheme covers employees and the self-employed.

URUGUAY

Mortality and morbidity: The country's health policy was enunciated in the national health plan approved in 1984. The policy is founded on the joint principles of attaining the highest possible level of health for all and the right of every citizen to health care. It is intended to strengthen maternal and child health programmes, with emphasis on infant mortality and complications of childbirth. There are also plans to improve basic medical and dental care to underserved rural and urban populations and programmes for the treatment and rehabilitation of the disabled. Immunization coverage is being expanded in order to vaccinate 95 per cent of all children under the age of one year.

Fertility and the family: With relatively low rates of fertility, a policy to boost fertility through a variety of incentives is being pursued. A maternity benefit of 100 per cent of wages payable for up to 12 weeks can be extended up to an additional five months if confinement occurs after the expected date or in case of illness. Dismissal from employment is prohibited and nursing breaks are provided. A family allowance of not less than 8 per cent of the monthly minimum wage is also available. Abortion is legal only to save the life of the mother, or in cases of rape or incest. The penalties for having an abortion, however, may be reduced or waived on grounds of economic hardship. The Government provides support for modern methods of contraception.

International migration: To increase rates of population growth, the Government pursues a policy of stimulating immigration, particularly for permanent settlement. In addition, the Government seeks to reduce emigration and encourage the large-scale repatriation of emigrants and political refugees. According to government estimates, some 350,000 Uruguayans left the country between 1968 and 1984. One of the Parliament's first acts, following the succession to power of the new Government in March 1985, was the adoption of a sweeping amnesty law which permitted the release of political prisoners and the return of all political exiles. Former civil servants who had fled the country were guaranteed reinstatement in their former jobs by another law passed in 1985. The National Repatriation Commission was established in 1985 to select and repatriate those exiles who could be reinstated in government employment or integrated into national development projects.

Spatial distribution/urbanization: The Government is concerned with reducing the primacy of the capital, Montevideo, revitalizing sparsely inhabited rural areas and populating the country's frontier regions. Government policy concerning internal migration consists of decelerating migration with comprehensive strategies aimed at slowing primate city growth and encouraging rural development. Strategies included regional development policies for lagging regions and border regions as well as land colonization schemes.

Status of women and population: Government objectives have included the incorporation of women into the development process while preserving the role of motherhood. The Instituto de la Mujer, an organization whose membership is composed of representatives from governmental and non-governmental agencies, is responsible for analysing the situation of women in Uruguay and undertaking the measures necessary to increase the participation of women in society.

VANUATU

DEMOGRAPHIC INDICATORS	CURRENT PERCEPTION
SIZE/AGE STRUCTURE/GROWTH Population: <u>1985</u> <u>2025</u> (thousands) 142 360 0-14 years (%) ... ... 60+ years (%) ... ... Rate of: <u>1980-85</u> <u>2020-25</u> growth 3.9 1.5 natural increase	The Government considers the rate of growth to be <u>satisfactory</u>.
MORTALITY/MORBIDITY <u>1980-85</u> <u>2020-25</u> Life expectancy ... ... Crude death rate ... ... Infant mortality	Current health levels are viewed as <u>unacceptable</u>. Infants and young children are of particular concern.
FERTILITY/NUPTIALITY/FAMILY <u>1980-85</u> <u>2020-25</u> Fertility rate ... ... Crude birth rate ... ... Contraceptive prevalence rate ... ... Female mean age at first marriage	Fertility levels are considered to be <u>satisfactory</u>.
INTERNATIONAL MIGRATION <u>1980-85</u> <u>2020-25</u> Net migration rate 0.0 0.0 Foreign-born population (%) 3.4 (1979)	Levels and trends of immigration and emigration are seen as <u>insignificant</u> and <u>satisfactory</u>.
SPATIAL DISTRIBUTION/URBANIZATION Urban <u>1985</u> <u>2025</u> population (%) 25.4 58.2 Growth rate: <u>1980-85</u> <u>2020-25</u> urban 7.7 2.7 rural 2.7 -0.1	Patterns of spatial distribution are considered to be <u>appropriate</u>.

GENERAL POLICY FRAMEWORK

<u>Overall approach to population problems</u>: The Government feels that in general it does not have a population problem, and thus no official policy of intervention to modify demographic variables has been formulated. The Government has acknowledged that population dynamics will eventually require Government attention.

<u>Importance of population policy in achieving development objectives</u>: Although the Government does not have a population policy, it is aware that the uneven distribution of its small population, the costly administrative infrastructure, the lack of basic facilities and services, and a limited supply of skilled nationals and substantial external budgetary support, all pose serious barriers to development objectives. The Second National Development Plan (1987-1991) seeks to alleviate some of those problems and the Vanuatu Vital Statistics Survey, undertaken in 1987-1988, will be instrumental in forming development objectives.

INSTITUTIONAL FRAMEWORK

<u>Population data systems and development planning</u>: A complete population census was conducted in 1979, while a census of urban areas was held in 1986. The most recent census was held in 1989. Census-taking is the responsibility of the National Planning and Statistics Office. During the period 1987-1988 the Government conducted a vital statistics survey to obtain estimates on fertility and mortality levels required for development planning. The Second National Development Plan (1987-1991), prepared by the National Planning and Statistics Office, is currently in effect.

<u>Integration of population within development planning</u>: The Government reports that no government agency formulates or co-ordinates population policy and that no machinery exists to integrate population into development planning. Guidelines for investment are determined by the Minister of Finance and the Central Bank of Vanuatu.

POLICIES AND MEASURES

<u>Changes in population size and age structure</u>: The Government has no policy to influence population growth. It acknowledges, however, the increasing demand placed on social services by a growing population and is concerned over the burden of a high dependency ratio on the productive sector. A National Provident Fund was established in 1987 and covers all those in regular employment over the age of 14 years who are not members of existing employers' schemes approved by the Board of the Fund, with the exception of those earning less than 3,000 vatu a month ($US 1 = 100 vatu).

VANUATU

<u>Mortality and morbidity</u>: The national strategy is based on developing primary health care with the involvement of local communities and pursuing decentralization that will give local authorities greater participation. The Government reports that the participation in health development of related Government sectors, and non-governmental associations such as those for women, young people and the churches, must be strengthened. The main obstacle to better co-ordination is the scarcity of nationals with sufficient managerial and technical capabilities. Economic and social factors, the geographical isolation of the communities and a scattered population have also impeded the development strategies. A Master Plan was prepared in the mid-1980s that was to serve as the basis for determining future allocations of resources for health development. The lack of up-to-date mortality data was expected to be remedied by the Vital Statistics Survey undertaken in 1987-1988. AIDS is considered to be a minor concern by the Government. The following measures have been adopted to prevent its occurrence: AIDS education, screening of blood donations, the promotion of condoms to "risk-groups" and epidemiological monitoring.

<u>Fertility and the family</u>: There is no policy to influence fertility. Family planning, which receives direct support from the Government, is included in health policy and is organized at the district level. To improve family well-being, particularly of mothers and children, a project was initiated in 1984 to upgrade maternal and child health care and services through family planning. Population education has been integrated into formal and non-formal education programmes. Abortion is permitted only to save the life of the mother or in the case of rape, incest or high-risk impairment. Sterilization is permitted and although there are no legal restrictions, in practice a woman must be at least 18 years old and have the consent of the spouse.

<u>International migration</u>: The Government considers that the only permanent residents of Vanuatu are its citizens. All other residents are subject to permit control. Permits to enter and reside in the country are issued only to those who can make a positive contribution to the economic development of Vanuatu. The Government seeks to maintain the flow of those entering on non-permanent work permits and of their dependants. At present there is no government policy towards emigration and the brain drain is not a concern for the Government.

<u>Spatial distribution/urbanization</u>: There is no explicit policy to modify population distribution; however, the Government's aim is to achieve a balanced distribution between regional and urban/rural areas. The main obstacle is the fact that the population is scattered across 40 islands that constitute the Republic of Vanuatu, making it difficult to establish an organized spatial distribution pattern.

<u>Status of women and population</u>: Measures relating to the status of women have been adopted indirectly through increased training programmes for women and programmes that emphasize nutrition and family health. The Women's Affairs Office (WAO) of Vanuatu, a branch of the Department of Social Development, was established in 1980 and seeks to improve the status of women by promoting changes in their role in Vanuatu society and working towards their full and equal participation in domestic, local and national affairs. WAO has

established programmes that stress education, health and the economic participation of women; it has also set up programmes to create trading opportunities and teach practical skills to women in rural areas, to encourage and strengthen the family as the most important social unit, and to improve the standard of pre-school education through a systematic national training programme. Information on the minimum age at marriage for women is not readily available.

Other issues: In 1988 Vanuatu was struck by two cyclones that severely damaged public infrastructure, private homes and roads in the northern and central islands. The number of people in the severely affected areas was estimated to be over 15,000 or about 10 per cent of the country's population. Provision of health and educational services was also handicapped. A previous cyclone in 1987 resulted in the loss of many lives and substantial damage to food and crops. Relief assistance was allocated by the United Nations for reconstruction and to establish educational, vocational and health programmes. However, the Government is aware that this natural disaster will have a long-term impact on the economy and development of the country.

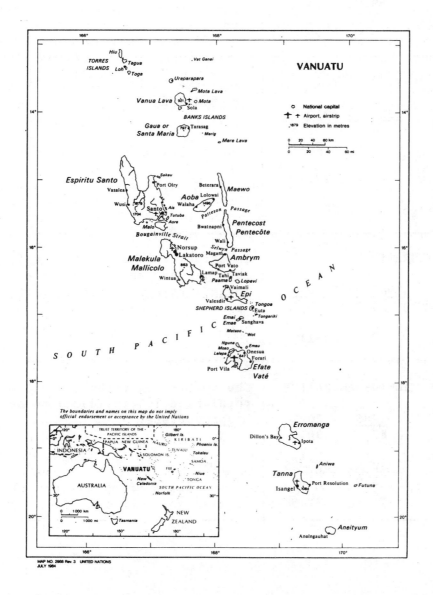

MAP NO. 2968 Rev. 3 UNITED NATIONS
JULY 1984

VENEZUELA

DEMOGRAPHIC INDICATORS	CURRENT PERCEPTION

SIZE/AGE STRUCTURE/GROWTH
 	
Population: 1985   2025
 (thousands) 17 317 38 000
  0-14 years (%) 39.5   27.8
  60+ years (%)   5.3   11.5
 	
Rate of: 1980-85 2020-25
 growth   2.8   1.4
 natural increase 27.4   13.8
	The Government perceives population growth as <u>satisfactory</u>.

MORTALITY/MORBIDITY 1980-85 2020-25 Life expectancy 69.0 73.7 Crude death rate 5.5 6.3 Infant mortality 39.0 20.0	Mortality and morbidity levels are perceived as <u>unacceptable</u>.
FERTILITY/NUPTIALITY/FAMILY 1980-85 2020-25 Fertility rate 4.1 2.6 Crude birth rate 33.0 20.1 Contraceptive prevalence rate 49.3 (1977) Female mean age at first marriage 21.2 (1981)	The level of fertility is felt to be <u>satisfactory</u>.
INTERNATIONAL MIGRATION 1980-85 2020-25 Net migration rate 0.0 0.4 Foreign-born population (%) 7.2 (1981)	Immigration is seen as <u>significant</u> and <u>too high</u> and emigration is perceived as <u>insignificant</u> and <u>satisfactory</u>.
SPATIAL DISTRIBUTION/URBANIZATION Urban 1985 2025 population (%) 87.6 96.0 Growth rate: 1980-85 2020-25 urban 3.9 1.5 rural -3.1 -0.2	The spatial distribution pattern of the population is considered to be <u>inappropriate</u>.

GENERAL POLICY FRAMEWORK

Overall approach to population problems: The Government does not intervene to influence population growth or fertility. Population concerns of fertility and health are viewed by the Government as an endogenous part of a wider social sector policy and in the general context of family welfare rather than separate objects of policy. As a result, Venezuela has produced a series of sectoral programmes and national development plans that have had an impact on population dynamics, although they were not specifically designed towards that end. Immigration, however, has been the object of explicit policy.

Importance of population policy in achieving development objectives: The Government has not formulated any explicit population policies with intended demographic objectives. Since the advent in 1958 of the country's formal planning institution, the Office for Co-ordination and Planning (CORDIPLAN), demographic concerns have been considered in the context of various sectoral plans involving health, the family and the economy. The Government has stated that development policies must be intimately linked to the demographic situation.

INSTITUTIONAL FRAMEWORK

Population data systems and development planning: Eight censuses have been conducted, with the most recent in 1981 and the next provisionally scheduled for 1990. Vital registration is considered to be incomplete. Demographic data collection is the responsibility of the Dirección de Estadística de Población. International assistance has been provided to train nationals in population census planning and the use of data in the policy-making process. The Seventh Development Plan for the period 1984-1988 prepared by CORDIPLAN is the latest available plan.

Integration of population within development planning: Population concerns have been systematically integrated into national development plans since 1960, as well as into various sectoral plans.

POLICIES AND MEASURES

Changes in population size and age structure: The Government has not attempted to influence the rate of population growth, although it supports programmes to modify fertility as a means of improving family well-being. Measures have been instituted that are directed at the elderly and include geriatric hospital services, geriatric residences and training for those involved in caring for the elderly. The social security scheme covers employees in public and private employment and excludes temporary and casual workers and the self-employed.

VENEZUELA

Mortality and morbidity: The country's health objectives are to facilitate access to high quality health services through the following programmes: protection of the environment, prevention of work-place health hazards, combating cancer and social problems including drug abuse, smoking and alcoholism, traffic accidents, mental illness and cardio-vascular disease, and improvement of care to mothers, children and adolescents. The Ministry of Education and the Ministry of Health and Social Welfare will incorporate health instruction into the education system. Academic training for family physicians and paramedical personnel is encouraged and hospital management is being improved. A special social outreach office has been established with several permanent programmes aimed at fostering community involvement in health programmes. Short- and medium-term research priorities for tropical diseases were established in 1985. In 1986 a programme in maternal and child health was begun that includes activities related to pre-natal health, obstetrics and post-natal care; and health of school children and adolescents. The approach is to train primary health-care professionals in maternal and child care, to motivate the use of family planning methods and to control diarrhoeal diseases more effectively.

Fertility and the family: While the Government has never actively supported a policy to reduce fertility for demographic ends, it has permitted the incremental and gradual expansion of family planning for health-related reasons. A family planning programme targeted at low-income urban areas had existed since 1963, and in 1974 a national family planning programme was created within the Maternal and Child Section of the Ministry of Health which continues to provide mainly urban services and family planning education. In 1987 the Ministry of the Family, representing the first and only institution of its type in Latin America, was created to co-ordinate sectoral programmes affecting youth, the elderly and women. Through the Ministry of Youth a project in the promotion of family life and sex education in the informal sector was begun in 1987. Abortion is permitted to save the life of the mother and sterilization is allowed only for medical or eugenic reasons.

International migration: Migration is the demographic variable that has received the most attention in Venezuela. The country has historically been a pole of attraction for immigrants; as a result, immigration has been controlled and at times restricted. In 1958 the open-door policy of the country was replaced by a more restrictive policy. Undocumented immigration, particularly of workers from Colombia, has remained a problem in the face of the country's deteriorating economic situation. Towards the end of the 1970s the problem of undocumented immigration was tackled by restrictions on visas, the reorganization of certain consulates in Colombia, increased deportation, and the extension of services identifying and controlling foreigners including the establishment of a general register of foreigners. At the same time, measures have been undertaken to guarantee immigrants to Venezuela the same rights as nationals with respect to education, employment, health services and social security. There is no policy with respect to emigration.

Spatial distribution/urbanization: The Government intervenes to adjust the spatial distribution of the population, particularly to reduce rural-to-urban flows. The Government's priority had been to establish a spatial distribution pattern appropriate to socio-economic development; comprehensive measures towards this end have included regionalization and decentralization of industry and administration. In 1988, research was undertaken to examine migration patterns and occupational structure in the industrial sector of two frontier districts to determine actual and potential labour force demand and training needs, to project short-term migration patterns and occupational structure, and to elaborate policy recommendations related to frontier migration, industrial employment and training.

<u>Status of women and population</u>: The Government has undertaken measures aimed at improving the status of women. In 1974 the Advisory Committee for Women to the Presidency was created to aid their incorporation into social development and to avoid discrimination. Subsequently, a Ministry for the Participation of Women in Development was created that achieved a reform of the Civil Code in 1982. Reforms included establishing equality of marital proprietary, residential and parental rights between men and women. The labour law is being reviewed with the aim of guaranteeing women work conditions equal to those of men. The General Sectoral Directorate for the Promotion of Women, of the Ministry of the Family, has the major responsibility for formulating, co-ordinating and supervising programmes to improve women's participation in socio-economic, cultural and political spheres. The minimum legal age at marriage for women is 18 years.

VIET NAM

DEMOGRAPHIC INDICATORS	CURRENT PERCEPTION

SIZE/AGE STRUCTURE/GROWTH
 	
Population: 1985   2025
 (thousands) 60 059 117 972
  0-14 years (%) 40.6   24.0
  60+ years (%)   6.8   10.7
 	
Rate of: 1980-85 2020-25
 growth   2.2   1.2
 natural increase 23.6   11.8
	The Government considers the growth rate to be <u>unsatisfactory</u> because it is <u>too high</u>.

MORTALITY/MORBIDITY 1980-85 2020-25 Life expectancy 58.8 73.1 Crude death rate 11.2 5.7 Infant mortality 76.0 19.0	Current levels and trends are perceived as <u>unacceptable</u>. Major concerns are the high incidence of malaria, acute respiratory infections and malnutrition.
FERTILITY/NUPTIALITY/FAMILY 1980-85 2020-25 Fertility rate 4.8 2.1 Crude birth rate 34.8 17.5 Contraceptive prevalence rate 53.2 (1988) Female mean age at first marriage	Fertility levels are viewed as <u>unsatisfactory</u> because they are <u>too high</u>.
INTERNATIONAL MIGRATION 1980-85 2020-25 Net migration rate 0.0 0.0 Foreign-born population (%)	Immigration is <u>insignificant</u> and <u>satisfactory</u>. Emigration is regarded as <u>insignificant</u> and <u>too low</u>.
SPATIAL DISTRIBUTION/URBANIZATION Urban 1985 2025 population (%) 20.3 46.7 Growth rate: 1980-85 2020-25 urban 3.3 3.0 rural 2.0 -0.3	The Government considers the spatial distribution of population to be <u>inappropriate</u>.

GENERAL POLICY FRAMEWORK

<u>Overall approach to population problems</u>: The Government's major policy objectives are to reduce population growth and to achieve a more balanced population distribution. Measures include the delivery of family planning services, information, education and communication campaigns, the use of incentives to encourage the two-child family norm, and voluntary resettlement schemes to redistribute population from the Red River Delta to the Central Highlands.

<u>Importance of population policy in achieving development objectives</u>: The Government ascribes major importance to population policy in achieving development objectives. In 1978, a national population policy was adopted to reduce population growth so as to avoid critical pressure on the supply of food, essential goods and services. In addition, the national population policy aims to alleviate unemployment and underemployment in cities and densely populated rural areas and optimize use of the country's natural resources by a more equitable distribution of the population.

INSTITUTIONAL FRAMEWORK

<u>Population data systems and development planning</u>: Prior to reunification in 1976, censuses had been conducted in the northern part of the country in 1960 and 1974. The unified country's first population census was conducted in 1979 and another census was held in 1989. Census-taking is the responsibility of the Demography Division of the General Statistical Office (GSO). GSO developed and tested an improved vital registration system in 1986-1987 in two rural provinces and will test the system in Hanoi and Ho Chi Minh City in 1988-1991. The Fourth Five-Year Development Plan (1986-1990), drafted by the State Planning Committee of the Council of Ministers, emphasized the need to integrate population planning into economic programmes. After the Sixth Party Congress in 1986 and as a result of the economic crisis, a revised development plan was implemented in 1987.

<u>Integration of population within development planning</u>: In 1984, the National Committee for Population and Family Planning (NCPFP) was established to strengthen the Government's capacity to implement population policies. It is chaired by the Vice-President of the Council of Ministers, with two Vice-Chairmen, the Ministers of Health and Labour, who are in charge of family planning and population redistribution, respectively. A network of NCPFP sub-committees has also been created at the provincial level. In the mid-1980s, the Population Documentation Information Centre was formed to improve monitoring of the national population policy and to evaluate its demographic impact and effectiveness. The Centre for Population Studies in the Ministry of Labour is being strengthened in order to undertake research on the implementation of the resettlement policy. The State Committee for Social Sciences is receiving international assistance for the purpose of co-ordinating research on the design and evaluation of population policy.

VIET NAM

POLICIES AND MEASURES

Changes in population size and age structure: The Government has repeatedly reiterated its commitment to reducing rates of population growth and has relied on voluntary family planning to achieve its goal. Measures undertaken to achieve lower growth include the provision of planning services throughout the country, development of information, education and communication campaigns and a policy of resettling population to other areas of the country. Specified targets were a population growth rate of 1.7 and a total population of 66 million by 1990. Information on the status of the national social security scheme is not readily available.

Mortality and morbidity: The Government is committed to reducing mortality and morbidity levels, with the major policy approach being the improvement of primary health care. Efforts have focused on expanding low-cost, high impact programmes on a national scale. The Expanded Programme of Immunization was adopted as a national priority in 1985 and the goal of universal child immunization by 1990 was set. The Diarrhoeal Diseases Programme, whose main strategy is oral rehydration therapy, has been accelerated, the maternal and child health and family planning network consolidated, and clean water supply and sanitation projects have been undertaken. Additional programmes deal with environmental health and campaigns against acute respiratory infections, malaria and venereal diseases. To determine the effectiveness of those programmes, hundreds of monitors have been trained in assessing the progress of the primary health-care programme.

Fertility and the family: The Government's objective is to to reduce fertility and it rigorously promotes the two-child family norm. The Sixth Party Congress in 1986 established a target rate of natural increase of 1.7 by the year 1990. The three main policy instruments used to achieve this objective are delivery of family planning services free of charge down to the commune and village level; development of information, education and communication activities in support of family planning through mass media, formal education systems and mass organizations; and use of incentives and disincentives. Education programmes stress spacing births at five-year intervals and delaying the first birth until age 22 for women in urban areas and age 20 for rural dwellers. Families with two or fewer children receive preference for promotions and bonuses, the opportunity to move to urban areas and the granting of rental subsidies. Female wage-earners are entitled to six months' maternity leave at full pay or to maternity allowances if they are members of a co-operative. Abortion, sterilization and the use of intrauterine devices (IUDs) are encouraged through a system of incentives. To reduce costs and increase self-reliance in the provision of contraceptives, local production of IUDs and pills is being expanded and a factory to produce condoms was completed in 1988. Abortion is available on request up to the twelfth week of pregnancy and is recommended for women aged over 35. Sterilization is available on request to married women over the age of 30 with two or more children.

International migration: Information relating to the insignificant level of immigration is not readily available. Regarding emigration under the Orderly Departure Programme, which was established in 1979 to provide a safe, humanitarian alternative to departure from Viet Nam, 172,000 people had left the country by mid-1989 for permanent residence abroad, while 109,000 Vietnamese were in camps in East and South-east Asia as of November 1989. Resettlement has not kept pace with new arrivals, eroding the understanding reached in 1979. In June 1989 an International Conference on Indo-Chinese Refugees was convened in order to reach agreement on a new comprehensive approach to the problem of refugees and asylum-seekers from Indo-China.

Spatial distribution/urbanization: An ambitious programme of large-scale population redistribution has been undertaken, with emphasis on reducing the pace of urbanization, particularly of Ho Chi Minh City, the major city in the south, the creation of new economic zones, and the opening up of additional land for cultivation, mostly in the south. The Fourth Five-Year Development Plan (1986-1990) set the goal of transferring 3 million persons, but the Government has acknowledged that such policies have not been well co-ordinated. Revised plans for 1988-1991 have targeted 2 million people for resettlement, mostly from the densely populated Red River Delta area to the more sparsely populated Central Highlands and valley areas. Resettlement within provinces and districts is receiving increasing attention.

Status of women and population: The 1980 Constitution guarantees equal rights for men and women in all respects, although a resolution passed by the Council of Ministers in December 1984 highlighted problems involved in promoting female status. The Women's Union, a mass organization that is highly active, has been mobilized for education and motivation activities. While the minimum legal age at marriage is 18 years for women, postponing marriage until age 22 is strongly recommended.

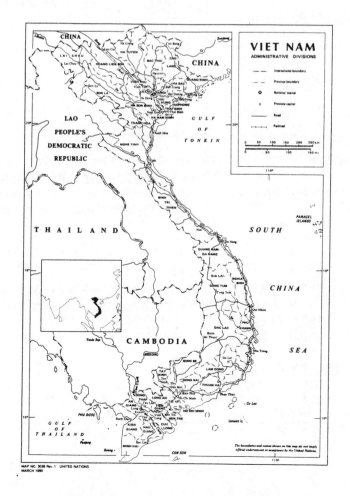

YEMEN

DEMOGRAPHIC INDICATORS	CURRENT PERCEPTION

SIZE/AGE STRUCTURE/GROWTH

Population:	1985	2025
(thousands)	6 888	23 338
0-14 years (%)	48.0	38.5
60+ years (%)	5.3	4.2

Rate of:	1980-85	2020-25
growth	2.8	2.4
natural increase	30.8	23.8

The Government perceives current growth rates as <u>satisfactory</u>.

MORTALITY/MORBIDITY

	1980-85	2020-25
Life expectancy	48.4	68.0
Crude death rate	17.8	5.0
Infant mortality	130.0	36.0

The Government views levels of mortality as <u>unacceptable</u>. Major concerns are high levels of infant and child mortality and poor maternal and child health.

FERTILITY/NUPTIALITY/FAMILY

	1980-85	2020-25
Fertility rate	7.1	3.6
Crude birth rate	48.6	28.8
Contraceptive prevalence rate	1.1 (1979)	
Female mean age at first marriage	17.8 (1981)	

Current fertility rates are regarded as <u>unsatisfactory</u> because they are <u>too high</u>.

INTERNATIONAL MIGRATION

	1980-85	2020-25
Net migration rate	0.0	0.0
Foreign-born population (%)	...	...

Levels of immigration are considered to be <u>significant</u> and <u>satisfactory</u>. Emigration levels are viewed as <u>significant</u> and <u>too high</u>.

SPATIAL DISTRIBUTION/URBANIZATION

Urban	1985	2025
population (%)	20.0	53.1

Growth rate:	1980-85	2020-25
urban	8.2	3.9
rural	1.6	0.8

The spatial distribution is considered to be <u>partially appropriate</u>.

GENERAL POLICY FRAMEWORK

<u>Overall approach to population problems</u>: The Government has no explicit policy to modify the high rates of population growth and natural increase, which are not seen as problematic. It is committed to lowering mortality rates, improving overall health and living standards and lowering fertility in order to improve maternal and child health. Government efforts to satisfy the population's basic needs continue to focus on the provision of water and basic services to the most disadvantaged rural population.

<u>Importance of population policy in achieving development objectives</u>: Although the Government has not formulated a population policy of direct intervention, it is increasingly aware of the links between population and development. Programmes and measures have been pursued to lower fertility and mortality in order to achieve the country's objectives for social and economic development. Poor health conditions are considered to be the most critical population problem and resources continue to be directed at addressing those needs, particularly through the extension of primary health care and improvements in water supply and sanitation. The Government has identified the availability of water as one of the most important pre-conditions for the success of the Third Five-Year Development Plan (1987-1991). The education system is being extended to develop human resources.

INSTITUTIONAL FRAMEWORK

<u>Population data systems and development planning</u>: The first census was conducted in 1975. Sample national surveys were taken in 1981 and 1982 and another census was held in 1986. Vital registration is incomplete, although a civil registration system set up in the early 1980s continues to be developed. International assistance has been received to develop a system of generating vital and migration statistics based on the recording of vital and migratory events. The Central Planning Organization is charged with development planning, to which other government ministries and departments contribute. The Third Five-Year Development Plan covers the period 1987-1991.

<u>Integration of population within development planning</u>: In 1980 a Population Centre was created in the Statistics Department, which is part of the Central Planning Organization (CPO). The Centre has the specific responsibility for incorporating demographic variables into development planning, preparing population projections and providing information on population-development interrelationships.

YEMEN

POLICIES AND MEASURES

<u>Changes in population size and age structure</u>: Although the Government does not intervene to modify rates of growth, it considers it necessary to monitor the rate strictly in the event that it begins to constrain the achievement of economic and social objectives. However, policies with implications for the growth rate are those to reduce morbidity and mortality levels, promote family planning and adjust spatial distribution patterns. A national social security scheme became operational in November 1988, covering all employees, both nationals and non-nationals, as well as Yemeni workers abroad.

<u>Mortality and morbidity</u>: As specified in the Third Five-Year Development Plan, priorities in the health sector include the strengthening and expansion of primary health-care services, with major emphasis on maternal and child health care, immunization and massive dissemination of oral rehydration therapy. Specific objectives are to increase accessibility of primary health-care services to the rural population and expansion and improvement of the training of middle-level health staff, the strengthening of maternal and child health care through the increased training and supervision of female primary health-care workers and traditional birth attendants, the provision of health education to at least 80 per cent of women, focusing on the promotion of breast-feeding, proper weaning and maternal nutrition, oral rehydration and immunization. Projects are under way to improve rural water supplies and environmental sanitation. Targets include full immunization of 80 per cent of all children under the age of three years and 80 per cent of all women in the child-bearing ages by 1991 and reducing infant and maternal mortality by one half by 1991. The Government has reported that health programmes have been constrained by the shortage of health personnel, which to some extent has been alleviated by expatriates.

<u>Fertility and the family</u>: The Government views fertility reduction as necessary to achieve social and economic development objectives. The policy is to encourage family planning activities, mainly to improve maternal and child health and family well-being. Measures take the form of strengthening maternal and child health programmes, direct Government support for the provision of contraceptives, the training of family planning volunteers, encouraging women's participation in the labour force and raising the educational status of women. Population education is being integrated into the formal and non-formal educational systems. Abortion is legal only to save the mother's life and sterilization is permitted.

<u>International migration</u>: Because of substantial out-migration, the country has depended heavily on the immigration of unskilled workers to compensate for its labour deficit. In addition, it is dependent upon expatriates to fill many professional positions. With international assistance, the Ministry of Social Affairs is attempting to provide for the basic needs of the estimated 78,000 refugees as of January 1989, many of whom are living in camps in remote provinces in Yemen. While the emigration of Yemeni workers represents a major source of income through their remittances, it has deprived the country of qualified workers and has depressed agricultural output owing to the departure of agricultural workers. The Government seeks the return of qualified Yemenis, although no measures to encourage their return have been specified.

Spatial distribution/urbanization: To reduce migration to Sana'a City, the largest metropolitan centre, and other urban areas, the Government's policy seeks to improve the provision of basic needs and the quality of life in rural areas, strengthen the agricultural sector, develop a more balanced regional infrastructure and establish more educational opportunities in small towns. The measures undertaken include soil improvement, road construction, agricultural education and training, potable water, electrification, telecommunications, urban development and industrial location.

Status of women and population: The Women's Bureau has been set up within the Ministry of Social Affairs to enhance women's active participation in development, especially in rural areas. Official policy accords equal rights and responsibilities to both men and women. Census data indicate low literacy rates, particularly among women. The Government has made efforts to improve access to both formal and non-formal education. The minimum legal age at marriage for women is 16 years.

Editor's note: On 22 May 1990 Democratic Yemen and Yemen merged to form a single State. Since that date they have been represented as one Member with the name "Yemen". The information provided above describes the situation prior to the merger.

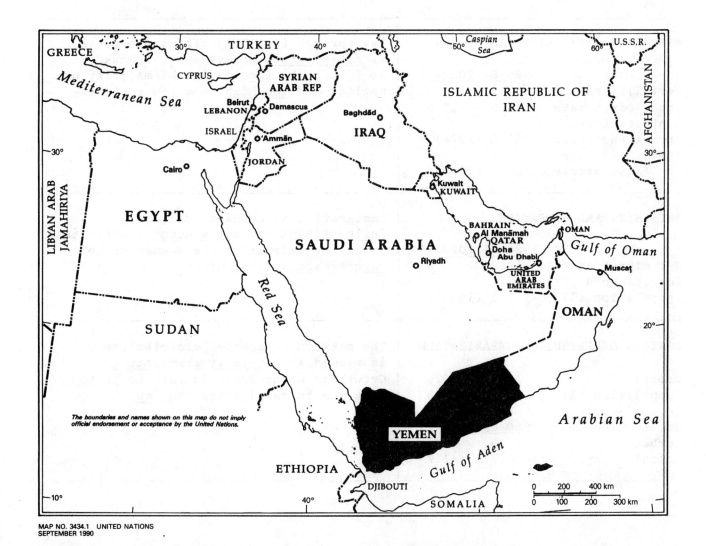

YUGOSLAVIA

DEMOGRAPHIC INDICATORS	CURRENT PERCEPTION

SIZE/AGE STRUCTURE/GROWTH
 	
Population: 1985   2025
 (thousands)   23 118   26 292
  0-14 years (%)   24.1   17.5
  60+ years (%)   12.5   24.3
 	
Rate of: 1980-85   2020-25
 growth   0.7   0.1
 natural increase   7.3   0.6
	The growth rate is considered to be <u>too high</u> in some regions and <u>too low</u> in others.

MORTALITY/MORBIDITY 1980-85 2020-25 Life expectancy 70.8 78.0 Crude death rate 9.2 10.9 Infant mortality 30.0 7.0	The Government views levels of mortality as <u>unacceptable</u>. There is concern over infant and child mortality.
FERTILITY/NUPTIALITY/FAMILY 1980-85 2020-25 Fertility rate 2.1 1.9 Crude birth rate 16.5 11.5 Contraceptive prevalence rate 55.0 (1976) Female mean age at first marriage 22.2 (1981)	The current fertility rate is perceived as <u>satisfactory</u> on average, although it is felt to be <u>too low</u> in the majority of regions and <u>too high</u> in a few regions.
INTERNATIONAL MIGRATION 1980-85 2020-25 Net migration rate 0.0 0.0 Foreign-born population (%) 1.3 (1981)	Immigration is considered to be <u>insignificant</u> and <u>satisfactory</u>, while the levels of emigration are deemed to be <u>significant</u> and <u>too high</u>.
SPATIAL DISTRIBUTION/URBANIZATION Urban 1985 2025 population (%) 46.3 72.3 Growth rate: 1980-85 2020-25 urban 2.5 0.8 rural -0.7 -1.7	The pattern of spatial distribution is viewed as <u>partially appropriate</u>. Growth in urban areas is felt to be <u>too high</u> and in rural areas <u>too low</u>.

GENERAL POLICY FRAMEWORK

Overall approach to population problems: The main goal of the Government's demographic policy is to reduce regional differences in population growth and fertility. A decrease in infant mortality and morbidity is also sought, as well as a reduction in the level of emigration.

Importance of population policy in achieving development objectives: A policy of integrating population variables into the development planning process has been adopted in order to narrow the differences among and within the individual republics. Therefore, specific population policies are formulated in each republic and province, while basic principles concerning fertility regulation and family planning have been adopted for Yugoslavia as a whole.

INSTITUTIONAL FRAMEWORK

Population data systems and development planning: Censuses were conducted in 1953, 1961, 1971 and 1981 and are the responsibility of the Federal Institute of Statistics. A census is scheduled for 1991. Vital registration is considered to be complete. In 1986 the Federal Assembly approved the Social Plan of the Socialist Federal Republic of Yugoslavia, 1986-1990 (medium-term plan). There is also a long-term plan until the year 2000. In addition, the Assembly annually adopted a resolution on implementing the policy established by the Social Plan.

Integration of population within development planning: In 1978 the Federal Institute for Development Planning was made responsible for taking into account population factors in development planning. The Demographic Research Centre of the Federal Institute of Statistics, established in Belgrade in 1963, is responsible for providing information on population-development interrelationships and for preparing population projections.

POLICIES AND MEASURES

Changes in population size and age structure: As a consequence of sharp regional differences in the rates of population growth, the Government pursues a policy of maintaining a moderate growth rate by harmonizing the differentials in regional rates. The Federal Committee for Labour, Health and Social Welfare has prepared a programme to implement the International Plan of Action on Aging, which includes basic principles to govern all activities concerning the aged in various areas such as socio-economic development, health care and nutrition, welfare services, pensions and disability insurance, town planning and population policy.

YUGOSLAVIA

Mortality and morbidity: The Government is particularly concerned with improving the state of health of the population in the following areas: (a) communicable and non-communicable chronic diseases, especially cancer and cardio-vascular diseases, preventive treatment, rehabilitation; (b) accidents in the workplace and among children aged 1-4; and (c) family planning with emphasis on the health protection of women, especially during pregnancy and delivery. A resolution adopted by the Federal Assembly of Yugoslavia in 1984 established guidelines for the further development of health by strengthening primary health care, safeguarding the environment, developing primary health care more rapidly, protecting at-risk groups and preventing and controlling cardio-vascular diseases, malignant neoplasms and other non-communicable diseases. Measures to implement the resolution were elaborated in the strategy for development of health care and health services to the year 2000, which specified programmes to lower infant mortality, reduce morbidity and combat drug abuse and AIDS. Various targets have been specified such as an infant mortality rate of 17 per thousand by the year 2000, as well as for specific types of cancer. Within the republics and provinces, all health-care activities are carried out at the commune level, with each commune organizing its own health services, prescribing health-care measures and establishing new health facilities unless this is the responsibility of other levels.

Fertility and the family: The Government's fertility policy aims to reduce fertility differentials within the country. Policy measures in favour of higher fertility are promoted in low fertility regions (Vojvodina, Slovenia, Croatia, Serbia) while adoption of measures aimed at reducing fertility was under consideration in 1988 for high fertility provinces (Kosovo, Bosnia and Herzegovina, Montenegro, Macedonia). Maternal/child health and family planning programmes have been implemented as well as campaigns to promote public awareness of population issues. Provisions concerning the length of maternity leave vary according to republic and province; it is payable at 100 per cent of earnings. Family allowances are granted and include payments to unemployed women with the same benefits as those who are employed. Access to modern methods of fertility regulation is not limited and direct Government support is provided. Specific measures to improve the distribution of contraceptive information and supplies and encourage less reliance on abortion were being considered in 1989. Sterilization for contraceptive purposes is permitted in certain regions (Croatia, Slovenia) for women above the age of 35. Abortion is permitted on request up to the tenth week of pregnancy and beyond 10 weeks with the approval of a medical commission. In 1988 the Government indicated that the possibility of establishing fertility targets was under consideration.

International migration: The insignificant level of immigration is not an active policy concern of the Government. The Law on Conditions for Entry and Stay of Foreigners and the Law on Employment of Foreign Nationals regulate the residence and employment of non-nationals. Concerning emigration, policies have been implemented to lower the level of emigration and encourage the return of Yugoslavs living abroad. Programmes in the field of socio-economic development of the regions of origin as well as measures concerning employment, tax credits and housing aim to encourage the return of Yugoslavs. The country's scientific and technological development, it is felt, will eventually lead to a reduction of emigration and the return of skilled

professionals. The Government also attempts to improve further the living and
employment conditions of Yugoslavs working abroad as well as the social and
educational links through education, vocational training and provision of
information in their mother tongue.

Spatial distribution/urbanization: To influence internal migration and the
pattern of spatial distribution, a number of measures have been implemented
and include public infrastructure subsidies, grants, loans and tax incentives
to new industries and persons who have relocated, decentralization of
administrative and educational research functions, migration assistance and
employment subsidies and provision of housing and social services. Since the
mid-1980s development of rural resources and management of rural change have
been integrated into the national development strategy and have resulted in a
number of specific policy initiatives and several proposed constitutional
amendments designed to enhance rural policy formulation and implementation.

Status of women and population: The measures adopted by the Government that
aim to improve and equalize the status of women involve the promotion of
education, female employment, benefits for working mothers, and other
measures, taken by the competent authorities in the republics and autonomous
provinces. The legal minimum age at marriage for women is 18 years in all
republics, but a lower limit of 16 years has also been authorized under
certain circumstances.

ZAIRE

DEMOGRAPHIC INDICATORS	CURRENT PERCEPTION
SIZE/AGE STRUCTURE/GROWTH	Levels are viewed as <u>satisfactory</u>.

Population: 1985   2025
(thousands) 30 712 99 512
  0-14 years (%) 46.1 38.4
  60+ years (%) 4.1 5.6
 	
Rate of: 1980-85 2020-25
 growth 3.0 2.3
 natural increase 29.3 22.6	

MORTALITY/MORBIDITY	The mortality and morbidity levels are considered to be <u>unacceptable</u>. Particular concerns are infant and child mortality as well as maternal health.
1980-85 2020-25 Life expectancy 50.0 66.5 Crude death rate 15.8 6.4 Infant mortality 107.0 43.0	
FERTILITY/NUPTIALITY/FAMILY	Fertility rates are perceived as <u>satisfactory</u>.
1980-85 2020-25 Fertility rate 6.1 3.6 Crude birth rate 45.1 29.1 Contraceptive prevalence rate ... ... Female mean age at first marriage 20.1(1975/76)	
INTERNATIONAL MIGRATION	The <u>significant</u> immigration levels are considered to be <u>satisfactory</u>. Emigration is considered to be <u>insignificant</u> and <u>satisfactory</u>.
1980-85 2020-25 Net migration rate 0.0 0.0 Foreign-born population (%) 2.2 (1984)	
SPATIAL DISTRIBUTION/URBANIZATION	Patterns of spatial distribution are viewed as <u>inappropriate</u>.
Urban 1985 2025 population (%) 36.6 64.1 Growth rate: 1980-85 2020-25 urban 4.4 3.3 rural 2.3 0.6	

GENERAL POLICY FRAMEWORK

<u>Overall approach to population problems</u>: Policies have been implemented to improve national welfare, promote public health, establish training, education and information programmes on population, promote the status of women and encourage child-spacing activities.

<u>Importance of population policy in achieving development objectives</u>: In mid-1989 a draft population policy was adopted by the National Population Committee (CONAPOP) and sent to the Executive Council for approval. The Council requested various clarifications and as of October 1989, CONAPOP was preparing to resubmit the draft to the Council. National development policies, plans and programmes are based on an integrated approach, which takes into account the relationship between population, resources and the environment.

INSTITUTIONAL FRAMEWORK

<u>Population data systems and development planning</u>: The country's first population census was conducted in 1984. Previously, only sample surveys had been undertaken. Vital registration of births and deaths is incomplete. Projects are under way to improve the vital registration system and develop a permanent registry containing data on population movements. Demographic research is conducted by the Department of Demography of the University of Kinshasa and the National Institute of Statistics. Implementation of the country's first Five-Year Development Plan (1986-1990), prepared by the Département du Plan, has been hampered by prevailing economic conditions.

<u>Integration of population within development planning</u>: The National Population Committee, an advisory agency of the Executive Council, is responsible for assisting the Council in drafting and implementing a population policy. In addition, it evaluates population-related programmes and projects concerning the impact of demographic growth on meeting basic population needs, the influence of demographic evolution on the fulfilment of economic and social development objectives and the integration of demographic variables in development planning. The Co-ordination Unit for Population Activities functions as the co-ordination branch of the National Population Committee. To assist the Government in the implementation and formulation of population policies and in the integration of demographic variables in development planning, international assistance was initiated in 1988 for the creation of a population planning unit.

ZAIRE

POLICIES AND MEASURES

Changes in population size and age structure: While the Government has not reported any policies intended to influence population growth directly, various policies with demographic consequences have been implemented. Such policies include the Desired Births Programme, the goal of which is the improvement of child-spacing practices and the reduction of infant mortality. The national pension scheme covers employed persons, while voluntary coverage is available to the unemployed under certain conditions.

Mortality and morbidity: The strengthening of a unified and integrated health system based on the primary health-care approach is the foundation for the country's national health strategy. The objective is to increase primary health-care coverage to 60 per cent of the population. It was hoped that by 1990, the country would be divided into 306 health districts, with each district providing preventive and curative health care. A health manpower development plan was formulated in the mid-1980s. One of the goals was to increase health-care personnel from 21,000 in 1982 to 35,000 by 1990. A target of 80 per cent immunization coverage of all children under the age of one by the year 1991 has been specified. In 1987 the Government launched an extensive anti-AIDS campaign which placed particular emphasis on education and information campaigns, as well as medical training for health personnel, the improvement of case identification and the protection of blood supplies, epidemiological surveillance and the improvement of laboratory diagnosis of AIDS and treatment for patients who have contracted the disease.

Fertility and the family: The Government does not intervene to influence the level of fertility. However, it recognizes the need to assist families in achieving the desired spacing of births and desired family size. Two components of the Desired Births Programme, the Rural Health Project undertaken in 1982 and the Desired Births Service Project undertaken in 1983, are providing family planning services. The Government gives direct support for the provision of contraceptive services. Abortion is illegal and considered to be an infraction of the Penal Code.

International migration: Concerning the significant level of immigration, regulations were issued in 1987 that permit employers to recruit non-nationals only when a suitable national cannot be found. Firms hiring non-nationals must then train at least one national during the expatriate's period of employment. According to government statistics there were an estimated 345,000 refugees, mostly from Angola, living in Zaire and concentrated in the Shaba, Bas-Zaïre and Bandandu regions as of mid-1989. The Office of the United Nations High Commissioner for Refugees has been providing aid to about 54,000 refugees in the form of assistance for agricultural development in order to facilitate local integration.

Spatial distribution/urbanization: The country's spatial distribution policy is based on a strategy of "foyers de développement", which among other measures includes agricultural development in regions selected by the Departments of Planning and Agriculture. To improve the living conditions of the population, particularly in cities, a Department of Town Planning and Housing was created. As of 1988, a study was under way to ensure consistency between Zaire's Land Act, which governs land and land-use rights both for private individuals and the public sector, and town planning regulations. An eventual overhaul of the real estate taxation system is expected to ensure a better balance between taxation and the urban services provided.

<u>Status of women and population</u>: The Government reported in 1988 that in general, women in Zaire enjoy equality with men and that there is no major discrimination against women. The Research Bureau created within the Department of Women's Affairs is charged with studying women's living conditions and seeking appropriate solutions to the problems encountered by women. Its functions include assisting women, through appropriate means, to increase their financial resources and productive capacity in order to improve their living conditions. In addition, it attempts to lighten women's work-loads by developing and popularizing appropriate technology and persuading men to play a more active role in food production and crop transport, activities in which women are extensively involved.

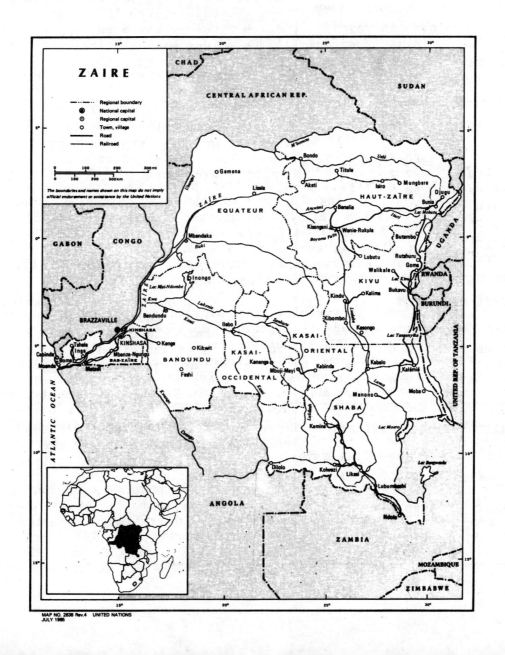

ZAMBIA

DEMOGRAPHIC INDICATORS	CURRENT PERCEPTION

SIZE/AGE STRUCTURE/GROWTH
 	
 Population: **1985**   **2025**
  (thousands) 7 007 25 466
   0-14 years (%) 48.7   38.0
   60+ years (%)   3.8   4.8
 	
 Rate of: **1980-85 2020-25**
  growth   4.0   .2.3
  natural increase 35.9 22.6
	The Government considers the rate of population growth to be <u>unsatisfactory</u> because it is <u>too high</u>.

MORTALITY/MORBIDITY **1980-85 2020-25** Life expectancy 51.4 67.2 Crude death rate 14.9 5.7 Infant mortality 88.0 31.0	Levels and trends are considered to be <u>unacceptable</u>. There is concern over the death rates of children, especially those in the first year of life.

FERTILITY/NUPTIALITY/FAMILY
 	
              1980-85 2020-25
 Fertility rate   7.2   3.6
 Crude birth rate 50.8   28.3
 Contraceptive
  prevalence rate ...   ...
 Female mean age
  at first marriage 19.4 (1980)
	The Government perceives the fertility rate as <u>unsatisfactory</u> and <u>too high</u> and expresses special concern over fertility among adolescents.

INTERNATIONAL MIGRATION
 	
              1980-85 2020-25
 Net migration rate 0.0   0.0
 Foreign-born
  population (%)   3.8 (1980)
	The level of immigration is considered to be <u>significant</u> and <u>too high</u>. The flow of refugees into the country is a concern. Emigration is perceived to be <u>insignificant</u> and <u>satisfactory</u>.

SPATIAL DISTRIBUTION/URBANIZATION
 	
 Urban   **1985**   **2025**
  population (%) 49.5   77.9
 	
 Growth rate: **1980-85 2020-25**
  urban   6.9   2.8
  rural   1.5   0.5
	Patterns of spatial distribution are considered to be <u>inappropriate</u>. Concern is expressed over rural migration to metropolitan areas.

GENERAL POLICY FRAMEWORK

Overall approach to population problems: In 1989 the Government assumed a more assertive role in dealing with population and adopted a population policy to lower population growth and fertility. In addition, the policy aims to improve maternal and child health, to reduce rural-to-urban migration, to strengthen the demographic data base and to integrate women more fully into the development process.

Importance of population policy in achieving development objectives: Recognizing the importance of population factors in the overall development process, a population policy was announced in 1989 as part of the new development plan for 1989-1993. To achieve its development objectives, the new policy among other things aims to integrate population into development planning and plan implementation.

INSTITUTIONAL FRAMEWORK

Population data systems and development planning: Since the country's independence, two national population censuses have been conducted, one in 1969 and the latest in 1980. A sample population census was undertaken in 1974. The next census had been scheduled for 1990. Vital statistics registration is considered incomplete. The Central Statistical Office, under the National Commission for Development Planning, is responsible for the collection and analysis of most population data. Four national development plans have been conducted since 1965. The National Development Plan for 1987-1991 was suspended and replaced by a New Economic Recovery National Development Plan for 1987-1988, which has been superseded by the Fourth Four-Year National Development Plan for the period 1989-1993.

Integration of population within development planning: Under the country's new population policy, the National Commission for Development Planning (NCDP) will serve as the secretariat of the newly created National Population Commission and will work closely with all ministries and private sector agencies involved in population activities to ensure that the policy is fully implemented. In May 1989 NCDP organized a National Conference on Population Policy as a first step in implementing the new policy.

POLICIES AND MEASURES

Changes in population size and age structure: Aware of the detrimental impact that high population growth rates were having on the country's development, a policy was implemented in 1989 to lower the rate of growth. Lower growth is to be achieved by expanding family planning programmes, improving maternal and child health, introducing population education into women's development

ZAMBIA

projects and integrating women more fully into the development process. The national pension scheme covers employed persons, including agricultural workers, domestic servants in urban areas, apprentices and public employees, while excluding casual workers, the self-employed and workers in co-operatives. Voluntary affiliation is available for those excluded from compulsory coverage.

Mortality and morbidity: A national health strategy has been undertaken to accelerate health-care delivery with community participation. Efforts to reduce mortality and morbidity have emphasized preventive rather than curative medicine. Programmes are under way in child immunization, oral rehydration therapy and prevention of communicable diseases. Provision of pre-natal, antenatal and post-natal care is being upgraded, as well as rural sanitation and potable water programmes. To promote primary health-care awareness and child survival programmes, the Ministry of Health has arranged theatre productions in towns, villages and schools. For victims of AIDS, various services are available such as individual counselling in clinics with follow-up and within the victims' family and community. For the purposes of promoting safe sex practices and to allay fears of transmission by casual contact, educational programmes have been established. A target has been specified to reduce infant mortality to 75 deaths per thousand live births by 1993.

Fertility and the family: One of the important components of the population policy adopted in 1989 is the reduction of fertility. This is to be accomplished by extending coverage of family planning services to all adults, increasing the percentage of family planning acceptors to 50 per cent, renovating 45 health centres, integrating family planning into the training curricula of all health personnel and increasing the number of family health nurses trained in family planning to 1,476. Information, education and communication campaigns are also under way. Population education has been introduced in schools and a programme in family life education has been widened to provide family planning in factories. Abortion is available on medical and social grounds. The target is a total fertility rate of 4.0 by 1993.

International migration: The Government is concernerd by undocumented migration and the substantial number of refugees in the country. As of mid-1989, there were some 137,000 refugees in Zambia. The Government recognizes most of the refugees and grants them either permanent or temporary status upon arrival, depending on circumstances. Government policy calls for the resettlement of all refugees at designated refugee centres, but this has not always been logistically possible. Many refugees remain spontaneously settled in rural areas. The emigration of professionals and skilled workers has also been acknowledged as an official concern.

Spatial distribution/urbanization: Since independence, population distribution has been a priority in development plans. The major problem faced by the Government is rural migration towards the metropolitan area and the Copper-Belt cities. In order to retain households in the widely scattered rural areas and to induce them to accept agriculture and other related activities as permanent employment, a policy of village regrouping has been conducted, knitting together isolated human settlements into viable community groups.

The Government also promotes agricultural co-operatives in the rural areas, controls industrial location, decentralizes administrative services and redirects investment from large urban centres to smaller towns and rural areas.

Status of women and population: The Government is concerned about the low levels of participation in education, employment and other socio-economic development activities among women. The Women's Unit within the National Commission for Development Planning is undertaking various studies on the status of women and their role in national development, for the purpose of providing planners and policy makers with the base-line data necessary to formulate policies and programmes dealing with women. It is expected that the findings will be reviewed and recommendations made by a national seminar in 1990. Subsequently, programmes to improve the status of women will be incorporated into the national development plan for 1993-1996. The minimum legal age at marriage for women is 21 years.

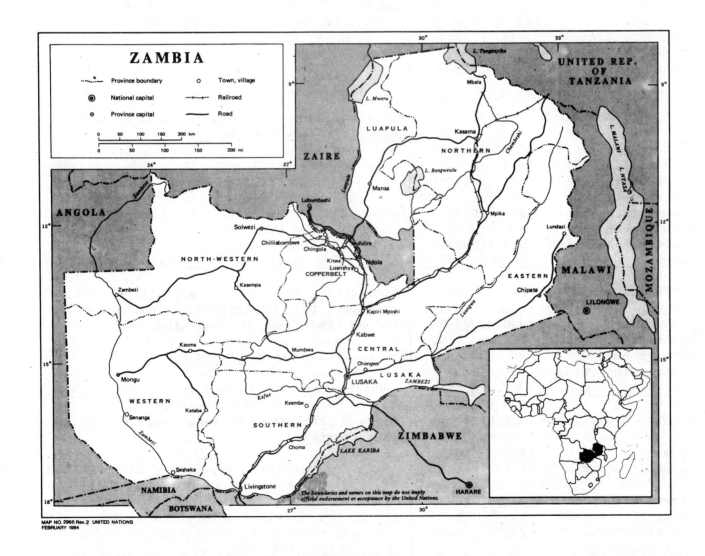

ZIMBABWE

DEMOGRAPHIC INDICATORS	CURRENT PERCEPTION
SIZE/AGE STRUCTURE/GROWTH Population: 1985 2025 (thousands) 8 304 22 621 0–14 years (%) 46.3 30.5 60+ years (%) 4.3 7.4 Rate of: 1980-85 2020-25 growth 3.0 1.6 natural increase 30.8 16.0	The Government considers that its population growth rate is <u>unsatisfactory</u> because it is <u>too high</u>.
MORTALITY/MORBIDITY 1980-85 2020-25 Life expectancy 55.8 71.7 Crude death rate 11.7 5.0 Infant mortality 80.0 28.0	Levels and trends are considered to be <u>unacceptable</u>. Maternal and infant mortality are of particular concern.
FERTILITY/NUPTIALITY/FAMILY 1980-85 2020-25 Fertility rate 6.2 2.5 Crude birth rate 42.5 21.1 Contraceptive prevalence rate 38.4 (1984) Female mean age at first marriage 20.4 (1982)	Levels and trends are considered to be <u>unsatisfactory</u> and <u>too high</u>.
INTERNATIONAL MIGRATION 1980-85 2020-25 Net migration rate 0.0 0.0 Foreign-born population (%) 7.6 (1982)	Immigration is viewed as <u>significant</u> and <u>satisfactory</u>. Emigration is considered to be <u>significant</u> and <u>too high</u>.
SPATIAL DISTRIBUTION/URBANIZATION Urban 1985 2025 population (%) 24.6 54.1 Growth rate: 1980-85 2020-25 urban 5.3 3.0 rural 2.3 0.0	Current patterns are considered to be <u>inappropriate</u>.

GENERAL POLICY FRAMEWORK

Overall approach to population problems: The Government has expressed
concern over the country's demographic situation and has indicated its
desire to reduce the population growth rate by reducing fertility.
Measures are being taken to expand health services in rural areas and to
repatriate refugees.

Importance of population policy in achieving development objectives: The
Government believes that it must seek to achieve a definable relationship
between population growth and the country's capacity to provide its
growing population progressively with material requirements and other
essential services at an adequate level.

INSTITUTIONAL FRAMEWORK

Population data systems and development planning: The first comprehensive
census was carried out in 1982, which was followed by several household
surveys. A census has been provisionally scheduled for 1992.
Census-taking is the responsibility of the Central Statistical Office.
New regulations issued in 1989 to enable village headmen to verify births
and deaths should help to improve the vital registration system by
simplifying the registration process. The first Five-Year National
Development Plan for the period 1986-1990 was prepared by the Ministry of
Finance, Economic Planning and Development.

Integration of population within development planning: The Central
Statistical Office is responsible for taking into account population
variables in development planning, for making population projections and
conducting demographic surveys. A Population Planning Unit (PPU) was
established in 1986. The role of PPU is to furnish information on the
country's demographic dynamics to population planners and policy makers,
provide training for population planners and other officials, and promote
studies of key population and development interrelationships. It is
hoped that in the future PPU will act as a focal point for the dialogue
between the central planning organ of the Government and sectoral planning
ministries with a view to achieving harmony in the planning process and
promoting population activities in the country.

POLICIES AND MEASURES

Changes in population size and age structure: The policy to reduce the rate
of population growth is being implemented through measures to lower fertility
and infant and child mortality and to adjust the spatial distribution
pattern. In particular, family planning programmes have been expanded, a
major immunization campaign has been set up and a programme to upgrade 450
clinics to the level of health centres has been established by the Ministry of
Health. Information on the status of the national pension scheme is not
readily available.

ZIMBABWE

Mortality and morbidity: The Government is firmly committed to the goal of achieving Health for All by the Year 2000 and launched its primary health-care programme in 1982. The objective is for everyone to be within eight miles of a rural health centre. As of 1987, 163 health centres were constructed, while 450 primary health care clinics were being upgraded to rural health centres with facilities for the provision of mother and child care, delivery of complicated births, family planning, immunization, environmental sanitation and curative care. Village Health Workers (VHW) selected by the local communities are the link between the community and the local health service and are responsible for preventive and educational activities as well as for the treatment of simple conditions. AIDS is considered by the Government to be a major concern.

Fertility and the family: The Government has established the Family Planning and Child Spacing Council, which deals with information on birth control, the need for child-spacing and its benefits to the mother and the general well-being of the family. A project was undertaken to increase the availability of family planning services, improve the health status of mothers and children, and strengthen the Government's institutional capacity to plan, manage and evaluate maternal and child-health and family planning services. A major concern is fertility among adolescents, which has led to the establishment of the following programmes: youth counselling and advisory services and family life education in schools. Harare Hospital is now providing family planning services and home visits for high-risk patients. Abortion is legal only in cases where the life or health of the mother is at risk or in the case of rape, incest or serious physical or mental impairment of the foetus. Sterilization for women is permitted depending on age, marital status and parity.

International migration: Zimbabwe is facing problems as a consequence of the influx of refugees who are living on the northern and eastern borders of the country under extreme conditions of poverty and starvation. It is estimated that as of mid-1989, 175,000 refugees, mostly Mozambican asylum-seekers, were in Zimbabwe. The Government is aware that it is unable to house and offer medical care and employment to those refugees and has thus set up the following measures to encourage repatriation: creating camps for displaced non-residents and arranging repatriation through the Ministry of Foreign Affairs; checking the status of refugees living in the country, especially those who are employed; and ensuring that visitors leave the country after their visit by issuance of appropriate restrictive permits. Concerning emigration, the Government does not have a policy of encouraging the return of citizens who have emigrated. Former citizens who held dual citizenship beyond November 1985 were deemed to have lost their citizenship by default, but retained their domicile in the country.

Spatial distribution/urbanization: The Government is striving to achieve a better balance between population and resources while decreasing migration into the metropolitan and urban areas. There has been a notable rural development campaign emphasizing reconstruction and the resettlement of thousands of people. To improve the living conditions of those in communal areas, land reform measures were envisaged that would lead to a more efficient use of land, while maintaining a balance between development and the protection of the environment. The first Five-Year Development Plan established a goal of resettling 15,000 families each year during the period 1986-1990.

<u>Status of women and population</u>: With increasing urbanization and modernization the role of women has taken on a new perspective. The Age of Marriage Act was introduced in 1985 which gives women the right to sue their husbands or lovers for damages and gives them the right to seek custody of their children. The Zimbabwean Institute of Management in collaboration with the Ministry of Community Development and Women's Affairs, conducted a workshop for female managers of development programmes. The minimum legal age at marriage for women is 18 years.

MAP NO. 3200 UNITED NATIONS
DECEMBER 1982

SELECTED REFERENCES

Except for the indicators mentioned below, the source of the demographic estimates and projections is World Population Prospects, 1988 (United Nations publication, Sales No. E.88.XIII.7). Additional information on demographic estimates and projections may also be found in the companion publications Global Estimates and Projections of Population by Sex and Age: The 1988 Revision (ST/ESA/SER.R/93) and Prospects of World Urbanization, 1988 (United Nations publication, Sales No. E.89.XIII.8). For several countries, recent political upheavals have had considerable impact on their demographic phenomena. Therefore, the demographic estimates and projections cited for such countries should be used with caution.

It should also be noted that the estimates of international migration are the most problematic of the demographic estimates due to the shortage of appropriate data. Even more uncertain are the projected rates of international migration, shown in this publication for the period 2020-2025. As international migration is influenced greatly by social, economic and political conditions in countries of origin and destination, projecting future trends in international migration is a highly risky undertaking. In the United Nations projections, it is assumed that the volume of net migration will progressively move to zero as time passes except for those countries for which the evidence strongly suggests a continuation of current migration levels for a considerable time into the future (for example, Australia, Canada, Mexico and the United States).

Replies from Governments to a United Nations questionnaire entitled "Sixth Population Inquiry among Governments: monitoring of Government perceptions and policies on demographic trends and levels in relation to development as of 1987", where received, constitute important sources for the individual country narratives. (Annex II lists those countries that have responded to the six questionnaires.) The results of the Sixth Population Inquiry have been published (ST/ESA/SER.R/104).

Figures on the contraceptive prevalence rate are from Levels and Trends of Contraceptive Use as Assessed in 1988 (United Nations publication, Sales No. E.89.XIII.4). The reader is advised to consult the country-specific notes given below for deviations from the standard age group of 15-49 years for the contraceptive prevalence rate. Information on national pension schemes has for the most part been taken from Social Security Programs Throughout the World - 1987, Research Report No. 61 (Washington, D.C., United States Department of Health and Human Services, Social Security Administration, 1988). The female mean ages at first marriage are from Patterns of First Marriage: Timing and Prevalence (United Nations publication, forthcoming). The source for the minimum legal age at marriage for women is First Marriage: Patterns and Determinants (ST/ESA/SER.R/76), which for some countries has been revised with more recent data.

- 235 -

OMAN

Economic and Social Commission for Western Asia (1987). The Human-Settlements
    Situation in the Sultanate of Oman.

Economic Commission for Western Asia (1981). The Population Situation in the
    ECWA Region: Oman.

Economist Intelligence Unit (1989). Country Report: Bahrain, Qatar, Oman,
    The Yemens, No. 1. London: Economist Publications, p. 24.

Oman Daily Observer, 27 July 1987, p. 2.

World Health Organization (1987). Evaluation of the Strategy for Health for
    All by the Year 2000: Seventh Report on the World Health Situation,
    vol. 6 (Alexandria).

PAKISTAN

United Nations (1988). Bulletin on Aging, vol. VIII, No. 3.

United Nations/United Nations Population Fund (1979). Population policy
    compendium: Pakistan.

United Nations Children's Fund (1988). Country programme recommendation:
    Pakistan (E/ICEF/1988/P/L.21).

United Nations High Commissioner for Refugees (1989). Fact sheet: Pakistan,
    vol. 3, No. 2 (October).

World Health Organization (1986). Evaluation of the Strategy for Health for
    All by the Year 2000: Seventh Report on the World Health Situation,
    vol. 4 (New Delhi).

PANAMA*

República de Panamá, Ministerio de Planificación y Política Económica (1986).
    Algunos antecedentes sobre la Comisión Nacional de Política Demográfica y
    Comité Técnico de Población.

United Nations (1984). Demographic Yearbook, 1983. Sales No. E/F.84.XIII.1.

_____, Committee on the Elimination of Discrimination against Women
    (1982). Initial reports of States Parties: Panama. CEDAW/C/5/Add.9.

---

* Contraceptive prevalence rate is for women aged 15-44.

_____/United Nations Population Fund (1979). Population policy
compendium: Panama.

United Nations Population Fund (1989). Assistance to the Government of
Panama: support for a comprehensive population programme. DP/FPA/CP/57.

World Health Organization (1986). Evaluation of the Strategy for Health for
All by the Year 2000: Seventh Report on the World Health Situation,
vol. 3 (Washington, D.C.).

PAPUA NEW GUINEA*

International Labour Office (1988). Labour and Population Activities in Asia
and the Pacific, No. 32 (June). Bangkok: ILO Labour and Population Team
for Asia and the Pacific.

United Nations/United Nations Population Fund (1984). Population policy
compendium: Papua New Guinea.

United Nations High Commissioner for Refugees (1988). Refugees, Special
issue (December), p. 36.

World Health Organization (1986). Evaluation of the Strategy for Health for
All by the Year 2000: Seventh Report on the World Health Situation,
vol. 7 (Manila).

PARAGUAY**

Pan American Health Organization (1986). Health Conditions in the Americas,
1981-1984, vol. II.

República del Paraguay (1984). Dirección General de Estadística y Censos.
Censo Nacional de Población y Viviendas, 1982.

United Nations (1984). Conferencia Mundial del Decenio de las Naciones Unidas
para la Mujer: cuestionarios para los gobiernos. Parte II: desarrollo
en zonas sectorales. Factores demográficos.

United Nations/United Nations Population Fund (1982). Population policy
compendium: Paraguay.

United Nations Population Fund (1988). Assistance to the Government of
Paraguay: support for a comprehensive population programme.
DP/FPA/CP/43.

---

* Foreign-born population: 1980 census data as cited in Government
reply to the United Nations Demographic Yearbook questionnaire.

** Contraceptive prevalence rate is for women aged 15-44.

PERU

International Planned Parenthood Federation, Western Hemisphere Region (1988). Forum (April).

Pan American Health Organization (1986). Health Conditions in the Americas, 1981-1984, vol. II.

Peru, Consejo Nacional de Población (1988). Boletín, No. 13 (junio).

United Nations (1984). Demographic Yearbook, 1983. Sales No. E/F.84.XIII.1.

_____, Committee on the Elimination of Discrimination against Women (1988). Initial reports of States Parties: Peru. CEDAW/C/5/Add.60.

_____/United Nations Population Fund (1979). Population policy compendium: Peru.

PHILIPPINES*

Philippines, Department of Labor (1989). Philippine Labor (February), p. 24.

United Nations/United Nations Population Fund (1980). Population policy compendium: Philippines.

United Nations High Commissioner for Refugees (1989). Fact sheet: South East Asia, vol. 3, No. 2 (October).

United Nations Population Fund (1989). A new population programme in the Philippines, Populi, vol. 16, No. 1, pp. 4-13.

_____ (1989). Assistance to the Government of the Philippines: support for a comprehensive population programme. DP/FPA/CP/49.

POLAND**

Holzer, Jerzy (1990). International transmission of population policy experience in Eastern Europe. In International Transmission of Population Policy Experience: Proceedings of the Expert Group Meeting on the International Transmission of Population Policy Experience, New York City, 27-30 June 1988. ST/ESA/SER.R/108.

---

* Contraceptive prevalence rate is for women aged 15-44. Foreign-born population: 1980 census data as cited in the Government reply to the United Nations Demographic Yearbook questionnaire.

** Contraceptive prevalence rate is for women under 45 years of age.

International Planned Parenthood Federation (1989). Poland. <u>People</u>, vol. 16, No. 3.

_____, Committee on the Elimination of Discrimination against Women (1989). Second periodic reports of States Parties: Poland. CEDAW/C/13/Add.16.

World Health Organization (1986). <u>Evaluation of the Strategy for Health for All by the Year 2000: Seventh Report on the World Health Situation</u>, vol. 5 (Copenhagen).

PORTUGAL*

Commission of the European Communities (1988). <u>Social Europe</u> (July). Brussels, pp. 38 and 39.

Council of Europe (1986). National replies to the questionnaire: recent developments in family structure and future perspectives, Portugal. Strasbourg.

Organisation for Economic Co-operation and Development (1988). <u>New Trends in Rural Policymaking</u> (Paris), pp. 105-111.

United Nations High Commissioner for Refugees (1988). <u>Refugees</u>, No. 52 (April), pp. 8-12.

QATAR

AL-Najjar, B. S. (1988). Population policies in the countries of the Gulf Co-operation Council: politics and society. <u>Population Policies in the Third World</u>. Twenty-fifth Anniversary Commemorative Conference of Cairo Demographic Centre, 15-18 October.

Economic and Social Commission for Western Asia (1987). <u>Highlights of the Human Settlements Situation in Qatar</u>.

Economic Commission for Western Asia (1980). <u>The Population Situation in the ECWA Region: Qatar</u>.

World Health Organization (1987). <u>Evaluation of the Strategy for Health for All by the Year 2000: Seventh Report on the World Health Situation</u>, vol. 6 (Alexandria).

---

* Foreign-born population: 1980 census data as cited in the Government reply to the United Nations <u>Demographic Yearbook</u> questionnaire.

REPUBLIC OF KOREA*

Economist Intelligence Unit (1988). <u>Country Profile 1988-89: Qatar</u>. London: Economist Publications.

Kim, W. B. (1988). Population redistribution policy in Korea: a review. <u>Population Research and Policy Review</u>, vol. 7.

Song, K-Y. (1988). Health resources and management in Korea: development in the past, current issues and perspectives. <u>Journal of Population and Health Studies</u>, vol. 8, No. 1 (July).

United Nations (1984). <u>Demographic Yearbook, 1983</u>. Sales No. E/F.84.XIII.1.

_____/United Nations Population Fund (1980). Population policy compendium: Republic of Korea.

United Nations Children's Fund (1988). Country programme recommendation: Republic of Korea. E/ICEF/1988/P/L.24.

World Health Organization (1986). <u>Evaluation of the Strategy for Health for All by the Year 2000: Seventh Report on the World Health Situation</u>, vol. 4 (New Delhi).

ROMANIA*

Economic Commission for Europe (1987). La recherche démographique en Roumanie et la collaboration internationale dans ce domaine. Paper presented at the Regional Meeting on Population and Development, Budapest (Hungary), 24-27 February. ECE/AC.16/R.2/Add.2.

International Planned Parenthood Federation (1989). <u>People</u>, vol. 16, No. 3, pp. 10-12.

United Nations, Committee on the Elimination of Discrimination against Women (1987). Initial reports of States Parties: Romania. CEDAW/C/5/Add.45.

World Health Organization (1986). <u>Evaluation of the Strategy for Health for All by the Year 2000: Seventh Report on the World Health Situation</u>, vol. 5 (Copenhagen).

---

* Contraceptive prevalence rate is for women aged 15-44.

RWANDA*

Habimana Nyirasafari, Gaudence (1988). Politiques de population: cadre institutionnel et assistance technique. Paper presented at the African Population Conference, Dakar, 7-12 November.

O'Haire, H. (1988). Land of a thousand hills adopts a population policy. _Populi_, vol. 15, No. 1, pp. 27-34.

United Nations (1984). _Demographic Yearbook, 1983_. Sales No. E/F.84.XIII.1.

_____, Committee on the Elimination of Discrimination against Women (1988). Second periodic reports of States Parties: Rwanda. CEDAW/C/13/Add.13.

United Nations Children's Fund (1988). Country programme recommendation: Rwanda. E/ICEF/1988/P/L.5.

United Nations Population Fund (1987). Assistance to the Government of Rwanda: support for a comprehensive population programme. DP/FPA/CP/29.

World Health Organization (1987). _Evaluation of the Strategy for Health for All by the Year 2000: Seventh Report on the World Health Situation_, vol. 2 (Brazzaville).

SAINT KITTS AND NEVIS**

Population Reference Bureau (1984). St. Kitts/Nevis: yesterday, today and tomorrow. PRB Occasional Series: The Caribbean. Washington, D.C.

United Nations (1984). _Demographic Yearbook, 1983_. Sales No. E/F.84 XIII.1.

United Nations Population Fund (1989). _Inventory of Population Projects in Developing Countries Around the World 1987/88_. Sales No. E.89.III.H.1.

World Health Organization (1986). _Evaluation of the Strategy for Health for All by the Year 2000: Seventh Report on the World Health Situation_, vol. 3 (Washington, D.C.).

---

* Contraceptive prevalence rate for women aged 15-50.

** Contraceptive prevalence rate for women aged 15-44.

SAINT LUCIA*

Caribbean Community Secretariat (1985). 1980-1981 Population Census of the Commonwealth Caribbean: St. Lucia, vol. I.

United Nations Development Programme (1986). Second country programme for St. Lucia. DP/CP/STL/2.

United Nations Population Fund (1989). Inventory of Population Projects in Developing Countries Around the World 1987/88. Sales No. E.89.III.H.1.

World Health Organization (1986). Evaluation of the Strategy for Health for All by the Year 2000: Seventh Report on the World Health Situation, vol. 3 (Washington, D.C.).

SAINT VINCENT AND THE GRENADINES*

Caribbean Community Secretariat (1985). 1980-1981 Population Census of the Commonwealth Caribbean: St. Vincent and the Grenadines, vol. I.

United Nations Development Programme (1986). Second country programme for St. Vincent and the Grenadines. DP/CP/STV/2.

United Nations Population Fund (1989). Inventory of Population Projects in Developing Countries Around the World 1987/88. Sales No. E.89.III.H.1.

World Health Organization (1986). Evaluation of the Strategy for Health for All by the Year 2000: Seventh Report on the World Health Situation, vol. 3 (Washington, D.C.).

SAMOA

Economic and Social Commission for Asia and the Pacific (1985). Development Planning Newsletter, No. 2 (August), pp. 1-3.

United Nations (1987). Directory of National Focal Points for the Advancement of Women in Asia and the Pacific.

_____ (1984). Demographic Yearbook, 1983. Sales No. E/F.84.XIII.1.

United Nations Population Fund (1989). Inventory of Population Projects in Developing Countries Around the World 1987/88. Sales No. E.89.III.H.1.

World Health Organization (1986). Evaluation of the Strategy for Health for All by the Year 2000: Seventh Report on the World Health Situation, vol. 7 (Manila).

---

* Contraceptive prevalence rate is for women aged 15-44.

SAN MARINO

United Nations (1984). <u>Demographic Yearbook, 1983</u>. Sales No. E/F.84.XIII.1.

World Health Organization (1986). <u>Evaluation of the Strategy for Health for All by the Year 2000: Seventh Report on the World Health Situation</u>, vol. 5 (Copenhagen).

SAO TOME AND PRINCIPE*

Economist Intelligence Unit (1989). <u>Country Report: Angola, Sao Tome and Principe</u>, No. 3. London: Economist Publications, pp. 19 and 20.

United Nations Population Fund (1989). <u>Inventory of Population Projects in Developing Countries Around the World 1987/88</u>. Sales No. E.89.III.H.1.

World Health Organization (1987). <u>Evaluation of the Strategy for Health for All by the Year 2000: Seventh Report on the World Health Situation</u>, vol. 2 (Brazzaville).

SAUDI ARABIA

Economic and Social Commission for Western Asia (1987). <u>Highlights of the Human Settlements Situation in Saudi Arabia</u>.

International Labour Organisation (1988). <u>Social and Labour Bulletin</u>, 4/88, pp. 511-513.

United Nations/United Nations Population Fund (1980). Population policy compendium: Saudi Arabia.

World Health Organization (1987). <u>Evaluation of the Strategy for Health for All by the Year 2000: Seventh Report on the World Health Situation</u>, vol. 6 (Alexandria).

SENEGAL

Fonds des Nations Unies pour les activités en matière de population (1989). <u>Rapport de mission sur l'évaluation des besoins d'aide en matière de population: Sénégal</u>. Rapport numéro 96.

Institut du Sahel, Centre d'études et de recherche sur la population pour le développement (1989). <u>Pop Sahel</u>, Numéro 9 (mai), pp. 20-24.

---

* Foreign-born population: 1980 census data as cited in Government reply to United Nations <u>Demographic Yearbook</u> questionnaire.

République du Sénégal (1983). <u>Recensement général de la population d'avril 1976</u>.

United Nations/United Nations Population Fund (1980). Population policy compendium: Senegal.

World Health Organization (1987). <u>Evaluation of the Strategy for Health for All by the Year 2000: Seventh Report on the World Health Situation</u>, vol. 2 (Brazzaville).

SEYCHELLES

Economist Intelligence Unit (1988). <u>Country Profile 1988-89: Seychelles</u> London: Economist Publications, pp. 39-48.

United Nations (1984). <u>Demographic Yearbook, 1983</u>. Sales No. E/F.84.XIII.1.

United Nations Population Fund (1989). <u>Inventory of Population Projects in Developing Countries Around the World 1987/88</u>. Sales No. E.89.III.H.1.

World Health Organization (1987). <u>Evaluation of the Strategy for Health for All by the Year 2000: Seventh Report on the World Health Situation</u>, vol. 2 (Brazzaville).

SIERRA LEONE*

John, G. (1986). Sierra Leone: country statement on the status of discussions, developments on population policy. Paper presented at the Rapid II Workshops on Population Policy/All-Africa Parliamentary Conference on Population and Development, Harare, Zimbabwe, 10-16 May.

United Nations Development Programme (1987). Fourth country programme for Sierra Leone. 22 October. DP/CP/SIL/4.

United Nations Population Fund (1989). <u>Inventory of Population Projects in Developing Countries Around the World 1987/88</u>. Sales No. E.89.III.H.1.

United Nations/United Nations Population Fund (1982). Population policy compendium: Sierra Leone.

World Health Organization (1987). <u>Evaluation of the Strategy for Health for All by the Year 2000: Seventh Report on the World Health Situation</u>, vol. 2 (Brazzaville).

---

* Foreign-born population: 1974 census data as cited in the Government reply to the United Nations <u>Demographic Yearbook</u> questionnaire.

SINGAPORE*

Economic and Social Commission for Asia and the Pacific (1987). <u>Directory of National Focal Points for the Advancement of Women in Asia and the Pacific</u>.

Population Council (1987). Lee Kuan Yew on marriage, education and fertility in Singapore. <u>Population and Development Review</u>, vol. 13, No. 1 (March), pp. 179-185.

United Nations (1984). <u>Demographic Yearbook, 1983</u>. Sales No. E/F.84.XIII.1.

_____/United Nations Population Fund (1982). Population policy compendium: Singapore.

World Health Organization (1986). <u>Evaluation of the Strategy for Health for All by the Year 2000: Seventh Report on the World Health Situation</u>, vol. 7 (Manila).

SOLOMON ISLANDS

Economic and Social Commission for Asia and the Pacific (1987). <u>Directory of National Focal Points for the Advancement of Women in Asia and the Pacific</u>.

_____ (1988). <u>Population Headliners</u> (August), p. 4.

United Nations (1984). <u>Demographic Yearbook, 1983</u>. Sales No. E/F.84.XIII.1.

_____/United Nations Population Fund (1985). Population policy compendium: Solomon Islands.

World Health Organization (1986). <u>Evaluation of the Strategy for Health for All by the Year 2000: Seventh Report on the World Health Situation</u>, vol. 7 (Manila).

SOMALIA

United Nations, General Assembly (1989). Emergency assistance to Somalia: report of the Secretary-General. A/44/261.

_____/United Nations Population Fund (1984). Population policy compendium: Somalia.

United Nations Children's Fund (1988). Country programme recommendation: Somalia. E/ICEF/1988/P/L.6.

_____

* Contraceptive prevalence rate is for women aged 15-44.

United Nations High Commissioner for Refugees (1989). Fact sheet: Somalia,
    vol. 3, No. 2 (October).

World Health Organization (1987). _Evaluation of the Strategy for Health for_
    All by the Year 2000: Seventh Report on the World Health Situation,
    vol. 2 (Brazzaville).

SOUTH AFRICA*

Economist Intelligence Unit (1988). _Country Report: South Africa_, No. 1.
    London: Economist Publications, pp. 9 and 10.

Republic of South Africa, Department of Development Planning (1989).
    Annual Report, 1988.

_____ (1988). _White Paper on Urbanisation._

World Health Organization (1987). _Evaluation of the Strategy for Health for_
    All by the Year 2000: Seventh Report on the World Health Situation,
    vol. 2 (Brazzaville).

SPAIN**

Gobierno de España (1985). _Censo de Población de 1981. Resultados_
    Nacionales, tomo I.

International Labour Organisation (1989). _Social and Labour Bulletin,_ 1/89,
    pp. 88 and 89.

Naciones Unidas, Comité para la Eliminación de la Discriminación contra
    la Mujer (1989). Segundos informes periódicos de los Estados Partes:
    España. CEDAW/C/13/Add.19.

Organisation for Economic Co-operation and Development (1988). _New Trends in_
    Rural Policymaking. Paris, pp. 55-60.

United Nations High Commissioner for Refugees (1988). _Refugees_, No. 50
    (March), pp. 8-12, 42 and 43.

World Health Organization (1986). _Evaluation of the Strategy for Health for_
    All by the Year 2000: Seventh Report on the World Health Situation,
    vol. 5 (Copenhagen).

---

     * Contraceptive prevalence rate is for women under 50 years of age.
Foreign-born population: 1985 census data as cited in the Government reply to
the United Nations _Demographic Yearbook_ questionnaire.

     ** Contraceptive prevalence rate is for women aged 18-49.

SRI LANKA

United Nations (1984). <u>Demographic Yearbook, 1983</u>. Sales No. E/F.84.XIII.1.

_____, Committee on the Elimination of Discrimination against Women (1989). Second periodic reports of States Parties, Sri Lanka. CEDAW/C/13/Add.18.

_____/United Nations Population Fund (1979). Population policy compendium: Sri Lanka.

United Nations Population Fund (1989). <u>Inventory of Population Projects in Developing Countries Around the World 1987/88</u>. Sales No. E.89.III.H.1.

World Health Organization (1986). <u>Evaluation of the Strategy for Health for All by the Year 2000: Seventh Report on the World Health Situation</u>, vol. 7 (Manila).

SUDAN*

United Nations/United Nations Population Fund (1979). Population policy compendium: Sri Lanka.

United Nations High Commissioner for Refugees (1989). Fact Sheet: Sudan, vol. 3, No. 2 (October).

United Nations Population Fund (1987). Assistance to the Government of the Sudan: support for a comprehensive population programme. DP/FPA/CP/22.

_____ (1989). <u>Inventory of Population Projects in Developing Countries Around the World 1987/88</u>. Sales No. E.89.III.H.1.

World Health Organization (1987). <u>Evaluation of the Strategy for Health for All by the Year 2000: Seventh Report on the World Health Situation</u>, vol. 2 (Brazzaville).

SURINAME

Pan American Health Organization (1986). <u>Health Conditions in the Americas, 1981-1984</u>, vol. II.

United Nations High Commissioner for Refugees (1989). Fact sheet: South America, vol. 3, No. 2 (October).

_____ (1987). <u>Refugees</u>, No. 38 (February), pp. 9 and 10.

United Nations Population Fund (1989). <u>Inventory of Population Projects in Developing Countries Around the World 1987/88</u>. Sales No. E.89.III.H.1.

---

* Contraceptive prevalence rate is only for the northern part of the country.

SWAZILAND

United Nations (1984). Demographic Yearbook, 1983. Sales No. E/F.84.XIII.1).

_____/United Nations Population Fund (1985). Population policy compendium: Swaziland.

United Nations Children's Fund (1988). Country programme recommendation: Swaziland. E/ICEF/1988/P/L.7.

United Nations High Commissioner for Refugees (1989). Fact sheet: Swaziland, vol. 3, No. 2 (October).

World Health Organization (1987). Evaluation of the Strategy for Health for All by the Year 2000: Seventh Report on the World Health Situation, vol. 2 (Brazzaville).

SWEDEN*

Council of Europe (1986). National replies to the questionnaire, recent developments in family structure and future perspectives: Sweden. Strasbourg.

Organisation for Economic Co-operation and Development (1988). New Trends in Rural Policymaking. Paris, pp. 117-123.

United Nations, Committee on the Elimination of Discrimination against Women (1987). Second periodic reports of States Parties: Sweden. CEDAW/C/13/Add.6.

United Nations High Commissioner for Refugees (1989). Fact sheet: Nordic countries, vol. 3, No. 2 (October).

World Health Organization (1986), Evaluation of the Strategy for Health for All by the Year 2000: Seventh Report on the World Health Situation, vol. 5 (Copenhagen).

---

* Contraceptive prevalence rate is for women aged 20-44. Foreign-born population: 1985 census data as cited in the Government reply to the United Nations Demographic Yearbook questionnaire.

SWITZERLAND*

Organisation for Economic Co-operation and Development (1988). <u>New Trends in Rural Policymaking</u>. Paris, pp. 117-123.

United Nations (1984). <u>Demographic Yearbook, 1983</u>. Sales No. E/F.84.XIII.1.

United Nations High Commissioner for Refugees (1989). <u>Refugees</u>, No. 61 (February), pp. 14-16.

World Health Organization (1986). <u>Evaluation of the Strategy for Health for All by the Year 2000: Seventh Report on the World Health Situation</u>, vol. 5 (Copenhagen).

SYRIAN ARAB REPUBLIC

United Nations/United Nations Population Fund (1980). Population policy compendium: Syrian Arab Republic.

United Nations Population Fund (1985). <u>Report of Second Mission on Needs Assessment for Population Assistance: Syrian Arab Republic</u>. Report No. 77.

_____ (1987). <u>Population</u> (November).

World Health Organization (1987). <u>Evaluation of the Strategy for Health for All by the Year 2000: Seventh Report on the World Health Situation</u>, vol. 6 (Alexandria).

THAILAND

Chamrathrithirong, A. (1987). Case study of national policy and implementation. Thailand. Paper prepared for the International Forum on Population Policies in Development Planning, Mexico City, 4-7 May. M/WD/E/10.

Thailand, National Economic and Social Development Board (1986). <u>Summary: The Sixth National Economic and Social Development Plan (1986-1991)</u> (Bangkok).

United Nations (1984). <u>Demographic Yearbook, 1983</u>. Sales No. E/F.84.XIII.1.

_____ (1987). <u>Population Growth and Policies in Mega-cities: Bangkok</u>. Population Policy Paper No. 10. ST/ESA/SER.R/72.

----

* Contraceptive prevalence rate is for a sample of women married between 1970 and 1979.

United Nations High Commissioner for Refugees (1989). Fact sheet: South East Asia, vol. 3, No. 1 (April).

United Nations Population Fund (1987). Assistance to the Government of Thailand: support for a comprehensive population programme. DP/FPA/CP/1.

_____ (1988). Report of Third Mission on Needs Assessment for Population Assistance: Thailand. Report No. 92.

World Health Organization (1986). Evaluation of the Strategy for Health for All by the Year 2000, Seventh Report on the World Health Situation, vol. 4 (New Delhi).

TOGO*

United Nations/United Nations Population Fund (1985). Population policy compendium: Togo.

United Nations High Commissioner for Refugees (1989). Fact sheet: West Africa, vol. 3, No. 1 (April).

United Nations Population Fund (1989). Population (July), p. 1.

World Health Organization (1987). Evaluation of the Strategy for Health for All by the Year 2000: Seventh Report on the World Health Situation, vol. 2 (Brazzaville).

TONGA

Economic and Social Commission for Asia and the Pacific (1987). Directory of National Focal Points for the Advancement of Women in Asia and the Pacific.

United Nations (1984). Demographic Yearbook, 1983. Sales No. E/F.84.XIII.1.

United Nations Population Fund (1989). Inventory of Population Projects in Developing Countries Around the World 1987/88. Sales No. E.89.III.H.1.

World Health Organization (1986). Evaluation of the Strategy for Health for All by the Year 2000: Seventh Report on the World Health Situation, vol. 7 (Manila).

_____

* Contraceptive prevalence rate includes post-partum abstinence.

TRINIDAD AND TOBAGO

Mynard, Glenda (1988). Case study on Trinidad and Tobago. Paper presented at the United Nations Expert Group Meeting on Social Support Measures for the Advancement of Women, Vienna, 14-18 November. ECM/SSMAW/1988.CS.14.

Pan American Health Organization (1986). Health Conditions in the Americas, 1981-1984, vol. II.

Republic of Trinidad and Tobago, Central Statistical Office (1983). Population and Housing Census, 1980, vol. 4.

United Nations (1989). Committee on Economic, Social and Cultural Rights concludes examination of reports of Trinidad and Tobago. Press release HR/3399 (21 February).

_____/United Nations Population Fund (1983). Population policy compendium: Trinidad and Tobago.

TUNISIA*

AL-Zarifa, E. and M. El-Zawaghi (1988). Some aspects of population policy in Tunisia. Population Policies in the Third World. Twenty-fifth Anniversary Commemorative Conference of Cairo Demographic Centre, 15-18 October.

International Labour Office (1988). Social and Labour Bulletin, 1/88, pp. 97-99.

République tunisienne, Institut National de la Statistique (1985). Recensement Général de la Population et de l'Habitat, 1984.

United Nations/United Nations Population Fund (1981). Population policy compendium: Tunisia.

World Health Organization (1987). Evaluation of the Strategy for Health for All by the Year 2000: Seventh Report on the World Health Situation, vol. 6 (Alexandria).

---

* Foreign-born population: data are reported by nationality rather than by place of birth.

TURKEY*

Organisation for Economic Co-operation and Development (1988). New Trends in Rural Policymaking. Paris, pp. 131-136.

United Nations (1990). Committee on Elimination of Discrimination against Women hears Turkey's response to questions. Press release WOM/537 (31 January).

_____/United Nations Population Fund (1980). Population policy compendium: Turkey.

United Nations Children's Fund (1988). Country programme recommendation: Turkey. E/ICEF/1988/P/L.30.

United Nations Population Fund (1988). Report of Second Mission on Needs Assessment for Population Assistance: Turkey. Report No. 97.

TUVALU

United Nations Development Programme (1988). World Development (November), pp. 25-28.

United Nations Population Fund (1989). Inventory of Population Projects in Developing Countries Around the World 1987/88. Sales No. E.89.III.H.1.

World Health Organization (1986). Evaluation of the Strategy for Health for All by the Year 2000: Seventh Report on the World Health Situation, vol. 7 (Manila).

UGANDA

United Nations High Commissioner for Refugees (1989). Fact sheet: Uganda, vol. 3, No. 2 (October).

United Nations Population Fund (1988). Assistance to the Government of Uganda: support for a comprehensive population programme. DP/FPA/CP/40.

_____ (1989). Population (November), p. 1.

World Health Organization (1987). Evaluation of the Strategy for Health for All by the Year 2000: Seventh Report on the World Health Situation, vol. 2 (Brazzaville).

---

* Contraceptive prevalence rate is for women under the age of 50.

UKRAINIAN SOVIET SOCIALIST REPUBLIC

United Nations, Committee on the Elimination of Discrimination against Women (1983). Initial reports of States Parties: Ukrainian SSR. CEDAW/C/5/Add.11.

_____ (1987). Second periodic reports of States Parties: Ukrainian SSR. CEDAW/C/13/Add.8.

World Health Organization (1986). Evaluation of the Strategy for Health for All by the Year 2000: Seventh Report on the World Health Situation, vol. 5 (Copenhagen).

UNION OF SOVIET SOCIALIST REPUBLICS

Demko, G. (1987). The Soviet settlement system – current issues and future prospects. Soviet Geography, vol. XXVIII, No. 10 (December).

International Labour Office (1986). Social and Labour Bulletin, vol. 2, p. 219.

Population Council (1987). Mikhail Gorbachev on women and the family. Population and Development Review, vol. 13, No. 4 (December), pp. 757-759.

United Nations, Committee on the Elimination of Discrimination against Women (1987). Second periodic reports of States Parties: Union of Soviet Socialist Republics. CEDAW/C/13/Add.4.

World Health Organization (1986). Evaluation of the Strategy for Health for All by the Year 2000: Seventh Report on the World Health Situation, vol. 5 (Copenhagen).

UNITED ARAB EMIRATES

Economic and Social Commission for Western Asia (1987). The Human Settlements Situation in the United Arab Emirates (E/ESCWA/HS/87/3).

Economic Commission for Western Asia (1981). The Population Situation in the ECWA Region: United Arab Emirates.

United Nations (1984). Demographic Yearbook, 1983. Sales No. E/F.84.XIII.1.

United Nations Population Fund (1986). Report of Mission on Needs Assessment for Population Assistance: The United Arab Emirates. Report No. 82.

World Health Organization (1987). Evaluation of the Strategy for Health for All by the Year 2000: Seventh Report on the World Health Situation, vol. 6 (Alexandria).

UNITED KINGDOM OF GREAT BRITAIN AND NORTHERN IRELAND*

Organisation for Economic Co-operation and Development (1988). New Trends in Rural Policymaking. Paris, pp. 112-116.

Silverman, J. and E. Jones (1988). The delivery of family planning and health services in Great Britain. Family Planning Perspectives, vol. 20, No. 2 (March/April).

United Nations (1989). Committee on Economic, Social and Cultural Rights examines report of the United Kingdom. Press release HR/3398 (17 February).

_____ (1984). Demographic Yearbook, 1983. Sales No. E/F.84.XIII.1.

Whitehead, Frank E. (1988). Population policy in the United Kingdom. Paper presented at the United Nations/International Union for the Scientific Study of Population Expert Group Meeting on the International Transmission of Population Policy Experience, New York, 27-30 June.

World Health Organization (1986). Evaluation of the Strategy for Health for All by the Year 2000: Seventh Report on the World Health Situation, vol. 5 (Copenhagen).

UNITED REPUBLIC OF TANZANIA**

United Nations (1989). Case Studies in Population Policy: United Republic of Tanzania. ST/ESA/SER.R/91.

_____, Committee on the Elimination of Discrimination against Women (1988). Initial reports of States Parties: United Republic of Tanzania. CEDAW/C/5/Add.57.

_____/United Nations Population Fund (1980). Population policy compendium: United Republic of Tanzania.

United Nations High Commissioner for Refugees (1989). Fact sheet: Tanzania, vol. 3, No. 2 (October).

Warioba, Christine (1988). Case study on Tansania. Paper presented at the United Nations Expert Group Meeting on Social Support Measures for the Advanvecement of Women, Vienna, 14-18 November. ECM/SSMAW/1988/CS.10.

---

* Contraceptive prevalence rate is for women aged 18-44.

** Foreign-born population: 1978 census data as cited in the Government reply to the United Nations Demographic Yearbook questionnaire.

UNITED STATES OF AMERICA*

Organisation for Economic Co-operation and Development (1988). New Trends in Rural Policymaking. Paris, pp. 61-65.

Pan American Health Organization (1986). Health Conditions in the Americas, 1981-1984, vol. II.

Sullivan, L. (1989). The health care priorities of the Bush Administration. New England Journal of Medicine, vol. 321, No. 2 (13 July).

United States, Department of Commerce (1984). 1980 Census of Population. Washington, D.C.

_____, Department of State (1989). World Refugee Report. Washington, D.C..

URUGUAY

Pan American Health Organization (1986). Health Conditions in the Americas, 1981-1984, vol. II.

República del Uruguay, Dirección General de Estadística y Censos (1988). VI Censo de Población y IV de Viviendas.

United Nations/United Nations Population Fund (1982). Population policy compendium: Uruguay.

United Nations High Commissioner for Refugees (1986). Refugees, No. 25 (January), pp. 28 and 29.

United Nations Population Fund (1987). Concern rises as Uruguay's birth rate falls. Population (December).

VANUATU**

United Nations Conference on Trade and Development (1989). The Least Developed Countries: 1988 Report.

United Nations Population Fund (1989). 1988 Report by the Executive Director of the United Nations Population Fund.

World Health Organization (1986). Evaluation of the Strategy for Health for All by the Year 2000: Seventh Report on the World Health Situation, vol. 7 (Manila).

---

* Contraceptive prevalence rate is for women aged 15-44.

** Foreign-born population: 1979 census data as cited in the Government reply to the United Nations Demographic Yearbook questionnaire.

VENEZUELA*

Colmenares, Maria Magdalena (1988). Case study on Venezuela. Paper presented at the United Nations Expert Group Meeting on Social Support Measures for the Advancement of Women, Vienna, 14-18 November. ECM/SSMAW/1988/CS.15.

Pan American Health Organization (1986). Health Conditions in the Americas, 1981-1984, vol. II.

Universidad Catolica Andres Bello (1986). Revista sobre Relaciones Industriales y Laborales, No. 18 (enero-junio). Caracas.

United Nations, Committee on the Elimination of Discrimination against Women (1989). Second periodic reports of States Parties: Venezuela. CEDAW/C/13/Add.21

_____/United Nations Population Fund (1982). Population policy compendium: Venezuela.

VIET NAM

Desbarats, J. (1987). Population redistribution in the Socialist Republic of Viet Nam. Population and Development Review, vol. 13, No. 1 (March), pp. 43-76.

United Nations/United Nations Population Fund (1982). Population policy compendium: Viet Nam.

United Nations Children's Fund (1988). Country programme recommendation: Viet Nam. E/ICEF/1988/P/L.25.

United Nations High Commissioner for Refugees (1989). Information paper prepared for the International Conference on Indo-Chinese Refugees, Geneva, 13-14 June.

United Nations Population Fund (1988). Assistance to the Government of Viet Nam: support for a national population programme. DP/FPA/CP/42.

Xuan, D. H. (1988). PHC in Viet Nam. World Health (August-September), pp. 23-25.

_____

* Contraceptive prevalence rate is for women aged 15-44.

YEMEN*

International Labour Office (1987). The role of international labour migration in the transformation of an economy: the case of the Yemen Arab Republic. International Migration for Employment, Working Paper No. 35. Geneva.

United Nations/United Nations Population Fund (1985). Population policy compendium: Yemen Arab Republic.

United Nations Children's Fund (1987). Country programme recommendation: Yemen. E/ICEF/1987/P/L.25.

United Nations Population Fund (1987). Assistance to the Government of Yemen: support for a comprehensive population programme. DP/FPA/CP/5.

World Health Organization (1986). Primary health care: first steps in the Yemen Arab Republic. World Health Forum, vol. 7, No. 4, pp. 355-359.

YUGOSLAVIA**

International Labour Office (1988). Social and Labour Bulletin, 4/88, pp. 513-514.

International Planned Parenthood Federation (1989). People, vol. 16, No. 3, pp. 16-18.

Organisation for Economic Co-operation and Development (1988). New Trends in Rural Policymaking. Paris, pp. 137-144.

World Health Organization (1986). Evaluation of the Strategy for Health for All by the Year 2000: Seventh Report on the World Health Situation, vol. 5 (Copenhagen).

---

* Contraceptive prevalence rate is for women under 50 years of age.

** Contraceptive prevalence rate is for women aged 15-44 who had used a method other than sterilization within the past six months. Foreign-born population: 1981 census data as cited in the Government reply to the United Nations Demographic Yearbook questionnaire.

ZAIRE

Population Reference Bureau (1989). Africa's expanding population:
old problems, new policies. _Population Bulletin_, vol. 44, No. 3
(November).

République du Zaïre, Commission Nationale du Recensement (1986). _Combien
Sommes-Nous. Résultats Provisoires_.

United Nations (1989). Additional information submitted by States parties to
the Covenant following the consideration of their reports by the
Committee on Economic, Social and Cultural Rights. E/1989/5.

United Nations High Commissioner for Refugees (1989). Fact sheet: Zaire,
vol. 3, No. 2 (October).

World Health Organization (1987). _Evaluation of the Strategy for Health for
All by the Year 2000: Seventh Report on the World Health Situation_,
vol. 2 (Brazzaville).

ZAMBIA*

Population Reference Bureau (1989). Africa's expanding population:
old problems, new policies. _Population Bulletin_, vol. 44, No. 3
(November), pp. 31 and 32.

United Nations Children's Fund (1987). Country programme recommendation:
Zambia. E/ICEF/1987/P/L.5.

United Nations High Commissioner for Refugees (1989). Fact sheet: Zambia,
vol. 3, No. 2 (October).

United Nations Population Fund (1988). Assistance to the Government of
Zambia: support for a comprehensive population programme. DP/FPA/CP/39.

World Health Organization (1987). _Evaluation of the Strategy for Health for
All by the Year 2000: Seventh Report on the World Health Situation_,
vol. 2 (Brazzaville).

---

* 1980 Census data as cited in the Government reply to the United
Nations _Demographic Yearbook_ questionnaire.

ZIMBABWE*

Government of Zimbabwe, Central Statistical Office (1985). Main Demographic Features of the Population of Zimbabwe.

United Nations Centre for Regional Planning (1988). Changing rural development policies in Zimbabwe. Regional Development Dialogue, Special issue.

United Nations High Commissioner for Refugees (1989). Fact sheet: Zimbabwe, vol. 3, No. 2 (October).

Wekwete, K. (1988). Development of urban planning in Zimbabwe. Cities, vol. 5 No. 1 (February).

World Health Organization (1987). Evaluation of the Strategy for Health for All by the Year 2000: Seventh Report on the World Health Situation, vol.2, (Brazzaville).

---

    * Foreign-born population: data are reported by nationality rather than by place of birth.

ANNEXES

Annex I

GLOSSARY

Contraceptive prevalence rate: percentage currently using contraception; usually based on married or sexually active couples with women in the reproductive age.

Crude birth rate: the number of births in a year per 1,000 mid-year population.

Crude death rate: the number of deaths in a year per 1,000 mid-year population.

Dependency ratio or age dependency ratio: the ratio of the combined child population under 15 years of age and adult population 65 years and over to the population of intermediate age per 100.

Foreign-born population: persons born outside the country or area in which they were enumerated at the time of the census.

General fertility rate: the annual number of births divided by the mid-year population of women aged 15 to 49 years multiplied by 1,000.

Gross reproduction rate: a measure of the reproduction of a population expressed as an average number of daughters to be born to a cohort of women during their reproductive age, assuming no mortality and a fixed schedule of age-specific fertility rates. More specifically, it is the sum of age-specific fertility rates for the period multiplied by the proportion of the total births of girl babies.

Infant mortality rate: the probability of dying between birth and age 1 multiplied by 1,000; commonly calculated as the number of deaths of infants under one year of age in any given calendar year divided by the number of births in that year and multiplied by 1,000.

Life expectancy at birth: a life-table function to indicate the expected average number of years to be lived by a newly born baby, assuming a fixed schedule of age-specific mortality rates.

Mean age at first marriage (females): the average age at which women marry for the first time.

Median age: the age which divides the population into two groups of equal size, one of which is younger and the other is older.

Natural rate of increase: the difference between the crude birth rate and the crude death rate, expressed per 1,000 of the mid-year population.

Net migration: the difference between gross immigration and gross emigration.

Net migration rate: the difference between gross immigration and gross emigration per 1,000 of the mid-year population.

Net reproduction rate: a refined measure of the reproduction of population expressed as an average number of daughters that a cohort of newly born girl babies will bear during their lifetime, assuming fixed schedules of age-specific fertility and mortality rates. In other words, it is the measure of the extent to which a cohort of newly born girls will replace themselves under given schedules of age-specific fertility and mortality rates.

Rate of growth: the exponential average annual rate of population growth, expressed as a percentage.

Sex ratio: the number of men per 100 women.

Survival ratio: the probability of surviving from one age to an older one; it is often computed for five-year age groups and a five-year time period.

Total fertility rate: the sum of the age-specific fertility rates over all ages of the child-bearing period; if five-year age groups are used, the sum of the rates is multiplied by 5. This measure gives the approximate magnitude of "completed family size", that is, the total number of children an average woman will bear in her lifetime, assuming no mortality.

Urban population: population living in areas defined as urban by national authorities.

Annex II

LIST OF COUNTRIES REPLYING TO THE FIRST, SECOND, THIRD,
FOURTH, FIFTH and SIXTH UNITED NATIONS POPULATION
INQUIRIES AMONG GOVERNMENTS

Country	Inquiry					
	First (1963)	Second (1968)	Third (1976)	Fourth (1978)	Fifth (1982)	Sixth (1988)
Oman	..	−	+	−	−	−
Pakistan	+	+	+	+	+	+
Panama	+	+	+	+	+	+
Papua New Guinea	..	..	+	+	+	−
Paraguay	−	−	−	−	+	−
Peru	−	+	−	+	+	+
Philippines	+	+	+	+	+	+
Poland	−	+	+	−	+	+
Portugal	−	−	+	−	+	+
Qatar	..	−	+	−	+	−
Republic of Korea	+	+	+	+	+	+
Romania	−	+	+	+	+	−
Rwanda	−	+	+	+	+	−
Saint Kitts and Nevis	..	..	..	..	..	−
Saint Lucia	..	..	..	..	−	+
Saint Vincent and the Grenadines	..	..	..	..	−	+
Samoa	+	−	+	+	−	−
San Marino	−	−	+	−	−	−
Sao Tome and Principe	..	..	−	−	+	−
Saudi Arabia	−	−	+	−	−	−
Senegal	−	−	+	+	+	+
Seychelles	..	..	..	+	−	−
Sierra Leone	+	−	+	+	+	+
Singapore	..	+	+	+	+	+
Solomon Islands	..	..	..	..	−	−
Somalia	−	−	+	+	+	+
South Africa	−	−	−	−	−	+
Spain	−	+	+	+	+	+
Sri Lanka	+	+	+	+	+	+
Sudan	+	−	+	−	−	−
Suriname	..	..	−	−	−	−
Swaziland	..	+	+	−	+	+
Sweden	+	+	+	+	+	+
Switzerland	−	−	+	+	+	+
Syrian Arab Republic	−	+	+	+	+	−
Thailand	−	+	+	+	+	+
Togo	−	−	+	+	+	−
Tonga	−	−	+	+	−	−
Trinidad and Tobago	−	+	−	−	−	−
Tunisia	+	+	+	−	+	+

Country	Inquiry					
	First (1963)	Second (1968)	Third (1976)	Fourth (1978)	Fifth (1982)	Sixth (1988)
Turkey	+	+	+	+	+	+
Tuvalu	..	..	..	..	–	–
Uganda	–	–	+	–	+	+
Ukrainian Soviet Socialist Republics	–	+	+	–	+	+
Union of Soviet Socialist Republics	+	+	+	+	+	+
United Arab Emirates	..	+	+	–	+	+
United Kingdom of Great Britain and Northern Ireland	+	+	+	+	+	+
United Republic of Tanzania	–	+	+	–	+	+
United States of America	+	+	+	+	+	+
Uruguay	–	+	+	–	+	–
Vanuatu	..	..	..	..	+	+
Venezuela	+	–	–	–	–	+
Viet Nam	–	+	–	–	–	+
Yemen	–	–	+	–	+	–
Yugoslavia	+	+	+	–	+	+
Zaire	–	–	+	–	+	–
Zambia	..	+	+	–	+	+
Zimbabwe	..	..	..	..	+	+

Source: Population Policy Data Bank, Population Division, Department of International Economic and Social Affairs, United Nations Secretariat.

Notes: A plus (+) indicates reply received.

A minus (–) indicates reply not received.

Two dots (..) indicate not applicable because the country was neither a State Member of the United Nations nor an Observer at the time of the Inquiry.

Litho in United Nations, New York   United Nations publication
24903—October 1990—5,100   Sales No. E.90.XIII.2
ISBN 92-1-151188-7   ST/ESA/SER.A/102/Add.2